HUIZHOU STUDIES:
A COLLECTION
OF PAPERS TRANSLATED
徽学研究经典文献选译

方传余 ◎ 编译

北京师范大学出版集团
安徽大学出版社

图书在版编目(CIP)数据

徽学研究经典文献选译/方传余编译. —合肥:安徽大学出版社,2017.11
ISBN 978-7-5664-1435-9

Ⅰ.①徽… Ⅱ.①方… Ⅲ.①文化史-研究-徽州地区 Ⅳ.①K295.42

中国版本图书馆 CIP 数据核字(2017)第 174208 号

Huizhou Studies: A Collection of Papers Translated
徽学研究经典文献选译
方传余 编译

出版发行:	北京师范大学出版集团 安 徽 大 学 出 版 社 (安徽省合肥市肥西路 3 号 邮编 230039) www.bnupg.com.cn www.ahupress.com.cn
印　　刷:	安徽省人民印刷有限公司
经　　销:	全国新华书店
开　　本:	170mm×230mm
印　　张:	13.5
字　　数:	250 千字
版　　次:	2017 年 11 月第 1 版
印　　次:	2017 年 11 月第 1 次印刷
定　　价:	40.50 元

ISBN 978-7-5664-1435-9

策划编辑:李　梅　李　雪　　　装帧设计:李　军
责任编辑:李　雪　　　　　　　美术编辑:李　军
责任印制:李　军

版权所有　侵权必究
反盗版、侵权举报电话:0551-65106311
外埠邮购电话:0551-65107716
本书如有印装质量问题,请与印制管理部联系调换。
印制管理部电话:0551-65106311

Acknowledgements

This collection of translated papers on Huizhou studies is the outcome of the research projects (Y01002219 and Y01002288) granted by Anhui University Huizhou Culture Inheritance and Innovation Center. Our heartfelt thanks go to the center, the authors of the individual papers originally in Chinese, and the journals and newspapers where the papers appeared. We should also wish to express our thanks to Guo Jihong, who offered suggestions as to what papers to translate, and to Zhou Xiaoguang, Wang Kaidui, Meng Fansheng, Hu Xuewen and Mi Xueqin, who helped in their own ways which make our work easier to go on.

The editor and the translators will share the responsibility for any shortcomings or mistakes that remain.

Fang Chuanyu

Contents

Part Ⅰ The Basics of Huizhou Studies ········· 1

Chapter 1 A Random Reflection on Huizhou Studies ········· 1

Chapter 2 A Discussion on Contemporary Huizhou Studies ········· 8

Chapter 3 The Object, Value, Content and Method of Huizhou Studies
  ········· 18

Chapter 4 Multi-disciplinary Values of Huizhou Studies ········· 30

Part Ⅱ Huizhou Culture ········· 36

Chapter 5 The Basic Concepts and Historical Status of Huizhou Culture
  ········· 36

Chapter 6 The Formation and Evolution of Huizhou Culture ········· 53

Chapter 7 The Position of the Huizhou Culture and the Trend of Its
  Development ········· 65

Part Ⅲ The Patriarchal Clan System in Huizhou ········· 78

Chapter 8 Three Issues Related to the Patriarchal Clan System in Huizhou
  ········· 78

Chapter 9 Genealogical Tree in the Ming and Qing Dynasties in Huizhou
  and Its Social Customs ········· 101

Part Ⅳ Huizhou Files ·· **117**

Chapter 10 A Review of the Research into Huizhou Files from the
             Late-1980s to the 1990s ·································· 117

Chapter 11 Huizhou Historical Files and Huizhou Studies ············ 139

Part Ⅴ Huizhou Merchants ·· **161**

Chapter 12 A Discussion on Some Issues in the Research of Huizhou
             Merchants ·· 161

Chapter 13 On the Formation and Development of the Huizhou Merchant
             Group ·· 184

Information of the Original Passages ·································· **207**

Part I
The Basics of Huizhou Studies

Chapter 1　A Random Reflection on Huizhou Studies

The late 1970s to mid-1980s saw another round of prosperity of academic research in China, and Huizhou Studies budded as a new research field of regional culture. With decades of the joint efforts of scholars inside and outside China, Huizhou Studies, or Huixue, took on an exciting development, hence a boom and, most likely, a crescendo of Huizhou Studies, so to speak.

As the name suggests, Huizhou Studies is the study of Huizhou prefecture or its culture. It is an integration of cultural phenomena in the six counties (Shexian, Yixian, Xiuning, Qimen, Jixi and Wuyuan) under Huizhou prefecture in history. While the counties share more or less similarities in cultures, each is unique in one way or another. Locally rooted and outwardly expanding, Huizhou culture fuses both small Huizhou and big Huizhou into a colorful and high-quality cultural treasure.

As a matter of fact, the term Huixue can be found in early literature of Huizhou, as in "Wengong is the master of Huixue". Nevertheless, Huixue in early literature refers to Xin'an Rationalism founded by Zhu Xi, thus different than what it denotes and covers today. While the old Huixue is mono-disciplinary, belonging to the history of academics, the new Huixue is about regional culture and therefore multidisciplinary.

As studies of regional culture, today's Huizhou studies is inclusive so much that it covers Xin'an① Rationalism, Xin'an medicine, Xin'an literature, Xin'an drawings, Xin'an clan community, Xin'an merchants, Huizhou academies, dialects, rituals, operas, dwellings, genealogies, land system, tenant system, contract documents, philology, engraving, seal cutting, architecture, bonsai, and even writing brushes, ink sticks, paper and ink slabs. All these, with either Xin'an or Hui in naming, are typical cultural specialties which represent the business and academic prosperity of Huizhou and thus constitute Huixue, a giant thesaurus of regional culture.

What may account for the colorful regional cultures in such a scarcely populated remote mountainous area? The answer lies in the cultures in the central plains, which served as the source or gene, and Huizhou merchant clans, which served as the catalyst of the development.

It has never been accidental for cultures in the central plains to be the source of Huizhou culture. Huizhou was historically an area of immigrants, who were mostly from the central plains, the birthplace of the Chinese civilization. This area, the middle and lower reaches of the Yellow River, used to be the political and cultural center of the country and suffered from the most frequent wars resulting from regime substitution, ruling class scrambling, warlords separatism, national conflicts, and peasant revolutions. Each war would drove out a considerable number of people, who mostly moved southward over the Huanghuai Plain and across the Yangtze River. With its unique geographic features, Huizhou was just an ideal place for these immigrants. According to local records, "half of the major national groups of people in Huizhou were immigrants from the north especially

---

① Xin'an prefecture is what Huizhou was known as in the Jin Dynasty and Xin'an was used thereafter to refer to the prefecture.

during Jin, Song and late Tang dynasties", others moved here either from the central plains or from other places during other periods in history. Many of the immigrant families "get into the officialdom and love the landscape, thus settling down here generation after generation" (*Minguo Shexian County Chronicles*, Volume 1). According to *Xin'an Chronicles of Noble Families* by Cheng Shangkuan in Jiajing, the Ming Dynasty, the number of "noble families" had amounted to 84 by the Mid-Ming Dynasty, among which about eighty percent were from the central plains by origin. These immigrants were of more or less the same sub-nations as the "Hakka people" who moved also from the central plains to the mountainous areas in Fujian, Guangdong and Jiangxi.

Apart from some common people, many of the immigrants from the central plains were of business, official or academic gentry with a noble family background. Settling down in Huizhou, they brought in the advanced culture and gradually gained dominance in social life.

What the immigrants brought in was above all the Confucian atmosphere. As recorded in the entry of Yixian in Hanshu, Geographic Annals, Huizhou is a mountainous area where the "south barbarian tribes" dwelled. Before Six Dynasties, Huizhou was a land of prevalent martialism and undereducated people. With the immigration of people from the central plains, Huizhou became more Confucian than ever, especially in social morals as the atmosphere of valuing education and etiquette was brought in. The upsurge of reading was felt everywhere so that "the sound of reading could often be heard in mountain huts", as recorded in Kangxi, *Qimen County Annals*, Volume 1. The Confucian atmosphere in Huizhou was even more vigorous during the Ming and Qing Dynasties, which gave birth to multitudes of scholars and the thriving of Confucian classics studies (Daoguang, *Preface to the Revised Annals of Huizhou Prefecture*) so that Xin'an was generally regarded as a land of propriety and righteous in the southeast, as compared to the hometowns of Confucius and Mencus. Along with the prevalence of classics reading came the emphasis on such social morals as etiquette, harmony and frugality. As is noted in *Collected Works of Taihan*①, Xin'an was a land of etiquette and harmony. Even when the common people encountered each other on the country road, the younger would behave with courtesy towards the elder. Such social relic was so strong in Huizhou that it remained widely known for long. The relic, in fact, had as its source in none other the central plains and was passed down for later generations. Such social customs are vigorously embodied simply in some old couplets in Xidi village of Yixian County, for example, in which words like the five cardinal relationships, the six classics, reading, books, virtue, thrifty and others can be found. All these qualities originated from the central plains and perfectly fit into Huizhou and took root and flourished in Huizhou.

In addition to the Confucian atmosphere, the immigrants also brought in religious culture of the central plains. It is mostly in family clans that the immigrants from the north moved to Huizhou and settled down here, which helped keep each clan united against the bullying of other family groups and maintained the particular family rules under the patriarchal clan system. In some villages of the major family clans, in fact, there was not even one family of other clans. According to Volume 18 of *Random Records of Shexian County*②, all the major family clans in Huizhou have a long history and "many even last for hundreds of years ever since the Six Dynasties through Tang and Song Dynasties". They built their own ancestral temples where the clan members gathered on special occasions to hold sacrificial rites. In this way, the patriarchal clan system is impellingly rooted. In his *The Thoughts of Jiyuan*, Zhao Jishi, a Huizhou native in the late Ming Dynasty and early Qing Dynasty, mentions his elders' describing "many of the social customs in Xin'an as better than those in other areas", and "it is usually for hundreds of years, or generation after generation, that forefathers' tombs are sacredly maintained, family clans closely bonded,

---

① A book by Wang Daokun, a writer in the Ming Dynasty.
② A book by Xu Chengyao, a Jinshi in Shexian County during the Guangxu period.

family pedigrees orderly recorded, master-servant relations strictly emphasized." The generations of family inheritance succession is exactly the living specimen of the clan culture in the central plains.

Huizhou gave birth to a great Confucian in the Southern Song Dynasty, Zhu Xi, whose philosophy was profoundly influential in the area, yet it has to be noted that Zhu's learning is derived from that of Cheng Hao and Cheng Yi (generally known as the two Cheng's) in the Northern Song Dynasty, whose philosophy is typically part of the culture of the central plains. The source of Zhu's learning and its influence is documented in *Guangxu, Wuyuan County Annals*, Volume 3 and *Preface to Family Documents Wu's in Mingzhou, Xiuning*. With the enlightenment of Zhu's philosophical learning, human relations and social customs in Huizhou continuously inherited and developed the Confucianism in the central plains. Just as Zeng Guofan comments in Volume 4 of his *Complete Works*, Huizhou, as Zhu Xi's hometown, has a repertoire of historical and cultural heritage which dwarfs many other areas. With Zhu's influence found everywhere, Huizhou has indeed grown into a culturally refined land after Zhu's era.

With the above-mentioned long-term accumulation of the culture in the central plains, Huixue, or Huizhou culture experienced a healthy growth. At the same time, in the course of social and historical generation, the absorption of elements of other cultures also added to the depth of the cultural deposits of Huizhou culture.

It is the Huizhou merchant clans, with the great fortune they made, that served as the catalyst of the development of Huizhou culture. Historically, economy is the foundation of culture, and without a strong economic support, a culture can hardly grow into high quality. Huizhou was a barren land of mountains, yet as the large number of immigrants moved in and settled down one generation after another, the farming land became scarcely enough to support the ever-increasing population. To better their living, many people had to give up farming and switch to business instead. Since the Ming Dynasty, the number of businessmen in Huizhou had grown to more than twice as many as farmers, and such a high businessman proportion could hardly be found in any other areas. Moreover, many of the businessmen had a scholastic background, which enabled them to make good judgments in the competitive business world. Shrewd as they were, the businessmen were also hard-working and, with their unique spirit generally known "camel spirit of Huizhou merchants", many soon became wealthy. They generally accumulated their wealth to the middle level in five years' time and to the upper level in ten. A considerable number of the Huizhou merchants had their deposits around a million *qiang*, a currency unit at that time, some even up to ten millions. Large in number of people, amount of wealth, business scope and scale, Huizhou merchants had grown into a leading clan in the south of the Yangtze River by the Mid-Ming Dynasty. With the great profit they made, they gradually brought the whole area out of poverty, making Xin'an even the most prosperous place in the south of the Yangtze River.

Much of a Confucian turn of mind, Huizhou merchants were generous in financing local educational and cultural undertakings as they got rich. The building and repairing of schools, temples and academies in Huizhou during the Ming and Qing Dynasties were mostly financed by the merchants, especially the academies of higher level of classic learning enjoyed a much better growth over earlier times both in number or scale. According to *Daoguang, the Revised Annals of Huizhou Prefecture*, Volume 3, "there are scores of academies is Huizhou, and Ziyang Academy is the largest." To rebuild Ziyang Academy, some of the merchants of Shexian County who did salt business on both sides of the Huaihe River even offered as much as 30 million *liang* of silver, another merchant in Yixian County donated up to 2,400 *jin* at his county fellows' proposal to build an academy, similar donators were not rare in every other county of Huizhou. Thanks to the thriving of academies, each of the triennial imperial exams saw as many as a thousand candidates from each of the counties.

The Huizhou merchants attached more importance to their children's education. In fact, they would spare no expense in hiring teachers for their children once they became rich enough. The keen enthusiasm of Huizhou merchants in general for their children's bright future can be best exemplified by "what's the use of saving the fortune without spending it timely on children's education" as asked by Bao Baiting, a merchant himself, and quoted in *Genealogical Sub-tree of the Bao's, Shexian County* (Volume 3). It's no wonder therefore that many famous scholars and officials in the Ming and Qing Dynasties were from business families in Huizhou, such as Wang Daokun, Xu Guo, Jin Sheng, Cao Wenzhi, Cao Zhenyong, Dai Zhen, Cheng Jinfang, Cheng Yaotian, Ling Tingkan, Wang Maoyin, to name just a few.

The focus of the development of Huizhou Studies is Study. It was the academies and schools and hundreds and thousands of students that made it possible for the region to be able to boast so many learned scholars. With the scholars' joint efforts, common goal and unique creativity, different groups with their own characteristics came into being in each field. Besides, it was just with the involvement of the Huizhou merchants, direct or indirect, that many of the cultural phenomena in Huizhou developed into schools with their own characteristics, such as drawing, opera, carving, architecture, gardening and even medicine. In fact, as the local historical records show, Huizhou culture developed just while the business was thriving.

The schools in Huizhou culture are so varied and inclusive that they fall into such academic fields as philosophy, history, sociology, economics, linguistics, art, education, genealogy, architecture, medicine, folklore and other interdisciplinary fields. The academic and practical value of all these fields is immeasurable in the course of carrying forward traditional culture and developing local cultural resources. Huizhou Studies has so far just opened its gate and a probe into its mystery will need the joint efforts of all people concerned.

Published in *Guangming Daily*, Mar. 24, 2000
Written by Zhang Haipeng
Translated by Fang Chuanyu

Chapter 2 A Discussion on Contemporary Huizhou Studies

Ⅰ. Objects of Contemporary Huizhou Studies

What are the objects of Huizhou Studies? Scholars give different definitions to Huizhou Studies and thus provide different answers to this question. Some say the object of Huizhou Studies is Huizhou's social history, or "it is a comprehensive discipline whose object is the history of Huizhou"; or " Huizhou Studies is a historical discipline whose objects are Huizhou documents, Huizhou's history and culture; whose aim is to expose social realities and laws of late feudal China"; or "Huizhou Studies is a series of concepts and theories whose objects are Huizhou's society, economy, culture, thoughts, arts, technology, etc. ".

It is academically known that the distinction of disciplines is based on different research objects, which are always about some particular phenomenon in a particular field.

In fact the expression "Huizhou Studies" appeared in documents long ago. In history, the expression could refer to "Xin'an Neo-Confucianism", or "Huizhou Academia", or "Huizhou culture", or "the study of Huizhou culture".

Today, "Huizhou Studies" is a new concept, but the new concept is also related with the old one because it still contains Xin'an Neo-Confucianism, Huizhou Academia and the study of Huizhou culture. We should see the connection between the new and the old, but more importantly, we should distinguish the new from the old.

Then what is the "new" Huizhou Studies? We think it is a discipline that uses historical documents and other materials, that studies the development and change of Huizhou's society, economy, culture, that exposes Huizhou people's activities in other places and Huizhou culture's development in neighboring areas, and that discusses relative social movements in late feudal China.

What are the differences between the old and the new Huizhou Studies? First, the old one only used materials in the four traditional categories of Chinese writings (Confucian classics, historical records, philosophical writings, miscellaneous works), while the new one uses not only those materials but also historical documents and files. Second, the old one only emphasized social consciousness, but not social existence; and it only studied spiritual culture, but not material culture. The new one emphasizes both social consciousness and existence, studies both spiritual and material culture, and even studies the inner relationships in the above two pairs and their laws. Third, the old one only studied the history of the rulers, but not of the ruled; the new one studies both of them and emphasizes the history of the ruled.

There are five points about study objects which need more explanation. First, we think historical files of Huizhou are not only materials, but also a research object. As materials, they have unique academic values; however, as a research object, they are as important as clans, land systems, merchants of Huizhou. Second, Huizhou has a long history, in which Xin'an period and Shezhou period were the origins. We should not cut off the history, but we focus our study on Huizhou from the Song Dynasty, because every scientific expression can only reflect the most basic, the most important contents. What about the most important contents of contemporary Huizhou Studies? We think they are about Huizhou's society, economy and culture from the Song Dynasty; about Huizhou people's activities in other places and Huizhou culture's development in neighboring areas. Third, we think the aim of contemporary Huizhou Studies is similar to that of other historical studies. They both hope to expose social realities. If there is any difference in this aspect, that must be the distance to social realities—from which some historical studies are a little far and to which Huizhou Studies are much near. Fourth, the geographical scope of our study is not only Huizhou.

Huizhou people's activities in other places and Huizhou culture's influence in neighboring areas are also study objects. Fifth, we think Huizhou Studies can only discuss some social problems of late feudal China. If we want to expose the development of late feudalism in China, we should make a comprehensive study on the whole history of Chinese feudalism.

What kind of discipline should contemporary Huizhou Studies be? We think it is a historical discipline. The main contents of the Studies are the history of Huizhou's society, economy, culture; Huizhou people's historical activities in other places and Huizhou culture's historical development in neighboring areas. Can we say they do not belong to history discipline? Of course the history of Huizhou's society is also included in sociology, the history of Huizhou's economy economics, the history of Huizhou's culture culturology, the history of Huizhou's philosophy philosophy and so on. However, Huizhou Studies cannot be said to belong to these disciplines, because these contents are not the main part of these disciplines. So we think Huizhou Studies, as a whole, belong to the discipline of history, and the specific objects of Huizhou Studies can belong to two or three disciplines. Undoubtedly this expression is different from the idea that Huizhou Studies is a comprehensive discipline. Can this put Huizhou Studies in a proper academic position?

Here we also want to point out that world history and Chinese history are in the same academic position. Can we say that the two are rather comprehensive disciplines than historical ones?

II. Characteristics of Contemporary Huizhou Studies' Objects

It was documented that Huizhou was an immigrant society. From late Eastern Han Dynasty, notable families and clans immigrated from Central Plains area into Huizhou for varied reasons. They brought advanced technology and culture into this region and consequently Huizhou saw its first historic leap in society in the Song Dynasty. "Famous officials emerge in large numbers" "Vulgar customs gradually turn to elegance". Huizhou's education, book-engraving, medicine, philosophy, ink-stone industry, ink-stick industry were all in flourishing conditions.

Since the Mid-Ming Dynasty, with the development of commercial economy and the sprout of capitalism, a lot of people left Huizhou to other places and became merchants instead of farmers or Confucian scholars at home. These merchants occupied the leading position in the whole country for more than three centuries. At that time, there appeared the second historic leap—advanced education, flourishing business, prosperous culture, great achievements in imperial examinations etc. The merchants established their nets in many places and brought their culture to over half of China.

Then, what about the characteristics of their activities in other places and their culture's development in neighboring areas and of Huizhou's society, economy and culture?

1. Rich Contents   What can be studied in this discipline is very rich. All the following should be included: clans, education, historical relics, customs, files and documents, land systems, merchants, forestry, book-engraving, technology, medicine, philosophy, painting, architecture, opera, dialect, cuisine, ink-stone, ink-stick, carving arts, etc. The objects of Huizhou Studies can be divided into many categories and in each category the contents are all very rich. According to records, education in Huizhou was very advanced, which had a complete system and a reasonable structure. Besides government schools, there were 120 local schools in Shexian County, 140 in Xiuning County, 140 in Wuyuan County, 27 in Qimen County, 13 in Yixian County, 30 in Jixi County (totally 470 local schools). Meanwhile private schools scattered everywhere. "In mountains and valleys where there are people living, there are teachers and students." "Even in a small village of 10 families, students can be heard reading and reciting." In addition, academies were an outstanding landscape in Huizhou. According to incomplete statistics, there were 104 schools named "academy". Since the Song-Yuan Dynasties, book-engraving industry had flourished and become

one of the four centers in China. Several hundred engravers had left their names behind such as Cheng Dachang, Zhu Xi, Wang Gang, Zhu Mu, Fang Hui, Zheng Yu, Zhu Sheng, Wang Tong, Cheng Minzheng, Bi Maokang, Wu Mianxue, Wang Daokun, Hu Zhengyan, Zhang Chao. To the Ming-Qing Dynasties, the number of book engravers reached 419. In a village of Shexian County, several clans made a living by this for generations. Within only Huang clan there were 329 engravers, tens of whom even got national reputation. Consequently numerous books were left in Huizhou.

Another object of Huizhou Studies is Xin'an Medicine. It was so prosperous in history that 745 doctors left their names behind, wrote or published 615 medical books. Huizhou was also a land of painters. Xin'an Art School fostered many talented artists. It was recorded that even in Jiang village of Shexian County, there were as many as 20 painters. Hong Ren (whose original name was Jiang Tao), Zha Shibiao, Sun Yi, Wang Zhirui were four early famous painters of Xin'an School. Wang Pu, He Wenyu, Cheng Ming, Huang Zhen, Jiang Rong, Seng Xuezhuang, Lian Xi were late famous ones. This school had great influence in Chinese painting history. Ancient books is another object of Huizhou Studies. It was recorded that except Xiuning County, there were 1,852 writers and 4,715 written books in Huizhou. In Jiang Yuanqing's *A Record of Books Written by Anhui People*, we can find about one third of over 6,000 Anhui writers and a quarter of 17,000 books were from Huizhou. The National Library of China has collected 458 ancient genealogies, among which over half were of Huizhou. So in this sense Huizhou was called "a land of books".

2. Splendid Achievements According to statistics, there were 860 "Jinshi" (a successful candidate in the highest imperial examinations) from Huizhou in the Song Dynasty, which occupied 2.04% of the total number; 492 in the Ming Dynasty, 1.95% of the total; 782 in the Qing Dynasty, 2.97% of the total. It was recorded that there were 5 "Zhuangyuan" (one who came first in the highest imperial examination), 2 "Bangyan" (one who came second in the highest imperial examination), 1 martial Bangyan, 8 "Tanhua"

(one who came the third in the highest imperial examination), 5 "Chuanglu" (one who came first in the second highest imperial examination), 3 "Huiyuan" (one who won the first place in metropolitan imperial examination), 13 "Jieyuan" (one who won the first place in provincial imperial examination), 296 Jinshi, and about 1,000 "Juren" (a successful candidate in the highest imperial examinations at the provincial level). There were 24 Zhuangyuan from Huizhou since the Five Dynasties such as Su Ya, Lu Zhen, Zhang Heng, Wu Qian, Ren Hentai and Tang Gao. There were 4 martial Zhuanyuan: Li Zhicheng, Cheng Mingfeng, Cheng Ruochuan and Huang Geng. There were 54 capital officials from Shexian County in the Qing Dynasty. There were as many as 17 prime ministers since the Song Dynasty who came originally from Huizhou such as Wang Boyan, Wang Che, Wu Yuan, Cheng Yuanfeng. As for Huizhou merchants, they rose in the Mid-Ming Dynasty. *Shexian County Records, the Republic of China Volume* said: "Among eight biggest salt merchants, half were always from clans of our county such as Jiang, Wu, Huang, Cheng, Wang, Xu, Zheng, Xu, Cao, Song, Bao, Ye." "The fortunes of these biggest salt merchants were calculated by millions or ten millions." Huizhou merchants got great achievements and occupied the leading position for more than three centuries. As for Huizhou Academia, its representative Dai Zhen was from Xiuning county and achieved outstandingly in such fields as mathematics, astronomy, hydrology, linguistics. Scholar Wang Zhong said: "Dai Zhen has learned and mastered the knowledge which has lost for a thousand years." Because of his merits, "Huizhou Academia became independent and flourishing." In the Qing Dynasty Dai Zhen stood in the first place of Qian-Jia School and was very influential. There were also other ten famous scholars such as Jing Bang, Cheng Yaotian and Ling Tingkan. As for Xin'an Medicine, famous doctors emerged continuously. Doctor Zhang Gao wrote a book *On Medicine*, which was the earliest medical book recording doctors' biographies and medical materials. Jiang Guan wrote *Cases of Famous Doctors*, the first book to summarize historical cases of medicine. Wu Cheng created a new theory; Cheng Wenyou published the first excerpt of medical theories. Zheng Honggang and Zheng Shufu created a new therapy for diphtheritis. In the Mid-Ming Dynasty, engraving industry rose abruptly and outstandingly. Hu Zhengyan, a famous engraver from Xiuning County, created two new technical methods and triggered a revolution in this field. With the help of the new methods, he created two art works, which pushed Huizhou engraving to a higher level.

3. Typical Phenomena   Since the Song Dynasty, many social, economic and cultural phenomena in Huizhou were very typical. From historical records, we can find that clans prevailed and this region was a typical clan society. These clans had 8 basic characteristics: having the same ancestors, being connected with blood, having a clear order, having a settled living area, taking up some certain collective activities, having a certain organization form, having clan rules, owning some common fortune. Most clans emphasized education and they aimed at being successful in imperial examinations. This pursuit of life was very typical at that time. Some people from these clans might try the examinations many times, sometimes they failed but did not regret. Ye Fengnian, a man of Ye clan from Yixian County in the Qing Dynasty, was a good example. He tried the examinations even in his 80s, but failed. Emperor Qianlong heard of this and "honored him a title". *Customs of Shexian County Records*, published in the reign of Emperor Wanli, gave a vivid description of Huizhou at different times. In the reign of Emperor Hongzhi, "everything is in its order—people are contented for they have houses, land, gardens, wood, etc. There is no theft, no disorder, but only harmony in the society." Of course, it was a little overstated. In the Mid-Ming Dynasty, great changes took place. In the reign of Emperors Zhengde and Jiajing, "more people became merchants instead of farmers. The old balance was broken—some people became rich while others poor. Competition was severe." Later, "the rich became richer and the poor poorer. Fortunes had their owners, but did not have eternal owners. Business disputes rose frequently." In the reign of Emperor Wanli, "one person in a hundred was rich while nine people in ten were poor. The poor

could not resist the rich, the few could control the majority. Money was the only god and people were all under its ruling." Here the flourishing of commercial economy and its consequences, the sprout of capitalism were reflected, thus the social trend of late feudal China was reflected too. Through large quantities of files, historians and economists discover the change of land system in Huizhou—more frequent land buying and selling, land ownership splitting becoming more serious, tenancy system becoming more popular, more farmers becoming free tenants. These economic phenomena were all typical. Many researchers point out the feudality of Huizhou merchants and their capital. Huizhou merchants put a large part of profits into building ancestral temples and archways, fixing genealogies, buying land, supporting feudal rulers' civil construction or military transportation or celebrations. This was also a common phenomenon for the movement of commercial capital in Chinese feudal society. The historical files tell us that Huizhou merchants are the most typical ones in late feudal China.

Joseph Mcdermott published in *Asia Culture Studies* an article "Huizhou Original Materials—the Key to Study Society and Economy of Late China Empire". Why do these files become the key? Because by using these materials, scholars can expose the development of Huizhou society and economy, and thus can expose in some degree the development of late feudal China.

4. Extensive Influences   Huizhou culture was a regional culture, but it had extensive influences over more than half of China. For Huizhou merchants established nets in many places such as Shanghai, Hangzhou, Suzhou, Nanjing, Beijing, Guangzhou and Wuhan. There was even a proverb in Yangtze River Valley, "No Huizhou merchants, no towns." With the footsteps of Huizhou merchants, Huizhou culture also spread to those places and became influential in the whole country. For instance, Xin'an Neo-Confucianism originated from Huizhou, but its representative Zhu Xi influenced the whole China with his idea. Huizhou Academia originated from Huizhou, but its representative Dai Zhen influenced the whole country. Xin'an Medicine originated from Huizhou, while its doctors could be seen in many

other places. Doctor Wu Qian, one of the top three doctors in the early Qing Dynasty, wrote a 90-volume medical book which was a must one for doctors at that time. Books written by doctors such as Zhang Gao, Wang Ji, Sun Yikui, Jiang Guan were also printed many times and were spread all over the country, or even to other Asian countries such as Korea and Japan.

III. The Shaping of Contemporary Huizhou Studies

How do Contemporary Huizhou Studies get into shape?

The process is as follows. In 1950s, several hundred thousands of folk files and documents were found in Huizhou. They included land leases, title deeds, lease agreements, contracts, written pledges, tax lists, account books, letters, bulletins, genealogies, etc. These materials are kept in Chinese National Library, the Chinese Academy of Sciences Institute for Economic Research and Institute of History, Chinese History Museum, Tianjing Library, Nanjing University, Nanjing Museum, Anhui Library, Anhui Museum, Anhui Provincial Archives, Huangshan Museum, Qimen Museum, Xiuning Archives, Huangshan College Library, Anhui University Huizhou Studies Center, etc. As to the volume of materials at region-level, no place can match Huizhou.

Mr. Zhou Shaoquan once said, these materials have 5 characteristics—suggestiveness, continuity, concreteness, genuineness, typicalness—and "have attracted many researchers to study them with devotion, and then consequently emerges a new discipline: Huizhou Studies". It is not an overstatement that without the discovery of these materials, there would be no contemporary Huizhou Studies.

However, some scholars only admit the importance of this discovery, but do not admit the importance of Huizhou historical performance in shaping this discipline. For example, Mr. Zhou Shaoquan said: "Some think Huizhou Studies emerge because Huizhou culture has rich contents, splendid achievements and have attracted thousands scholars home and abroad to study. Is it convincing? We can compare Suzhou with Huizhou.

Suzhou culture also has rich contents and splendid achievements, and also has attracted thousands scholars home and abroad to study. Why isn't there a discipline called 'Suzhou Studies'?"

We think in the shaping of Huizhou Studies, the above mentioned discovery is the decisive factor, while Huizhou's splendid performance since the Song Dynasty is the foundation. If there was only a decisive factor, without the foundation, there would be only a Huizhou Paleography. Huizhou Paleography is obviously different from Huizhou Studies, which has been academically acknowledged. We think the two are both essential in the shaping of contemporary Huizhou Studies. But we admit that the using of historical materials in studying Huizhou makes a great jump in this field. Why should we say so? Because in the past the materials scholars used were partly first-handed, partly second-handed or even third-handed. The newly-discovered materials are completely original, first-handed, so there would be a natural leap in study. The leap can be seen in three aspects: first, the new materials enable us to have a deeper, more comprehensive study over such objects as patriarchal clans, land system, renting, merchants, laws. Second, Confucian classics and books of history, philosophy and literature are mostly records about the activities of the rulers, while the new materials are records about activities of the ordinary people as well as of the rulers. Using these new materials will enable us to expose especially the activities of the ordinary people. Third, what historians pursue is to expose historical reality. With these new materials, we can approach historical reality more closely.

Published in *Journal of Anhui University*, Vol. 28, No. 5, 2004
Written by Zhao Huafu
Translated by Wang Yangwen

Chapter 3 The Object, Value, Content and Method of Huizhou Studies

Huizhou Studies are about the whole history of Huizhou district. This paper will discuss values, contents and research methods of Huizhou Studies. The discussion is about Huizhou Studies, but may also be of help to regional history study. Any comments and criticism are welcome if there are some mistakes or inappropriateness in the discussion.

I. Values of Huizhou Studies

1. The research approach of Huizhou Studies is different from that of traditional history science. The latter is centered by the study of politics and the emperor system, while the former jumps out of the circle and learn the whole country by analyzing a region of the country. Professor Wang Yuquan pointed out regional history study should be encouraged and said it was a new international trend when he attended the meeting of the Ming Dynasty Economic History in November, 1983. In the past we focused on the study of central governments, laws and institutions; we seldom considered the interaction between center and locality. In fact, different regions varied widely in executing the central government decrees because they differed greatly in their distances from the central government, economic development, customs, geography, products, ethic compositions, etc. Only if regional history has been deeply researched can we learn the interactions between a country's center and its regions, and then push Chinese history study to a new level.

2. Huizhou Studies have typical values for the study of traditional China. Huizhou is a good example to learn traditional China because it was different from agriculture-dominated regions and was a relatively developed region in many aspects. Economically, it had outstanding trading industry as well as agriculture. Through Huizhou merchants we can see the function of commercial

capital in traditional society, the relationship between commercial capital and social changes. Socially, it kept clan systems, which had disappeared in Central Plains area from the Tang-Song Dynasties. Through its clan systems, genealogies, ancestral temples, clan fields, tenant-servants, we can see clearly about Chinese traditional society. Culturally, Huizhou philosophy was prosperous, and the ancestral home of Zhu Xi (the representative of Xin'an Neo-Confucianism) was Huizhou. Through Xin'an Confucianism We can see how rationalism inherited the Orthodox Confucianism after Song Dynasty, how Huizhou merchants united with Confucian culture and their psychology. The above three aspects could be all hardly seen in other regions.

Huizhou had established a special regional system—merchants, clans and philosophy always interacted with each other and complemented each other. Clan culture was the core of its philosophy. Clans depended on imperial examinations in order to get the ability to survive and develop in the limited mountainous region. Merchants offered the funds for clan clustering and education. The power of clan structure and clan culture made merchant gangs extremely solid and competitive. With the help of clans, merchants got funds and hands, did commercial activities, controlled shop clerks, took refugee in the feudal regime, etc. Merchants invested in education, schooled their children to become officials and finally got commercial priorities in return. The increase of general education level also equipped merchants with higher commercial qualities. In a particular situation, these three elements had formed a virtuous cycle. Huizhou merchants had occupied the leading place for several hundreds years; Huizhou people achieved top success in imperial examinations in the Ming-Qing Dynasties; Huizhou clans were as stable as what was described "a tomb does not move in a thousand years; a genealogy does not disorder in a thousand years; a family with a thousand people does not separate." Besides, Huizhou is a big dialect region (one of eight or ten dialect regions in China). In conclusion Huizhou was a both closed and open system—it was closed because mountains separated it from the outside world and made its society stable; it was open because Xin'an

River, Chang River, Qingyi River connected it with Jiangnan region, its merchants and officials made it closely related with the outside world and made its society sustainable. Briefly we can say it is hard to find elsewhere such a sample region as Huizhou to study Chinese traditional society.

3. Huizhou has kept tremendous historical materials, which is the reason for Huizhou Studies to become a discipline and which is the foundation for Huizhou Studies' values. Because this region was closed and seldom disrupted by war, a large quantity of materials (including relics) were preserved. The prevailing of clan system left many ancestral temples, memorial archways, coffin homes and also numerous pedigrees; advanced education left many relics of academy schools and Confucian temples, or literal notes, literal collections, dramas, stories, inscriptions, etc. The prosperity of business and economy made this place full of delicate buildings and gardens, and moreover left uncountable contracts and files. In 1985 the book *Selected Materials of Huizhou Merchants in Ming-Qing Dynasties* (partly compiled by me) was published by Huangshan Press and it was the first collection on Huizhou Studies. *Social and Economic materials of Huizhou in the Ming-Qing Dynasties, the Series—Volume I* was published by China Social Science Press in 1988 and *Volume II* in 1990. *Contracts and Documents of Huizhou in a Thousand Years* was published by Huashan Art and Literature Press in 1991. These are only a small part of Huizhou materials. Compared with Dunhuang materials which are mainly on Buddhism, Huizhou materials are much superior in quantity and diversity. Huizhou files and documents have become more and more important in studying later feudal China especially the Ming-Qing Dynasties, more and more materials will be published.

II. Contents of Huizhou Studies

Since the object of Huizhou Studies is the whole history of this region, the studies should cover all people, all activities and all phenomena in the region. The following is just a rough list. Economically, merchants, land system, tenant-servant system should be included. Culturally, philosophy, language, education, literature, technology, buildings, engravings should be included. Socially, clan system, civil organization, customs, social life, social classes and contradictions should be included. In recent years, these studies have become deeper and deeper, while more and more scholars join in the field simultaneously.

However, it should be pointed out that Huizhou Studies are about the history of the region, but should not be limited in the range of six Huizhou counties. There should be three geographical levels. The first level is the core—the six counties. The second level covers cities, towns and villages along Yangtze River and the Great Canal. In this level the central area is Jiangnan region "where Huizhou merchants can be seen everywhere". The third level covers the whole country or even overseas. If the first level region is called "small Huizhou", the second and third ones can be called "big Huizhou". Mr. Hu Shi had once brought forward the concept—"small Jixi and big Jixi". He pointed that the compilation of county records "should not only cover 'small Jixi', but also 'big Jixi'. Without big Jixi, small Jixi would not have been so influential." So we can also say, without "big Huizhou", Huizhou Studies cannot be influential either.

Why can our studies cover so big an area? It's because the footsteps of Huizhou merchants covered so big an area. These merchants could be said vehicles of culture. They brought clan systems, behavior patterns, cultural psychology of Huizhou to elsewhere. For instance, Huizhou had a custom that operas should be played in festivals and clan rituals. Under this condition, Huizhou Opera gradually became mature. Huizhou merchants in places as Yangzhou, Nanjing or Suzhou reared opera troupes at home, and used them to do social communications, business activities. Without the support of these merchants, Huizhou Opera troupes could not rise and spread to elsewhere. Later some famous troupes went to Beijing and finally developed into Beijing Opera. Another example is Huizhou Cuisine and Huaiyang Cuisine (which is derived from Huizhou Cuisine), two of eight famous cuisines in China. Also Huizhou-style buildings were brought elsewhere by these merchants. They built guilds and halls in cities and towns where they went. Besides, these merchants brought elsewhere their spirits such as diligence, endurance and honesty. As for other famous things, four treasures of the study (writing brush, ink stick, ink slab and paper) made in Huizhou were greatly welcomed by scholars and artists. Book engraving was very outstanding in the Ming-Qing Dynasties. Huizhou versions were very famous at that time. Merchants not only supported the engraving of genealogies, Confucian classics, but also the engraving of popular novels and dramas, which encouraged the spread and development of civil culture. Moreover, Huizhou scholars influenced the whole country's culture trend, from Zhu Xi, Dai Zhen to Hu Shi and Tao Xingzhi, etc.

Naturally this cultural radiation is bi-directional. "Big Huizhou" has also great influence over "small Huizhou". Huizhou was originally a living place for mountainous Yue people, while Han people from Central Plains region came here to avoid wars in the period of two Han Dynasties. To Song Dynasty the two people's cultures mixed into one—Xin'an culture. Neo-confucianism, an important part of Xin'an culture, obviously inherited and developed Central Plains Confucianism. The clan system was also brought and preserved by powerful families from Central Plains region though the system had disappeared in Central Plains region because of war. It can be said without clan's cohesive force, there would be no powerful Huizhou merchants. In several hundreds of years Huizhou merchants brought large fortunes back to "small Huizhou" and offered a solid financial support for cultural landscape in "small Huizhou". Huizhou-style buildings themselves absorbed many elements of Jiangnan-style dwelling houses. In addition, many subjects of Huizhou engravings were landscapes of merchants' living cities such as Suzhou and Hangzhou. All these above can tell us that "big Huizhou" is an essential part in Huizhou Studies and that it is essential to combine the study of regions and the whole country.

III. Methods of Huizhou Studies

Huizhou Studies involve the whole region's society, so we must use multi-disciplinary methods. In the following I will introduce some methods used in my study.

1. Collection of Huizhou Materials   The study of regional history is very different from that of Orthodox history. Materials needed in the research can not be easily found in history books, so pains should be taken to collect them. Here I will introduce the way I collected the materials of Huizhou merchants.

In the past, merchants' status was the lowest class in society, so they did not have a position in traditional history books. Fragments could be found in pedigrees, local chronicles, notes, novels, essays, inscriptions, documents and files, etc. In 1980s, we compiled *Selected Materials of Huizhou Merchants in the Ming-Qing Dynasties*, which was the first material selection of Huizhou and was published in 1985. This book divides materials into seven categories: Huizhou society in the Ming-Qing Dynasties, sources and accumulation of Huizhou merchants' capital, industries involved for Huizhou merchants, sphere of Huizhou merchants' activities and their business operation modes, outlets of Huizhou merchants' capital, Huizhou merchants' political attitudes, Huizhou merchants and academic culture. Each category is divided further. For instance, the category "outlets of Huizhou merchants' capital" is divided into: land-buying, helping to build ancestral temples and schools, charity devotion, taking part in road-building and water conservancy projects, raising orphans and giving aid to the poor, luxury consumption, property-investment, etc. From these materials a profile of Huizhou merchants can be easily recognized.

2. Investigation of Huizhou Historical Geography and Population   Though there are tremendous materials for study, how to use them is a big problem. Whatever documents or files they are, we must know about the space in which they had been used. On old maps counties were the lowest level.

However, under the county-level, there were still the du-level and the village-level. Only if the two levels are clearly described can we fix a clan's geographical position, then can search neighboring clans and finally can do a community study. In 1987 Dr. Keith Hazelton, who got his doctor degree for Huizhou studies in Princeton University, came to China and co-operated with me to do a study on three counties: Shexian, Xiuning and Jixi. We made 85 forms named as "A village's name change in about 400 hundred years", drew maps of these three counties to the du-level, calculated the area of every "du". Besides, we drew a map on the population of three "dus" and a map about famous clans, with the aid of computer.

3. System Approach Should Be Used in Huizhou Studies   In region study, what should be avoided is only discussing a part while neglecting the whole. A region vs China is part vs whole. In a narrow scope, a region vs a county, du, village, family, person is part vs whole. In a large scope, China vs the world is also part vs whole. Region study must be put in historical coordination, and must be found its position in time and space. Even small as a person or a family or a village, we should see their position in a county or a "du" or the whole country. During the Ming-Qing Dynasties China had met the lash of the west, so region study should be put into the world study in order to get the real characteristics of the region.

In the article "On Huizhou Sea Merchants and Sprout of Chinese Capitalism", I studied these merchants both in Chinese economic and social development and world market, overseas trading. Then I concluded that Huizhou sea merchants had encouraged the sprout of capitalism in China's Jiangnan region. It is generally spoken that China's capitalism sprouted in 16th century, resulting from the productivity development. Mr. Wu Chengming said, Chinese feudal productivity had been mature in the Song Dynasty and did not develop greatly in the Ming Dynasty, so economic structure could not be shaken. Without the structure's change, there would not be development of domestic market. It is well-known that only when the market develops, production scales will expand, and then production organization will change and new production mode will appear. In studying the sprout of China's capitalism, we should also notice the shaping of world market and the smuggling of Chinese sea merchants. It was that smuggling that broke the Ming Dynasty's sea trade prohibition, that related Jiangnan region with world market, and then caused a series of reactions to Jiangnan's society and economy. In world market the most needed were such goods as silk and china, and in these two industries capitalism sprouted first in Jiangnan region. In the reign of Emperors Jiajing and Long Qing, the most powerful merchants were from Huizhou. That these merchants got the leading position could be said a result of their strong blood and geographical relationships. From production to circulation, every part of overseas trading process could see Huizhou merchants, who made great contribution to the sprout of capitalism. In 1990 the journal *Researches in Chinese Economic History* published my paper and the editor added a note: "This article—Two Characteristics of Economic Operation in the Qing Dynasty—and the next one (my article) give some opinions on the sprout of capitalism. They discuss the nature and development level of commodity economy in later feudal China, the understanding economic development law of feudal China, and the relations between production & circulation, internal & external causes, economy & culture etc. We welcome more discussions on the topic." These three relations in fact all involve the relationship between part and whole.

Another example is about my study on Fang clan, which was also done in a macro view. Fang clan was a prominent family from Central Plains into Huizhou to avoid wars in late Western Han Dynasty. I used many local materials and studied the origin, migration, splitting or integrating, evolution of Fang clan in about two thousand years. Then I took a combined method of dynamic & static, micro & macro, studied the relationships between Fang clan and regional society, the relationships between regional society and traditional China. The vicissitude of traditional society contains three parts: one is periodic rise and fall of governing, among which there are always foreign invasions, peasant revolts, tangled fights; two is that traditional agriculture society was relatively static; three is that social transition is intersected with periodic rise and fall of governing, which makes social changes more complicated. My article is centered with these three aspects. First, Fang clan met all changes via changes: they dealt with social disorder by migration. Their migrations roughly synchronized with three large-scale migrations of Chinese prominent families to the South. These families from Central Plains developed Huizhou's culture as well as its economy. They migrated with clans and Huizhou mountains kept their clan system. Second, it was a relatively static society. "Relatively static" means that with population's natural increase, clans would have new migrations; when Fang clan settled in a new place, they quickly restored their clan system and became "static". Clans had also the function of "being static" over "being unrest". In the late Northern Song Dynasty the famous Fang La Uprising began with attacking clan's ruling power and ended with being attacked by clans' power. Then Fang clan quickly rebuilt its governing and restored its "static" condition. Third, the development of commodity economy in 16th century gave the clan an unprecedented shake, whose force exceeded any war or disaster. The clan began to change their migration direction from countryside to cities or towns and to change itself into the mode "big clan and small family". Those corresponding relationships displayed a historical picture of the clan and further of Huizhou society. Though Huizhou was a closed mountain region, every disorder in China in two thousand years would cause reaction in this place.

Another example is about the study of Hu Shi, a Huizhou figure, which also reflects partial and whole. The history of Hu Shi and his family was an epitome of Huizhou society, reflecting the trend of China's transition from traditional to modern society. So to study him is not only to study a man or a family, but to study a region and a country.

4. Cross-discipline Methods   Huizhou studies must avoid being closed and separate, so cross-discipline methods should be taken such as demography,

geography, anthropology, economics, sociology, culturology, linguistics and psychology. As long as methods are helpful, we can use them in study, but should use them properly. Here is an example for anthropology. Mr. Wang Yuquan wrote a letter to me in November 3, 1985 after he read my article "On Huizhou merchants and Feudal Clan Power". "The way of Huizhou merchants could be seen in early modern Chinese overseas. For when people left home and wanted to set their feet firmly in a foreign land, they must depend on each other. Among many relationships, clan was the most powerful. In America there are 'Chinatowns' and among Chinese their ancestral temples such as 'Wo Hing Temple (Chee Kung Tong)' are still kept. In 1939 Hu Shi made a speech about the phenomenon when he was the ambassador in America. He said, 'The spread of culture is like the water of a pound. Put a stone into it and the wave spreads from the center to the edge. Similarly the signs of central culture can be found at the edge.' Your article offers a very a good example for this idea." Huizhou, embraced by mountains, contains signs which disappeared in the center region of ancient China. A field research will help us understand those signs and restructure the past.

We can also use climetric method. The article "The Structure of Huizhou Families and Clans in the Ming-Qing Dynasty" used the method and the statistics told us that under clan system nuclear families were the center and linear families were the supplement in the family structure. Meanwhile clans also expanded and combination of clan branches appeared again and again. Merchants were the key to the shaping of the structure "small family, big clan". Over half of the population went out to do business instead of farming, which dispersed people and restrained population growth. Commercial development encouraged family splitting and avoided some conflictions of big family. Merchants stabled and expanded groups with blood relations for the need of cooperation. On the other hand, this family structure reacted to economy, made society structure dynamic and fluid which was also helpful to keep social stability.

Method of social psychology is also helpful. "Huizhou merchants' Psychology in the Ming-Qing Dynasty" discusses the relationship between psychological integration and the shaping of merchant groups. The two were almost in synch. In 1560 the establishing of Shexian County Guild in Beijing was the symbol of merchants having been combined into gangs, the symbol of group psychology's shaping. The core of psychological intergration was value intergration. Merchants reconstructed old values into a new value which emphasized "business success" and was finally accepted by the whole Huizhou society. Though these merchants differed in family background, knowledge, profession, fortune, status, they had the same psychology—shared values and sense of belonging. We can easily distinguish them from other merchants according to their pursuit of "business success" and "imperial examination success", their behavior of "group help group", their close union of blood and region.

However, what should be paid attention to is that proper methods should also be used properly and suitable for the study objects.

5. Reinforce International Academic Communication and Encourage the Development of Huizhou Studies   Huizhou Studies have become world famous, scholars are attracted to do the research from Europe, America, Japan, Korea, etc. In November, 1983 I attended a meeting on Economy History in the Ming Dynasty and submitted an article "On Huizhou Merchants Being Both Businessmen and Confucians" (co-authored), published in the journal *Chinese History Study*. Professor Yu Yingshi from Princeton University quoted my opinions many times in his article "Shi' and Chinese Culture—Religious Ethics and Merchant Spirits in Early Modern China". In 1987 American scholar Dr. Keith Hazelton (He Jie, his Chinese name) came to China and studied with us for 10 months. This cooperation enabled us to learn better American scholars' methods of sociology or anthropology. Later more foreign scholars came to China and communicated with us, such as Professor Usui Sachiko from Tokyo University of Foreign Studies and Professor Piao Yuanhao from Korea University. Different

methods and perspectives will always trigger inspirations. I have commented Professor Usui Sachiko and regard her perspective valuable to see Chinese social development in breaking the time of 1940. Professor Piao is a vigorous scholar, who I met at an academic meeting. We discussed many problems and learned a lot from each other and have kept in touch with each other after that. Two years after *History Study* published my article on Fang clan, the journal also published Professor Piao's article on "Fang clan", which reached a high level. We should realize this field is also competitive. The center of Huizhou Studies should be in China and more communication will be helpful.

6. Region-comparing Study Suzhou is a good case. This city and Huizhou had been in Jiangnan administrative region for a long time. The two interacted and communicated with each other deeply in the social transition from 16th to 19th centuries. Economically, Suzhou's social structure gradually changed and slowly entered in a transition with the development of economy and population. While in Huizhou, the prevailing clan system constrained its transition. Huizhou merchants' business activities encouraged Suzhou's transition, but their behavior of carrying fortunes back to their hometown consolidated the old order. Culturally, the two were both advanced in education and philosophy. Huizhou merchants brought Suzhou's city culture into Huizhou and changed Huizhou society, at the same time they brought clan system or other cultures into Suzhou, which permeated into Suzhou's social life. Region-comparing study is very meaningful. Even two regions are in the same zone, they will differ greatly in economy and social development for their inner structure, culture, values, behavior patterns, etc. Discussing these differences and causes will provide us a new field for Region History Studies and help us learn the whole country more deeply too.

Published in *History World*, No. 3, 1999
Written by Tang Lixing
Translated by Wang Yangwen

Chapter 4 Multi-disciplinary Values of Huizhou Studies

Huizhou culture is a typically feudal folk culture which originated from Huizhou region (six counties Shexian, Xiuning, Yixian, Qimen, Jixi, Wuyuan are included and had been governed by Huizhou House from the year 1120 to 1949), and had a great influence on whole China. It is the sum of material and spiritual civilization created by Huizhou people. Huizhou Studies whose objects are Huizhou culture rose in 1920s, developed in 1980s and become internationally known today.

Huizhou Studies are not only regional studies, or history studies. Because the Studies' objects have outstanding characteristics, the Studies have also very important values in many disciplines such as philosophy, ethics, aesthetics, law, cultural anthropology. In the following we will discuss it further.

Ⅰ. Huizhou Culture after the Song Dynasty

After the Song Dynasty China stepped into a new phase—late feudalism. Politically, the centralization of power was reinforced, imperial examination system was fully implemented and the process of civilianization quickened. Ideologically, Cheng-Zhu Neo-Confucianism was made official philosophy, while the Enlightenment and anti-rationalism uprised in the Ming-Qing Dynasties. Culturally, the invention of movable-type printing encouraged cultural secularization. Economically, the development of commercial economy brought the sprout of capitalism and social transition. Most noticeably, China's center was in the North before the Song Dynasty, but moved to Jiangnan region after that. This move made Jiangnan region full of vigor in economy and culture. Huizhou culture rose under such background, had its ups and downs with feudalism's development and decline. In a thousand years it had great performance in philosophy, arts, literature, technology, publication, medicine, language, etc. What had been acknowledged as influential by society and history are Xin'an Confucianism, Xin'an Medicine, Xin'an Painting, Huizhou Academia, Huizhou book-engraving, Huizhou dialects, Huizhou buildings and gardens, Huizhou-style Bonsai Art, Huizhou merchants, Huizhou Opera, Huizhou Cuisine, etc.

Huizhou culture is not only a regional culture, but a culture having more values and a higher status.

First, it is an epitome of late feudal China. Its achievements were all essence of corresponding fields and reflected mainstream culture in these fields, so it has the value of "sample". For instance, Neo-Confucianism is Confucianism's performance in this period. The ancestral home of its two founders (Cheng Hao and Cheng Yi) and its representative Zhu Xi is Huizhou. Xin'an Confucianism aimed at defending, inheriting and developing Zhuxi's theory, so to study it is to typically study Cheng-Zhu's ideas. As for Huizhou academia, a theory of plain-learning, had a very high position for over three hundred years and even had influence in May Fourth period, especially Hu Shi. Another example is Xin'an Painting School, which was the representative one of Chinese painting after the Song Dynasty. To study it is to study Chinese painting's development, influence and inheritance. Similarly to do Huizhou studies is to study a sample of late feudal China.

Second, Huizhou culture is a real reflection of rural society and folk culture of late feudal China. China was an agricultural country, whose main areas were rural and whose population was mostly in the countryside. Huizhou was a typically rural region, mountainous region, far away from emperors and nobility. Its culture developed from folk people's work and life, and so reflected the real situation of Chinese countryside. The culture's initial motive was rather for people themselves and their survival than for the ruling class. The creation was rather for man's comfort than for eternity and greatness. So the culture was not imperial, academic or civil, but rural in this sense.

Third, Huizhou culture is quite systematic in structure. In a thousand years people here had created a complete cultural system. All elements in this system were dependent on each other or interrelated with each other. On the other hand, this unity could be also found in its duration. This culture rose in the South Song Dynasty, peaked in the Ming-Qing Dynasties and declined in the late Qing Dynasty.

Moreover, Huizhou culture has a great charm based on a fact that it is not a culture based on ruins, legends, archaeological discoveries, but based on live reality. For it has a large quantity of cultural legacies. Besides technology and customs there are still two kinds of important relics: one is over 5,000 surface relics—old villages, towns, houses, ancestral temples, towers, bridges, memorial archways, etc. Among them two old villages Xidi and Hongcun were even listed in World Cultural Heritages by UNESCO. The other one is numerous documents and files. In 1950s over 100,000 documents were discovered and called "the fifth discovery in 20th century" (the others are Oracles, Bamboo Slips and Silks, Dun Huang Documents, Files of the Ming-Qing Dynasties). In late 20th century libraries, museums, colleges, institutions collected about 250,000 Huizhou documents, while there are still 10,000 ones scattering in some other places. These original materials recorded people's production, communication and life from the South Song Dynasty to 1980's. Third, a large number of legends and oral materials are still circulated in people's mouth. Though Huizhou culture declined in the late Qing Dynasty, its history didn't end at that time. For ideology and culture always have a strong inertance, so even now this region still keeps many resources for field research.

II. Value of Huizhou Culture on Other Disciplines

These characteristics of Huizhou culture decide that it is not only valuable for Huizhou Studies, but for many other disciplines. It provides us the potential to do real and live research in many other fields and discover new academic room. The following are some typical disciplines which can absorb nutrition from Huizhou Studies.

1. Philosophy   Philosophy is not only philosophers' ideas but the reflection of an age's spirit which is based on mass consciousness. Therefore we study philosophy, we should study the base at the same time. Huizhou Studies give us a way to learn late feudal China's the most basic ideology. By doing this, we can base our research on the concept of "the masses are the real makers of history", and so cover traditional study's shortage of only focusing on representatives or masters.

2. Ethics   In ethics, moral norm and moral judgment are the two most important questions. In ancient China, human relations were decided by Confucian ethics which was officially acknowledged. But when it came to peasants and the rural areas, ethic practice performed differently in different levels and showed great diversity. This problem should be studied in Chinese ethics research. Huizhou is a very good example for a down-to-earth study instead of a from-top-to-down study. In this sense our study can show a real picture of Chinese feudal ethics, which has historical and practical significance.

3. Aesthetics   We can study Chinese traditional aesthetics through some giants and their works such as Liu Xie's *The Literary Mind and the Carving of Dragons* or Wang Guowei and his ideas. However these can only represent aesthetic consciousness and judgment of scholars, but not of ordinary people. While through Huizhou culture and its legacies, we can learn better ordinary people's aesthetics in a concrete way. Thousands of ancient ancestral temples, ancient folk houses were designed and built by native craftsmen, and directly reflected folk people's aesthetic interest and pursuit. There are also numerous brick carvings, wood carvings and stone carvings created by folk people. Furthermore, why Huizhou-style Bonsai Art and Xin'an Painting were so popular in the Ming-Qing Dynasties, these questions provide new room for aesthetic study on folk people.

4. Law   Ancient Chinese laws were rulers' laws, such as "Criminal Laws of the Ming Dynasty" or "Laws of the Qing Dynasty". Making laws and how to carry out them are different stories. From the state to officials to

folk people, every time the laws were carried out in a different way. What is more important, there were always customary laws which was the real ruling laws among folk people. Even state laws would finally turn to customary laws. This phenomenon attracted academic attention long ago. Huizhou is a good case in this sense. It was a "land of rites", also a "contract society" and a "litigation society". In the past Huizhou people would not solve their conflicts by violence, but by negotiation. Their disputes would always be mediated first by contracts, then by clan rules or village rules, then at last by law suits. Its society had been stable for over a thousand years partly because it had a complete inner mediation system. As a result, numerous contracts and documents were left in Huizhou's history, which is a large fortune to study customary laws and the way how state laws were carried out.

5. Cultural Anthropology   Located in the south of Anhui province, Huizhou has a good natural condition—Xin'an River, Mount Huangshan, Guniujiang Nature Reserve, Qiyun Mountain, etc. With a relatively separate and closed geography, a population of about a million, and with an area of only 10,000 square kilometers, Huizhou developed an outstanding culture, which had commonness with general Chinese culture and showed its uniqueness on the other hand. For instance, Huizhou-style building art. It not only kept traditional Chinese living habits, reflected traditional Chinese concept of "Unity between man and nature", but also contained Huizhou people's pursuit and understanding toward human environment, natural environment and the unity of the two. More examples (such as Xin'an Medicine, Huizhou-style Bonsai Art, Three Huizhou-style Carvings, Huizhou Four Treasures of the Study, Huizhou Cuisine) can also be found to have both national characteristics, practical or aesthetic values, and at the same time to be closely related with this region's geography and natural resources. Besides, there is also an interesting phenomenon "one clan living together"—people in a village having a same surname, different villages having different surnames, every village having its own story of change or

development, villages with different surnames having communication or disputes with each other. These examples are all valuable for cultural anthropology study.

In a word, Huizhou culture is a regional culture, but not only regional; Huizhou Studies are regional studies, but not only regional. That is why they attract scholars from many other countries to study and have become more and more internationally known.

Published in *Exploration and Contention*, No. 9, 2004
Written by Liu Boshan
Translated by Wang Yangwen

Part II
Huizhou Culture

Chapter 5 The Basic Concepts and Historical Status of Huizhou Culture

Huizhou Studies focus on the history of the Huizhou society.[①] Despite the fact that it is currently popular among both domestic and foreign academic circles, they still don't have a clear understanding of its definition and status. This paper is attempting to make some efforts at it.

I. The Definition of Huizhou Culture

To study Huizhou Culture, we should first have a clear definition of it, on which the academic circle still has not reached an agreement. According to the author's understanding, the so-called Huizhou Culture is about the typical feudal culture which occurred and existed in the history of Huizhou area as well as its influence in other places. Thus Huizhou Studies at least cover the following four aspects.

At first, the so-called Huizhou Culture refers to the culture within the scope of Huizhou region in history. Its geographical area covers 6 counties,

---

[①] Cao Tiansheng, Overview of Domestic Hui Studies in the 20th Century [J], *Journal of Renmin University of China*, 1995(1).

namely, Shexian, Xiuning, Yixian, Qimen, Jixi and Wuyuan.

Secondly, the history of Huizhou at least includes five or six thousand years. This period is also classified as the time span of Huizhou Culture. But its typical stage refers to the period after the third year under the reign of Emperor Xuan He in the Northern Song Dynasty (AD 1121). At that time, the emperor set up Huizhou Prefecture. Then the culture developed rapidly here and reached its summit during the Ming and Qing Dynasties. However, when we speak of Huizhou Culture nowadays, we can't depart it from its earlier formation and later development.

Thirdly, Huizhou Culture covers not only the local culture in Huizhou area, but also the culture that originated from Huizhou. The foundation of it is that people must have a strong identity of Huizhou. Take Zhu Xi as an example. Although he lived in Fujian and also completed his main work there, he still regarded Huizhou as his hometown and always called himself "Zhu Xi from Xin'an area" (an alternative name of Huizhou, translator's note). Meanwhile, people in Huizhou were all proud of Zhu Xi and were, consciously or unconsciously, deeply influenced by him in many aspects, such as ideology, morality, ethics, and social behaviors. Therefore, his thoughts and academic activities can be seen as part of Huizhou Culture.

Fourthly, Huizhou Culture is a general concept in fact, which not only refers to academic theory, but also involves business, patriarchal ethics, spiritual beliefs, customs, literature, social economy, land system, historical figures and so on.

This definition of Huizhou Culture considers the historical culture of Huizhou as an independent entirety with specific geographic space, limited time span and definitive contents. In this way, the object of Huizhou Studies can be clearer. Thus the author is against the opinion that Huizhou Studies (or Huizhouology) is only concerned about the occurrence, the rise and fall of the culture with five characters (rich, brilliant, unique, typical and local) in the poverty-stricken mountain area named Huizhou during the late period of the Chinese feudal society. ①

It is unwise to abandon the historic part before the Song Dynasty or after the First Opium War for Huizhou Studies. If we do it that way, people will be confused about the origin of Huizhou Culture and how it turned to be what it was later. History is an organic whole, and thus the span from the Southern Song Dynasty to the Late Qing Dynasty is just part of Huizhou Culture rather than the whole story.

In fact, Huizhou Culture means a developing process of the history and culture of Huizhou area. At an early stage, the aboriginal inhabitants were Yue People and the earliest form of culture here was what the author called "the early Yue Culture of Jiangnan area", with the specific time span from the ancient times to the Spring and Autumn Period and the Warring States Period. At the beginning, it was hard to distinguish the historic culture of Huizhou area from the national culture of ancient China. But then the Shanyue Culture occurred in the Middle and Late Warring States Period and then evolved gradually. Until the Three Kingdoms Period, the society and culture of Huizhou began to separate from the national culture. However, Huizhou Culture once suffered a dead period when Yue People went into the mountains and farmed in a 'slash-and-burn' way. Those Yue People were brave and aggressive, marked with the trace of semi-primitive jungle society. This special period was also called "The Dark Days". ② Then the Xin'an Cultural Period came. It covered more than 1,000 years from the last years of Eastern Han Dynasty to the Southern Song Dynasty. At that time, the society and culture of Huizhou developed fast, benefiting from the numerous immigrants who brought about a variety of changes in population, economy, culture and so on. After a long time, Han People integrated local

---

① Zhao Huafu. The Object and Significance of Hui Studies [J], Compiled by Zhang Maixian, Liu Boshan, et al. *Proceedings of Hui Studies*[C], 1994(10).

② Ye Xian'en, *The Rural Society and Tenant System of Huizhou Area in the Ming and the Qing Dynasties* [M], Hefei: Anhui People's Publishing House, 1983.

Yue People finally in the Southern Song Dynasty. Then people in Huizhou demonstrated obviously feudal features. Meanwhile, the small-landed but densely-populated circumstance led to the Second Moving wave in Huizhou, a process of migration. It worked mainly through two ways—imperial examination and business activities. People paid great attention to education those days. "During the time of Huang Chao Uprising, many gentries from the Central Plain moved into Huizhou to escape from wars. Then some of them chose to settle here and gave publicity to the importance of education. During the Song Dynasty, Huizhou turned to be both a cradle of talents and a district of culture."① Thanks to the immigrants, Huizhou became famous for numerous talented people and highly-developed literature. In those days, the education was so popular in Huizhou that students, teachers and books seemed to be everywhere...Thus Huizhou enjoyed the cultural fame as "Southeast Zoulu".② In addition, Huizhou was also the cradle of Neo-Confucianism of Cheng-Zhu. That's why people also considered this place as the hometown of Cheng and Zhu.③ And Neo-Confucianism of Cheng-Zhu, especially the theories of Zhu Xi, was the core of Huizhou Culture. Therefore, Huizhou Culture is only a stage of the long history of Huizhou. Within it, Xin'an culture is the base, but not the whole.④

Ⅱ. The Basic Contents of Huizhou Culture

Huizhou Culture arose from the Southern Dynasty, developed in the Yuan Dynasty, and flourished in the Ming and the Qing Dynasties. Its complete system, rich contents, unique characteristics are demonstrated at least in the following four respects.

---

① Chun Xiluoyuan, The 1st Volume of *Xin'an Chorography* [Z].
② Zhao Fang, *The Diaries in Shangshan Academy* [G].
③ Liu Boshan, The Origins of Neo-Confucianism of Cheng-Zhu [J], *Exploration and Free Views*, 2000(3).
④ Liu Boshan, The Rise of Cultural Studies on Huizhou: Some Ideas of the Study[J], *Huizhou Academy of Social Sciences*, 1989 (1).

Firstly, after the Southern Song Dynasty, people in Huizhou made achievements almost in all cultural fields and created remarkable cultural wealth. Besides, they established their own features and styles. For example, in business, Huizhou Merchants were very successful. In philosophy, the Neo-Confucianism of Zhu Xi was the best representative. This theory was named after its creator, Zhu Xi. There were also some other typical scholars in this circle, like Cheng Xun from Wuyuan County, Cheng Yongqi, Wang Shen, Cheng Dachang (all from Xiuning County). "In the Ming and Qing Dynasties, Neo-Confucianism of Zhu Xi was prevalent all around China. But those who learned it best mostly came from Xin'an area". ① Speaking of textology, the Huizhou Puxue, or Jiang-Dai Puxue, had extremely great influence. Jiang Fan, a scholar in Qing Dynasty, once said, "Three-Huizhou Studies became popular in the Wu language-speaking area, then Jiang Yong and Dai Zhen improved it. Thanks to them, the sinology became prevalent again."② In the field of painting, Xin'an Painting, established by Jiang Tao from Shexian County, was a famed branch that time. Huang Binhong, also from Shexian County, was a representative in modern times. According to statistics, there occurred more than 60 famous painters only in the history of less than 200 years from the reign of Emperor Wan Li in the Ming Dynasty to that of Emperor Qian Long in the Qing Dynasty. Huang Binhong once said that the skills of these painters even surpassed those from Jiangnan Area. ③ Saying seal cutting, it was flourishing in Huizhou during the Ming and Qing Dynasties, with some outstanding artists like He Zhen and Huang Shiling. ④ And the Huizhou-style book-carving, beginning at the Southern Song Dynasty and peaking at the Ming and Qing Dynasties, was another extraordinary

---

① *Xiuning Chorography* [Z]. The edition in the Reign of Emperor Kang Xi in the Qing Dynasty.
② Jiang Fan, *The Chronological Record of Scholars in the Qing Dynasty* [G].
③ Li Minghui, On Xin'an Painting [J], *Anhui Wenbo*.
④ Zheng Qingtu, He Zhen and Hui Seal Cutting [J], *The Inaugural Issue of the Serial Journals of Hui Studies*.

cultural achievement. At that time, if people need engrave books, they would give priority to a craftsman from Shexian County.① The Huizhou-style book-carving was one the "Top Three Engraving Books", with the others from Changzhou area and Suzhou area respectively. For block print, Huizhou also took unique position in the history of it. During the reign of Emperor Wan Li, people even stated, "all stories in operas can be the subjects print" and "the best craftsmen of it usually came from Shexian County, among them, the first choice was those from Huang's Family". The statistics displayed there were more than 100 people in Huang's Family only from Qiu village in Shexian County, making a living by block print during the period under the reign of Emperor Wan Li in the Ming Dynasty to the early Qing Dynasty.② Referring to opera, Huizhou Opera could never be missed. Under the reign of Emperor Qian Long in the Qing Dynasty, Four Huizhou Opera Troupes, as the predecessor of Peking Opera, were summoned into Beijing. Their performance shocked the whole city later. Then by the reign of Emperor Dao Guang, Huizhou Opera had become a regular play in performances.③ With regard to architecture, Huizhou-style Architecture was excellent. And in the field of traditional Chinese medicine, Xin'an Medicine played an important role. Records show that there were at least 668 famous doctors in Huizhou from the Eastern Jin Dynasty to the last years of the Qing Dynasty, and 225 of them wrote 461 medical books in total. These doctors made huge contribution to the Chinese medical history.④ For weiqi (a traditional Chinese chess game, translator's note), numerous weiqi players came from Huizhou. During the Ming and Qing Dynasties, Xin'an

---

① *Huizhou Chorography* [Z], The Edition in the Reign of Emperor Jia Jing in the Ming Dynasty.

② Zhou Wu, *The Proceedings of Woodcut Painting of Huizhou* [C], Anhui People's Publishing House, 1983.

③ Operatic Stories, *In the Reign of Emperor Daoguang of the Qing Dynasty* [G].

④ Li Jiren & Hu Jianbei, *Famous Doctors in Xin'an* [M], Anhui Science and Technology Publishing House, 1990.

School in weiqi was as famous as Yongjia School and Jiangshi School. Cheng Ruliang, from Shexian County, was a first-class weiqi player of Xin'an School. Wang Shizhen (a well-known litterateur in the Ming Dynasty, translator's note) even called Cheng Ruliang "the best player in the Ming Dynasty" in his book. Another man named Cheng Lanru from Shexian County was one of "The Four Grand Masters" in this circle while the others were Fan Xiping, Shi Dingan and Liang Weijin'.① In modern times, the brothers named Guo Tishen and Guo Xuchu became the new masters. In addition, the traditional crafts in Huizhou enjoyed a widespread reputation and covered various fields. For examples: Huizhou owned two kinds of crafts of The Four Treasures of Chinese Study. They were Huimo and Sheyan. Before the Yuan Dynasty, Cheng Xing Paper and Wang Libo Brush had also been the precious heritage of traditional crafts. Speaking of Cooking, Huizhou Cuisine, as one of The Excellent Eight Cuisines in China, was famous for paying great attention to the quality of the food and its unique techniques. And talking to carving, the high level of block-carving, wood-carving and stone-carving here won themselves the name of "The Three Outstanding Carvings of Huizhou". What's more, Huizhou Potted Landscape and some others crafts should all be mentioned. All these were significant parts of Huizhou Culture. Meanwhile, they were also the wealth in each circle and had represented the top level for a long time.

  Then, although some cultural fields in Huizhou didn't form their own styles, they still cultivated a number of prominent scholars and outstanding figures. For instance, natural science in Huizhou fostered a class of talents. In math, Cheng Dawei (1533—1606) from Tunxi area wrote the professional book *Suan Fa Zong Tong* and his biggest contribution was developing the calculation method in this book. Another achievement of him was to improve abacus rhymes, which radiated indelible light all over the world. In physics,

---

  ① Wu Xiaoting, The Study on the Xin'an School in Weiqi During the Ming and Qing Dynasties [J], *Huizhou Tongxun*.

Zheng Fuguang, a physicist from Shexian County, made tremendous contribution in optics. He also wrote the most critical book of optics in China which was called *Jing Jing Leng Chi*. Some people even claimed that the history of natural science of Huizhou could reveal that of Anhui Province. ① As far as poetry and literature are concerned, it is difficult to say that there once existed an independent school in Huizhou, but there was at least a poet-and-writer group. Zhu Xi, for example, was both a poet and litterateur. His poems represented the top level in the Southern Song Dynasty. ② More than 1,200 poems of him came down in history. Another person called Fang Hui from Qimen county established a similar style of heroic poetry with Xin Qiqi (one of the most famous Chinese poets, translator's note). Wang Daoku from Shexian County in the Ming Dynasty was a successful official and a gifted litterateur as well. The public regarded him as one of "the Five Representatives" of the classical school of literature in the Mid-Ming Dynasty. Besides, the grass-root poets were another influential source. Wang Shizhen thought Wu Feixiong and Cheng Mengyang, both from Xin'an area, were the best representatives in the Ming Dynasty. ③ During the Qing Dynasty, there were more than 200 poets and more than 10,000 poems in Huizhou area. In addition, Wang Maoying (1798—1865), as a brilliant economic expert from Shexian County, was the only man recorded in the book *Das Kapital* written by Marx. In 1337 A.D., he gave a famous piece of advice to Zhu Yuanzhang (the first emperor of Ming Dynasty, translator's note), saying, "Build higher walls, collect more army provisions and claim to be a king later". This suggestion played a vital role in the establishment of the Ming Dynasty. Moreover, Yu Zhengxie from Shexian County was a notable historian in the Qing Dynasty. And in the

---

① Zhang Binglun. The Development and Its Reasons of Anhui Science in the Ming and the Qing Dynasties [J], *The Inaugural Issue of The Serial Journals of Hui Studies*.
② Hu Yinglin, *Criticisms of Poetry* [G].
③ Poetry of Two Common Men [Z], The edition in the Qing Dynasty, stored in Qimen County Museum now.

field of opera, there were numerous remarkable drama writers like Zhang Zhizhen (1518—1595) from Qimen county and Wang Yanna (1573—1619) from Xiuning County. They, especially Wang Yanna, drew on others' strenghths and finally developed their own style. When it came to linguistics, such experts as Zhu Xi, Jiang Yong and Daizhen contributed a lot. In addition to them, a number of ordinary researchers also made some achievements. A typical example in recent days is the Center for Huizhou Studies of Anhui University. This center sets up a special collection room named "Boshan Library" for the research of the local dialect of Huizhou. ① A tremendous number of literal materials are reserved here, including the writings of Hu Zhaoqian and Jiang Xianglan, both from Wuyuan County. ② The clear classification and the rich materials prove that the research of Huizhou language is remarkable. What's more, Huizhou education boasts a long history with many eminent educators such as Zhu Xi, Zheng Yu (1298—1358), Zhao Fang (1319—1369) and Wang Kekuan (1304—1372). After them came Tao Xingzhi (1891—1946) from Shexian County and Hu Shi (1891—1962). Both of them once promoted the advancement of Chinese education. Thus their thoughts constitute not only Huizhou Culture but the international culture as well.

And the contents of Huizhou Culture should also consist of some unique local cultural phenomena because of its specific geographical conditions and some other factors. For instance, Huizhou was known as a contract society because hundreds of thousands of the well-preserved folk contracts had been left here. ③ The earliest pieces were from the Song Dynasty. The most famous contracts were, however, from the Ming and Qing Dynasties. And

---

① The writer once donated more than 11,000 Huizhou historical documents, collected before 2000, to Anhui University on May 19 in 2001, and then the university established "Boshan Study" to store those documents exclusively.

② All the four manuscripts belong to the same family in Wuyuan County. There are some other similar materials like manuscripts of Hu Zhaoqian and account books.

③ Liu Boshan, The Reserve and Protection of Huizhou Documents [N]. *Guangming Daily* (the Theoretical Edition), Nov. 11, 2001.

as far as the author knows, the latest three were signed in 1955, 1965 and 1985 respectively. ① The contents of these contracts involved land sale, work contract, convention, loan, etc. Their astonishing amount, wide time span and systematic contents made Huizhou a typical contract society and could help to reveal the social relationships of local residents better. In fact, most of the so-called Huizhou inhabitants were immigrants at that time. They lived together with the same clan members. Zhao Jishi from Xiuning County said, "Xin'an area was superior in dozens of customs. For example, people would never destroy an ancient tomb and even members from a sparsely-populated clan could unite as one. Furthermore, everyone was clear about his big family tree. The social stratification kept stable to make sure that a master was always a master just as a servant was always the same. ② People in Huizhou took the blood tie seriously. There was an old saying, "The ethics were the most critical things, and they depended on revising pedigree books". "If a man didn't revise the pedigree of his clan in time, he would be marked with impiety."③ In addition to all this, the social and economic structure, the special customs and beliefs, the unique local languages and the like should also be considered part of Huizhou Culture.

Ⅲ. The Reasons for the Rise of Huizhou Culture

Huizhou Culture could keep thriving for hundreds of years mainly for the following internal factors.

The first one is the economic base established by Huizhou Merchants, a group of merchants from Huizhou area. At the very beginning, they did business because of their harsh living conditions. It is known that Huizhou

---

① Liu Boshan, The Classification and Primary Research of the 1st Batch of Huizhou Historical Documents in Boshan Study (Volume I) [J]. *Hui Studies*, Hefei: Anhui University Press, 2001.
② Zhao Jishi, *Jiyuan Record* [G], Volumes I & II.
③ *The Pedigree of the Chen's in Wuxi area of Qimen* [Z], Stored in the Boshan Study of Anhui University.

was a mountain area and thus the lack of farmland was a common problem. "Even the rich were short of farmland." "This area was barren... Harvest was poor here. Therefore, it was impossible to survive here only by farming." ① The supply of food always depended on importing. And things became more serious after the Tang Dynasty and the Southern Song Dynasty. Two big waves of immigrants caused by the wars led to the sharp increase of the population. Therefore, people were forced to go outside seeking resources as a businessman. ②"While the majority of residents in ancient China were engaged in farming, people from Huizhou area relied on trading." ③ There was a saying that a man who was born in Huizhou for the present life must have done evil in his previous existence. When he grew up to about 13 years old, he had to leave home and learned to be a businessman. Another reason for the emergence of Huizhou Merchants was connected with the local economic structure and the developed water systems. The economic structure made people unable to live a self-sufficient and self-contained life, so they were engaged in trading to meet their basic needs. ④ In early times, Huizhou Merchants mainly exchanged rice, cloth, salt and other things with tea, woods and such products as lacquer ware, tusche, Xuan Paper and inkstone, just within Huizhou area. After the Ming Dynasty, they began to do business all over China and developed to an influential business group. In the Qing Dynasty, Huizhou Merchants played the leading role in The Ten Great Trading Groups in ancient China. They mainly traded salt, lumber, tea and pawning. At that time, Huizhou Merchants' trail could be found almost everywhere. It seemed that there was no town without Huizhou

---

① Gu Yanwu, *The Political Geography of Different Chinese Regions During the Ming Dynasty* [G].

② Xu Chengyao, *The 28th Volume of Essays of Shexian County* [G].

③ *Huizhou Chorography* [Z], The edition in the Reign of Emperor Kang Xi in the Qing Dynasty.

④ Liu Boshan. *The Introduction to Hui Merchants* [C], Compiled by Huangshan People's Political Consultative Committee of Literature and History, Huangshan: Huangshan Publishing House.

Merchants. One major point to distinguish them from other merchants was that they paid great attention to education and took the Confucian moral as their own standard of behaviors. Their management was greatly influenced by Confucianism and they always took honesty and integrity as the business moral. In this way, they got ahead in business and accumulated remarkable wealth. "It seemed that talented merchants were very common in Huizhou area, and even the business giants were not rare." With their assets they extended reproduction, joined in art or literary activities, and invested in education. In fact, education became so important to Huizhou Merchants that they even thought if a rich man didn't care about education, it was meaningless for him to possess money. ① So they devoted to developing education for the sake of enriching the knowledge and moral spirits of their children and others. Above all, they were also fond of building their hometowns. All this actually laid a solid economic foundation for the development of Huizhou Culture.

Another factor was the well-developed education in Huizhou area. There were numerous educational institutions here in history. Take academy for an example. Statistics showed that there were more than 260 academies successively from the Song Dynasty to the Qing Dynasty here. Most of them were built in the Ming and Qing Dynasties, with only 11 built in the Song Dynasty and 21 in the Yuan Dynasty. ② In January of the 8th year under the reign of Emperor Hong Wu in the Ming Dynasty, the emperor issued an order about establishing village schools to spread Confucian culture and civilize the common people. At that time, Huizhou set up 462 village schools. ③ Then up to the reign of Emperor Kang Xi in the Qing Dynasty, the number

---

① The 2nd Volume of *The Pedigree of the Bao's in Shexian County*.
② Liu Bingzheng, *The Transforming History of Huizhou Academies* [C], The 1st Volume of the Proceedings of Hui Studies.
③ The Educational Notes of Huizhou [J], *The Supplementary Issue of Huixue Tongxun*.

had increased to 562.① In addition, old-style private schools were more universal. "Even people who lived in remote places also learned hard. You could hear the sounds of reading wherever there were people." Thanks to the developed education, the talented came out successively. According to Ye Xian'en, an expert in Huizhou Studies, the number of Jingshi (an appellation of advanced scholar in the past, translator's note) had reached 624 in the Song Dynasty, 392 in the Ming Dynasty (1.55% of the total) and 226 in the Qing Dynasty(0.86% of the total) in the range of Huizhou natives.② If those who lived here temporarily were also taken into consideration, there would be more. Meanwhile, the number of Zhuangyuan (No. 1 in the imperial examination, translator's note) was also astonishing. For instance, there came 17 Zhuangyuan in the Qing Dynasty, which took up 14.9% of the total.③ In those years, Huizhou boasted the second largest number of Zhuangyuan while the No. 1 area was Suzhou. So it was common that several advanced scholars just came from the same big family. The highly-developed education gave birth to Huizhou Culture.

The next key reason was Neo-Confucianism. Huizhou was known as the "Southeast Zoulu" and was the birthplace of Neo-Confucianism of Cheng-Zhu. Its philosophy could be found in the book *The Cradle of Neo-Confucianism of Cheng-Zhu* and was popular in the Ming Dynasty, but venerated most in Shexian County. Neo-Confucianism of Cheng-Zhu developed from Cheng Brothers' Neo-Confucianism. Since both Cheng Brothers and Zhu Xi were closely related to Huizhou, it was regarded as

---

① The 7th Volume of *Huizhou Chorography* [Z], the Edition in the Reign of Emperor Kang Xi in the Qing Dynasty.

② Ye Xian'en, *The Rural Society and Tenant System of Huizhou Area in the Ming and the Qing Dynasties* [M], Hefei: Anhui People's Publishing House, 1983.

③ Wu Jianhua, The Zhuangyuan from Huizhou in the Qing Dynasty [J], *The Supplementary Issue of Huizhou Tongxun*.

their hometown.① Relatively speaking, Zhu Xi's philosophy was more significant to Huizhou area. Zhu Xi went back to Huizhou twice in his life and paid tribute to his ancestors. During the days in Huizhou, he delivered lectures. He cultivated at least 12 excellent scholars among his students. Zhu Xi also wrote poems or inscriptions for those from Zhu Family. The author has kept a precious stone inscription with the words "yuan fei yu yue" (playing one's proper role, translator's note) written by him. In Huizhou, people regarded Zhu Xi as their common teacher and were proud to be his followers.② Huizhou Merchants also respected him very much. Not only did his theory work on officials, students and merchants, but also on the public. Thus Confucian thoughts, together with Buddhism and Taoism, made Huizhou more feudal. Thus Neo-Confucianism was the core of Huizhou Culture.

Finally, Huizhou Culture has formed its unique characteristics for at least three reasons. First of all, it is affected by the specific local geographical conditions. Secondly, the immigrant culture contributes a lot to it. And the different aspects of Huizhou Culture itself also influence one another.

Ⅳ. The Historic Position of Huizhou Culture

Huizhou Culture, as a regional culture, is a product of the fully-developed feudal society. Therefore, feudalism is one of its essential characteristics. And Huizhou Merchants, as a basic part of Huizhou culture, are typical of a feudal business group. Many of their behaviors reflected the feudal culture. For instance, they combined Confucianism with their business and kept strong blood tie. In ancient times, the education in Huizhou could generally be regarded as a miniature of the feudal education. The choice of teaching materials, the arrangement of courses or teaching aims all met the requirements of

---

① The Preface to *The Hometown of Cheng-Zhu* [G], the Edition in the Reign of Emperor Yong Zheng in the Qing Dynasty, stored in Huangshan City Museum now.
② The Preface to *Wu's Family Rules* [Z].

the Chinese feudal society. A good example was that Neo-Confucianism of Cheng-Zhu, the core of Huizhou Culture, was the official philosophy at that time. Obviously, Huizhou Culture served the Chinese feudal society foundamentally. As a result, it declined with the demise of the feudal society in the last years of the Qing Dynasty. Its glory has become the past.

However, Huizhou Culture, which once remained prosperous for hundreds of years, can't be ignored in the history of the Chinese culture. The feudal culture was the crucial part of the traditional Chinese culture and when it reached its peak in the Southern Song Dynasty, the so-called Huizhou Culture thrived again. So Huizhou Culture was typical of both a projection and an epitome of the late period of the Chinese feudal society. That's to say, Huizhou Culture was a specimen of the feudal culture. This could be well proved by the inherent correspondence between the development of the Chinese feudal philosophy and the Huizhou local philosophy.

Confucian culture was always the subject of the traditional Chinese philosophy and its development went through several stages. Originally, it was mainly about the thoughts of Confucius and Mencius. The next stage was the theory of Manifest Destiny created by Dong Zhongshu (a great thinker, politician and educator in the Western Han Dynasty, translator's note). Then in the Song Dynasty, Dong's theory was challenged by Buddhism. To compete with the foreign theory, a new theory, namely Neo-Confucianism, was born. ① It was more systematic and rigorous than those before. Although its founders were Cheng Hao and Cheng Yi, it was Zhu Xi who epitomized the thoughts. After this stage, Confucianism declined, while the enlightenment thought and anti-Confucianism became the new mainstream. The last stage kept for hundreds of years and could also be divided into two periods. The former one was the birth period of the enlightenment thought, which was fighting against Confucianism and Feudalism indirectly. The latter period was the May 4 New Cultural Movement Period. The main difference lay in

---

① Lyu Simian, The Outline of Confucianism [J], *Confucianism of Sanyuan School*.

the fact that people were against Confucianism directly and asked for science and democracy explicitly.

From the above-mentioned stage of Neo-Confucianism, Confucian culture started to have affinity with Huizhou. This area, as the hometown of Zhu Xi and Cheng Brothers, gave birth to a new branch, namely Xin'an Neo-Confucianism. It was aimed at inheriting and developing Neo-Confucianism of Cheng-Zhu and could be seen as the typical epitome and projection of the former. At the early stage of the enlightenment movement, Huizhou inhabitants opposed Confucianism and Feudalism but often under the name of the feudal culture. Among those opponents, Dai Zhen was the most recognized figure. Duan Yucai once said, "Dai Zhen did his best to fight against Cheng-Zhu's Neo-Confucianism". ① Liang Qichao thought Dai Zhen was trying to replace rationalism philosophy with emotion philosophy, which was similar with the essence of Renaissance thought. ② Duan considered the thoughts of Dai a revolution in the ideological circle during the period of 800 years and the voice was buried in 2,000 years. ③ Sun Shuping also pointed out that Dai Zhen was the one who fought with the feudal ethics most firmly before the May 4 New Cultural Movement. ④ Then in this movement, Hu Shi, a native resident of Huizhou, was one of the leaders. With Ph. D degrees from 30 different fields, he devoted himself to the advancement of literature and the combination between the Chinese culture and the Western civilization. Another achievement of him was introducing Pragmatism to China. His thoughts and works benefit several generations and he is considered the most outstanding leader of this cultural movement. Thus the philosophy in Huizhou after the Song Dynasty was well-developed, and reflected the traces and contents of the late Chinese feudal philosophy.

---

① Duan Yucai, the 7th Volume of *Jing Yun Essays* [G].
② Liang Qichao, *The Academic Introduction of the Qing Dynasty* [M].
③ Liang Qichao, *The Origin of Dai Dongyuan Library* [Z].
④ Sun Shuping, *The Notes of Chinese Historiography* [M].

What's more, Huizhou Culture in other aspects was also a mirror of the Chinese feudal culture. For example, Huizhou Merchants were a representative business group due to the booming business in the late Chinese feudal society. They showed the same feudal characteristics as the others from the Ten Great Trading Gangs, either in combining Confucianism with their business, or in keeping strong blood relationship or in attaching importance to education. For another example, Huizhou was a typical specimen deeply affected by feudal ethics. For a woman here, Confucian chastity was so critical that she would protect it at any cost if a man tried to rape her. As Zhao Jishi from Xiuning County said, "The number of chaste females in Xin'an area was bigger than in any other region. It even took up half of the total in the whole province."① *The Local Gazetteer of Shexian County*, edited in the Republican Period, covered 16 books, and 4 of which aimed at recording chaste females. Besides, the number of chastity arches in Huizhou area was also the largest. In the 31st year under the reign of Emperor Guang Xu in the Qing Dynasty, a special chastity arch was built in Huizhou Prefecture in memory of 65,000 chaste women collectively. In a word, Huizhou was greatly influenced by feudal ethics.

It is obvious that the society and culture of Huizhou is a typical representative of the late Chinese feudal society and has a unique and vital position in the history of the Chinese society. Therefore, the studies of Huizhou Culture today is of great academic significance. ②

Published in *Journal of Anhui University*, Vol. 26, No. 6, 2002

Written by Liu Boshan

Translated by Cheng Hongzhen

---

① Zhao Jishi, *Jiyuan Record* [G].

② Liu Boshan, The Academic Significance of the Research on Hui Culture [J], *Xinhua Digest*, 1998(4).

Chapter 6   The Formation and Evolution of Huizhou Culture

Huizhou is located in the south mountain area of Anhui, involving Mt. Huang Shan and Mt. Baiyue (namely Mt. Qiyun nowadays, translator's note). This place enjoys a picturesque landscape. The remarkable nature breeds the remarkable people. And those hard-working residents create outstanding historic culture, which plays a leading role for more than one thousand years in ancient China. Huizhou Culture is usually marked with something broad and profound. On the one hand, it covers almost all aspects of the traditional Chinese culture and makes great contribution to philosophy, ethics, literature, science, crafts and so on. On the other hand, Huizhou Culture represents the top level at that time for its profound philosophy, fine craftsmanship and rich cultural connotation. Huizhou culture demonstrates some local characteristics. It can also be seen as a miniature of the main cultural stream and contributes a lot to the Chinese history. But how does such a great culture come into being? And how does it evolve?

The key is the unique geographical and humanistic environment there.

The geographical environment is a critical factor in the formation of Huizhou Culture. Huizhou in history was located in the mountain area. The scenery was beautiful, but the steep terrain made it extremely inconvenient to live here.① There was a serious shortage of farmland, as people often said, "Only 10 percent of the place is farmland while 70 percent consists of mountains." Although the natives made full use of the land for farming, the mountain topography was still a big problem for them to retain water. If there were no rainfalls in ten days, the lands would crack. However, with a heavy shower, flash floods may drown the grain seedlings. The condition was quite different in plain regions where farming was blessed. In those

---

① Luo Yuan, Xu Gong Fu, The 2nd Volume of *Xin'an Chorography* [Z].

agricultural days, Huizhou area was a terrible place to live in. But people there never gave up. Instead, they tried their utmost to fight against the harsh natural environment generation by generation. The long process steeled the residents and made them brave and strong. Zhu Yugui, a magistrate of Xiuning County in the Southern Song Dynasty, claimed that the steep mountains and the clean rivers contributed to the noble character and sterling integrity of the inhabitants so much. ① A well-known scholar named Luo Yuan said, "Huizhou is a cradle for honest and upright officials because of its steep mountains and clean rivers." ② Dai Zhen, a master of Huizhou Puxue in the Qing Dynasty also stated that the strong integrity view there attributed to the features of the mountains. ③ The natural environment shaped the residents' characters in many aspects. A typical one was their perseverance. It was easier to persuade them by rules than by force. Sometimes, they even fought against the local government to protect their territory. If one became an official, he usually would be upright and unbiased. And if one turned into a scholar, he would think independently and be creative. In conclusion, it was the unique geographical environment that shaped the locals' personalities.

    Cultural integration was another key factor in the history of Huizhou Culture. Before the Qin and Han Dynasties, Shanyue people had been the master on this land. These brave and tough natives lived here in a "slash-and-burn" farming way. Mountain migrating agriculture was their main life style. In general, it belonged to Southern Yue culture, the origin of Huizhou culture. Then Han Culture of the Central Plain fertilized this place after the establishment of Yixian County and Shexian County by the emperors in the Qin Dynasty. And During the early years of the Eastern

---

    ① Zhu Xi, The Essay of Taoist Monastery in Xiuning county [Z], Cheng Minzheng, *Xin'an Literary Chorography*. The Edition in the Ming Dynasty.
    ② Luo Yuan, Customs, The 1st Volume of *Xin'an Chorography* [Z].
    ③ Dai Zhen, *Dongyuan Essays* [G], All Essays of Daizhen, Hefei: Huangshan Publishing House, 1994.

Han Dynasty, some powerful families moved to Huizhou area to escape from wars. In the Chinese history, the vicissitudes of different dynasties always gave rise to frequent wars. To escape from those scary revolts, even some big clans had to migrate. For examples, Yong Jia Uprising in the late years of the Western Jin Dynasty, Huang Chao Uprising in the late years of the Tang Dynasty and the Song-Jin War all resulted in their immigration waves to Huizhou. After the migration, they lived together there and paid much attention to education and etiquette. Meanwhile, they brought civilization to Huizhou area. With the increase of population and the expansion of their groups, these immigrants turned to be the new master of the land. During that time, some outstanding scholars and officials tried to promote the etiquette and civilization, as Ren Fang and Xu Chi in the Southern Liang Dynasty or Xue Yong and Hong Jinglun in the Tang Dynasty. Then it became a social custom to follow Ren Fang and Xue Yong and be a well-cultivated man.[①] However, it didn't mean that this new culture had replaced Shanyue Culture completely. Lyu Wen, a remarkable litterateur in the Tang Dynasty, said that there were many Shanyue people in Shezhou (namely Huizhou) who were ambitious and aggressive. So it was a tough task to govern them.[②] Similar records could be found in the Ming and Qing Dynasties, which revealed that Shanyue Culture kept working there. Obviously, it was inevitable to have conflicts between Shanyue Culture and Central Plains Culture. But the mutual integration was the main trend. Central Plains Culture helped Shanyue Culture to be more polished while Shanyue Culture made the former more resolute. Some essence of Huizhou Culture, like paying attention to education and venerating Confucian-elegance, revealed the features of Central Plains Culture. And some other

---

① Wang Xiangzhi, the 20th Volume of *Yu Di Ji Sheng* [G], The 584th Volume of *Historic Geography of The Sequel of the Si Ku Quan Shu*, Shanghai: Shanghai Ancient Books Publishing House, 2002.

② Lyn Wen, The 5th Volume of *Essays of Lyn Wen* [G].

features, like being enterprising and hard-working, were the reflection of Shanyue Culture. They were reinforced mutually. And after the long process of cultural integration from the Qin and Han Dynasties to Sui, Tang and the Five Dynasties, the unique Huizhou Culture came into being. It was not just the heritage of Central Plains Culture but involved something new. For instance, the agricultural civilization of Central Plains Culture was originally a kind of settlement culture. In this cultural pattern, people would prefer to live in the same place rather than move frequently. However, Huizhou Culture was different. Grown-up men had to leave home for a living because of the lack of land resources, whether by taking the imperial examinations or by doing trades. However, the harsh geographical condition was only one reason, the moving floods also contributed to the pioneering spirit of Huizhou people.

In conclusion, the cultural integration and the unique geographical condition gave birth to the distinctive Huizhou Culture. Some basic spirits, including Confucian traditions, strong blood ties, being active and enterprising, all constituted the core part of Huizhou Culture. These cultural factors had great and far-reaching impact upon the advancement of Huizhou and provided a good starting point for it.

In the long history of China, a new stage appeared after the Song Dynasty. In the earlier time, the economic and cultural center of China was in the Yellow River valley, which was located in the north of China. But after the Song Dynasty, the center moved to the Yangtze River valley in the south of China. The moving process started from the Tang Dynasty and generally completed in the Song Dynasty. After that, the agricultural technology, productivity and produces in the south all exceeded those in the north. Meanwhile, the private ownership of land was well-developed. Commodity economy boomed and overseas trades thrived. With the southward shift of the economic center in Ancient China, the position of Huizhou raised. In fact, Huizhou was not in the heart of Yangtze River Delta, but not far from Hangzhou. So it was convenient for Huizhou to keep contact with other cities. After the southward migration of the Song Dynasty, Huizhou was so prosperous that it was considered the second capital in the Mid-Song Dynasty.① There was no doubt that Huizhou belonged to the most flourishing place of Jiangnan area. And with the development of its economy and culture, Huizhou became increasingly important for ancient China.

However, the formation and evolution of Huizhou Culture was not only limited to the local area. Hu Shi (a gorgeous scholar and thinker of China, translator's note) stated that there were two different concepts, namely "Huizhou in a regional sense" and "Huizhou in a cultural sense" respectively. The latter includes both the places inside Huizhou and the places outside Huizhou but influenced by its culture. Huizhou Culture was popular both in the native land and the whole nation. The limited space of Huizhou drove people to hunt for development outside. Originally, it was a helpless choice, but it turned to be a social tendency later. After the Song Dynasty, local residents kept contact with the outside world mainly through business activities and imperial examination system. And in the Ming and Qing Dynasties, the local residents communicated with people outside more frequently and they also influenced each other. With the help of the interaction, Huizhou achieved success both in economy and culture. Huizhou Merchants expanded their business almost everywhere and took a superior position in business. Men from Huizhou area also left their footprints by studying abroad or being officials in other regions. Thanks to them, the unique Huizhou Culture could spread all over the world. At that time, Huizhou acted as an economic and cultural center. In fact, Huizhou in a cultural sense contributed a lot to Huizhou Culture.

The imperial examination system was another critical factor for the advancement of Huizhou Culture. It sprang up in the Sui and Tang Dynasties and developed fully in the Song Dynasty. The emperors selected

---

① Luo Sichen, The New Town of Huizhou [Z]. The 13th Volume of *Xin'an Literary Chorography*. The Edition in the Ming Dynasty.

officials mainly by it at that time. Huizhou seized this historic opportunity successfully. More and more individuals joined in the political circle by the exam. The latest research revealed that there were 861 men in Huizhou who passed the imperial examinations in the Song Dynasty while the number was only 10 during the Tang and the Five Dynasties. Besides, More than 30 people from Huizhou once served as the forth-class ministers. ① Since the Song Dynasty was prosperous in culture, a lot of excellent officials appeared. ② During that time, Huizhou raised politically at first.

The popularity of Neo-Confucianism in the Song Dynasty raised Confucianism to a new height. It could be seen as a milestone in the history of the Chinese philosophy and culture. In the Northern Song Dynasty, Zhou Dunyi, Cheng Hao, Cheng Yi and some others created Neo-Confucianism. Then in Southern Song Dynasty, Zhu Xi promoted its development to a great degree. This theory took a dominant position in the history of the ancient Chinese ideology. The emperors in the Yuan, the Ming and Qing Dynasties all honored it and considered it the official ideology. It had impact not only on China, but also on the East Asia or even on some European countries. Since Huizhou was regarded as the hometown of Zhu Xi, Cheng Hao and Cheng Yi, it was no surprising that their theory influenced the region profoundly. On this basis, a new theory called Xin'an Neo-Confucianism emerged after the Yuan Dynasty. There was a saying, "Although Zhu Xi's theory was popular all over China, those from Xin'an (namely Huizhou) were the best to acquire it and practiced it."③

People from Huizhou were the models to support Neo-Confucianism in

---

① Fu Xuanzong (editor-in-chief), Gong Yanming & Zu Hui (Compilers), *The Essay of Imperial System in the Song Dynasty* [M], Nanjing: Jiangsu Education Publishing House, 2009. Yu Jing, The Study on Imperial System in the Song Dynasty [D], Zhejiang University, 2007.

② Luo Yuan, Customs, The 1st Volume of *Xin'an Chorography* [Z].

③ Zhao Fang, Essays of School Land of Shangshan Academy [Z], The 4th Volume of *Dongshan Essays*.

practice. They regarded Zhu Xin from Wuyuan county as Mencius from the ancient Zou area and Confucius from the ancient Qufu area. ① Emperor Xian Chun took Wuyuan county as the hometown of Zhu Xi in the fifth year of his reign in the Southern Song Dynasty. ② From then on, Huizhou were always called "the hometown of Cheng-Zhu" or "Southeast Zoulu". Since Huizhou was the cradle of Confucians in the late Chinese feudal society, it stood apart from other places.

After the Song Dynasty, Huizhou met with another historic opportunity, namely the boom of the commercial economy. It developed fast after the Song and the Yuan Dynasties, especially after the Mid-Ming Dynasty. Then the Chinese commercial economy reached a new peak. It was mainly reflected in the increased commercialization of commodities, the growth of long-distance trades, the increasing number of new commercial towns and the large commercial capital. In a word, a nationwide market was established. All this provided Huizhou Merchants with a good chance. However, the advancement of the commercial economy was only an objective condition, opportunities were equal to everyone. But why could Huizhou Merchants become the winner? One critical factor was Huizhou Culture. During that time, the majority of people were agriculture-oriented and hated migration. So if one attempted to do business he needed to challenge the tradition. Huizhou people did that successfully. The males usually chose to go out when they turned to about 14 years old. Actually, it was not an easy choice. But this open spirit constituted a significant part of Huizhou Culture. The geographical condition was another reason. The limited farmland resources drove people to go outside for a way out. But it didn't mean that business was the only choice. For example, in the Ming Dynasty, there were countless refugees

---

① Zhao Hong'en, The Rebuilding of the Ancestral Hall of Wen Gong, *Wuyuan Chorography* [Z], The Edition in the Reign of Emperor Dao Guang of the Qing Dynasty.

② The Zhu's [Z], The 14th Volume of *Wuyuan Chorography*, The Edition in the Reign of Emperor Dao Guang of the Qing Dynasty.

resulting from famine and conscription. Some of them made a living by begging; some worked as casual labors; some chose to be servants and the majority of them became vagrants. During the whole Ming Dynasty, it was a big challenge to manage them and there were no effective measures to solve the vagrant problem. However, at the same time, individuals from Huizhou chose to go outside as a businessman and achieved great success. An essential factor was their great attention to education. In Huizhou, education was widely spread even in a sparsely populated village. The education popularization provided necessary conditions for being successful merchants. Obviously, it was almost impossible for an illiterate person to do business outside. Even the vendors needed to acquire some cultural knowledge. And for the business giants who engaged in trades all over the nation, they must have higher cultural quality. In fact, many Huizhou Merchants were Confucians originally, and they regarded Confucian teachings as their business morals. Since they always did business in a Confucian way, they were called Confucian merchants. As Dai Zhen said, "Although they are merchants, their behaviors are similar to Confucian scholars." Consequently, the unique Huizhou Culture played an important role in the rise of Huizhou Merchants.

There were many records of Huizhou Merchants' achievements. Xie Zhaozhe, a famous official and writer in the Ming Dynasty once said, "The giants of the rich mainly come from Xin'an region within Jiangnan area or Shanyou region within Jiangbei area. Most successful businessmen from Xin'an are millionaires who engage in salt business. Those who possess hundreds of thousands of guan (an ancient monetary unit, translator's note) only belong to the middle-class businessmen."[①] Huizhou Merchants were active during the Ming and the Qing Dynasties. Their footprints were almost everywhere, from remote deserts to mysterious islands, or even to many foreign countries. They took control of several monopoly industries like salt

---

① Xie Zhaozhi, Geography, the 4th Volume of *Wu Za Zu* [G], Shanghai: Shanghai Bookstore Publishing House.

trade and pawnbroker and dominated the business world for hundreds of years from the Mid-Ming Dynasty to the Qing Dynasty. Their activities were not just commercial but economical, cultural and social as well. The development of the commercial economy in ancient China reached another peak after the Mid-Ming Dynasty. During that time, the commercial economy also displayed such new factors as the formation of a national market and the buds of new productive relationships. These factors demonstrated a shift from the traditional economic pattern to the modernization. In the process, Huizhou Merchants were both the beneficiaries and pioneers. It was an interactive relationship rather than a cause-and-effect one between the growth of the commercial production and the formation of the national market, and the rise of the business groups. In those days, Huizhou Merchants were famous for their characteristics. There was an old saying, "Huizhou Merchants, who are always hard-working and ready for any opportunity, sell almost everything and their business spreads almost everywhere in China. They took control of any commercial power."[1] The prosperity of business also promoted the growth of the commercial production and quickened the establishment of the nationwide market. In this process, such business groups as Huizhou Merchants made great contributions. Since Huizhou Merchants always played the leading role in the development of the commercial society, they were the pioneers of the era.

Huizhou Merchants' progress was based on the unique Huizhou Culture, and in the meantime, their economic success promoted the advancement of Huizhou Culture in return. The close interaction between economy and culture was a prominent feature in the history of Huizhou. Huizhou Merchants' great wealth laid a solid physical foundation for Huizhou Culture. They invested plenty of money in education, arts, architecture, public welfare, and so on. Their powerful economic power also played an important role in cultivating

---

[1] *Shexian Chorography* [Z], The Edition in the Reign of Emperor Wan Li in the Ming Dynasty.

talents. Thanks to it, Huizhou gave birth to a lot of talented people and it was the key to the glory of Huizhou Culture. A typical example was about the Wang's in Shexian County and Huizhou Puxue. This honorable family with a business background owned a private garden called Bushu Garden, which was the cradle of Huizhou Puxue. ① In the Ming and the Qing Dynasties, Huizhou Culture enjoyed its golden time and was flourishing almost in all cultural fields, like Huizhou education, Xin'an Neo-Confucianism, Huizhou Puxue, Xin'an Painting, Huizhou Opera and Huizhou Cuisine. The high level of its cultural development was universally acknowledged. There was no doubt that Huizhou Culture was valuable in the history of Chinese culture. It not only reflected the regional features but also represented the mainstream culture at that time. Consequently, Huizhou Culture was of both typicality and universality.

With the development of commercial economy and the success of Huizhou Merchants, people changed their traditional ideas. Wang Daokun, a literary leader in the late Ming Dynasty from Huizhou, said, "Xin'an is famous for the cultural relics from the south of the Yangtze River. The majority of people there choose to be scholars or merchants. In a word, a successful businessman is not overshadowed by a brilliant scholar."② He also said, "The ancient emperors were usually concerned about agriculture more than business, thus they taxed commerce more than farming. But I do not agree on this. Business is just as important as agriculture. In short, if each of them plays its role effectively, the importance of business will not be inferior to that of agriculture."③ Yu Zhengxie, an incredible scholar from Huizhou area in the Qing Dynasty, said, "Doing business is a proper choice for the commons. It is recorded in the Confucian book *Yi* that emperors in

---

① Wang Shiqing, Bushu Garden and Anhui Sinology [J], *Jianghuai Tribune*, 1997(2).
② Wang Daokun, The 10th Volume of *Taihan Essays* [G], The 118th Volume of *Si Ku Quan Shu*, Ji'nan: Qilu Publishing House, 1997.
③ Wang Daokun, The 65th Volume of *Taihan Essays* [G].

ancient times are also good at business. Another famous book *Shu* reveals that ancient emperors of the Yu and Xia Dynasties encourage people to improve their living conditions by trading."① All of the above were against the traditional idea that business was inferior to agriculture. Instead, the former was as important as the latter. This voice went against the old idea that the status of businessmen was the lowest among the ordinary people, which was a challenge to the deep-rooted tradition. Its significance went beyond the regional culture and represented the progressive voice of those days.

However, the solid foundation of Huizhou traditional culture also hindered its shift sometime. In modern time, Huizhou Merchants lost their leading status, and the social transformation of Huizhou was slow and hard. In spite of this, Huizhou Culture still played a role in the process of modernization. Dai Zhen, a master of Huizhou Puxue, was a Chinese materialist philosopher in the eighteenth century. His opinions were advanced and displayed something of early enlightenment. Yu Zhengxie, one of the Three Sages of the Chinese ideological circle, challenged the traditional voice before the Opium War. Some of his ideas, especially those about gender equality, indicated simple human rights. During the discord times under the reign of Emperors Xian Feng and Tong Zhi, Wang Shiduo, a scholar living in Huizhou temporarily, condemned such bad social customs as early marriage and expressed his preliminary ideas on population. He also opposed Confucian benevolent policy to some degree and advocated learning from the West in science and technology. Meanwhile, Wang Maoyin, an official originally from Huizhou area, proposed his own monetary theory and financial policy, which took a significant position in the history of the Chinese economic thoughts. He was also the only Chinese man mentioned in the world-famous book *Das Kapital* written by Karl Marx. Another figure named Huang Binhong was both a maverick genius and a representative person in painting, and promoted Xin'an Painting. In addition, Huizhou

---

① Yu Zhengxie, Opinions of Business Tax, *Gui Si Lei Gao* [G].

Opera was the origin of Peking Opera. Wang Lai, a mathematician from Huizhou, contributed a lot to the natural science and was even considered the predecessor of computer principles. Another man called Hu Shi was one of the leaders of the famous May 4 New Culture Movement. There was no doubt that his propositions were a great challenge to the traditional culture. However, from the perspective of criticism, he actually followed the ancient sages in Huizhou like Zhu Xi and Dai Zhen. No matter what great achievements those above made in the process of cultural transformation, it was a fact that they all benefited from Huizhou Culture to some degree.

The history and culture of Huizhou suggests the harmony between men and nature, the integration of different cultures and the interaction between economy and culture. Huizhou people hardened themselves and improved their cultural quality in hardships. Huizhou Culture was the product of the social development. The southward shift of the economic and cultural center and the boom of the commercial economy after the Song Dynasty provided Huizhou with an unprecedented good chance. Besides, Huizhou Culture took advantage of the resources in other places (namely, Huizhou area in a cultural sense). In conclusion, Huizhou Culture is ultimately created by the high-quality men there. It is those who seize the historic opportunities and breed the gorgeous Huizhou Culture.

Published in *Anhui History Studies*, No. 2, 2014
Written by Luan Chengxia
Translated by Cheng Hongzhen

Chapter 7　The Position of the Huizhou Culture and the Trend of Its Development

From the mid-1980s, Huizhou Studies is thriving rapidly. As the brilliant scholar Wang Guowei says, "a new kind of knowledge usually contributes to new findings." Obviously, the rise of Huizhou Studies is based on the discovery of numerous fresh materials. Those historical materials are more than 200,000, an astonishing number for the whole academic circle. They cover a wide range of contents, including contacts, letters, personal writings, account books and so on. Some of the documents are even from different ages, "belonging to one family".① In a word, these literal materials are precious because they are original, unique and time-honored. They deserve the name of the 5th Great Discovery. And they can be used alternatively with the 3,000 ancient books and more than 1,000 kinds of clan pedigrees of Huizhou. (Among the pedigrees preserved in the National Library in China, those of Huizhou occupy more than a half.) The relics on the ground also are rich. There are more than 5,000 historical relics and more than 200,000 pieces, involving the buildings, temples, memorial archways and the amazing Huashan Mysterious Grottoes. Mount Huang Shan, Village Hong and Village Xidi, as the most astonishing relics, are listed into the World Cultural Relic Reservation. So Huizhou can be called "Land of Historical Relics". However, the use of the rich materials is just at the beginning and they provide excellent conditions to do field work, monographic study or even interdisciplinary research. That is the reason why many foreign scholars are interested in Huizhou Studies. From nothing to something,

---

① The saying "belong to one family" means that the related people in the scattered contract documents belonging to the same family.

Huizhou Study rises only in 20 years. Now it is popular among the whole Chinese academic circle.

To promote the research of Huizhou Studies, the project "The Encyclopedia of Huizhou Culture", a huge cultural construction project, has been identified as the Social Science Key Project in 1999. *The Encyclopedia of Huizhou Culture* ("The Encyclopedia" for short) is about the cultural phenomena and their development, including the inner interaction between the different parts. The Encyclopedia is divided into 20 books with different topics, covering land relationship, nationhood society, Huizhou merchants, Xin'an Neo-Confucianism, etc. These books are written by 40 scholars respectively. In this way, each book can be independent so that diverse academic ideas can coexist. Each writer is an expert in the related field and each book is the essence of his wisdom and academic achievements. The Encyclopedia, as an all-inclusive cultural construction project, reflects the characteristics of current academy and represents the academic achievement to some degree.

After 6 years, *The Encyclopedia* is compiled, and published by Anhui People's Press. It is good news for the whole Chinese academic circle. So I am honored to be asked to write the preface to The Encyclopedia.

Huizhou culture is both a regional culture and a typical traditional Chinese culture. It reflects the essence of the traditional Chinese culture to a great extent.

The so-called Huizhou culture is a combination of all the valuable cultural phenomena in ancient Huizhou area where covers 6 counties, namely, She County, Yi County, Xiuning County, Qimen County, Jixi County and Wuyuan County. It is rooted in Huizhou area, but has a nationwide influence, especially in Jiangnan area (covering several cities as Suzhou, Songjiang, Changzhou and Hangzhou), Jianghuai area, Wuhu City and Anqing City. These regions which are so deeply influenced by Huizhou culture that they are called "Huizhou in the culture sense". The cultural integration gives birth to the formidable culture, which offers scholars with numerous chances to do the research on humanities, social science and natural science.

The reason why we take Huizhou culture as a kind of regional culture is that it shows obvious regional characteristics involving clan culture and the culture of Confucian Merchants. In this area, the clans are well-developed. And as for the Huizhou Merchants who rise from the Mid-Ming Dynasty, their influence is very broad, especially in Jiangnan area and the basins of The Beijing-Hangzhou Grand Canal. Huizhou Merchants and Shanxi Merchants, the two business giants, represent marine merchants and inland merchants respectively and demonstrate the two aspects of Chinese Geo-economy. In a word, Huizhou culture is marked by its special clans and business. Until today, tourists can more or less experience the cultural atmosphere here. The historical relics, as the ancient buildings, are not only the heritages of the traditional Chinese culture but also the proofs of the solid economical foundation of Huizhou Merchants. Besides, those relics are a kind of comprehensive art, including architecture, handwriting, painting and engraving. The unique regional culture of Confucian Merchants and clans can be traced almost everywhere, from the time-honored yards, streets, wells in the public space, from the paintings, handwritings, furniture in the private houses, or even from the numerous historical books and documents.

Originally, the traditional Chinese culture occurs from the central plain region. But to the Ming and Qing Dynasties, the southeast area becomes more powerful in culture. During those days, many people take Suzhou City and Hangzhou City as the new cultural centers. In fact, Huizhou area is the most typical area where the traditional Chinese culture is well-developed. Despite its regional features, Huizhou culture is still a representative of the splendid traditional Chinese culture.

As for the clan culture, though the clans of Huizhou are immigrants from the central plain land, they belong to the orthodox culture. The original patriarchal clan system made some adjustments to adapt to the social changes, but in nature it remains the same. Those powerful clans, before moving to Huizhou area, are hierarchical and still keep the strict systems later. The members of the same clan live together and are proud of their own clan. To foster the clan from age to age, they formulate the family rules. All the efforts are aimed at enhancing the patriarchal clan system. Relying on the power of the clan, they compete with the indigenous residents. On the one hand, they expand their land by force. On the other hand, they civilize the aborigines with their traditional culture, especially with the clan culture. Finally, they replace the indigenous people to be the master of the land. As time goes, more and more immigrants from the central plain move here so that the aborigines are assimilated by them. In the way of migrating, these honorable families get away from the wars and inherit their traditions successfully. Meanwhile, the others are diminished or even vanished because of the chaos caused by the wars, particularly by the Huang Chao Uprising. The immigrant clans form a patriarchal society after a long period of fighting in the remote and deserted land. The clan system lays the foundation of the local social structure.

After the Song Dynasty, the Neo-Confucianism of Cheng-Zhu emerges and has a far-reaching influence on this land. On the basis of this theory, clan ethics has been put to a higher place. Zhang Zai advises officials to control the public by clan rules. Cheng Yi thinks it is essential to enforce the management of clans by promoting the abilities of the head of the clan and bringing the common members to the justice. In his book *The Family Etiquette*, Zhu Xi established a series of clan ethics to enforce the clan system. Mixed with the Neo-Confucianism, clan systems have been better organized. The family tree must be clear and all the members should honor their own ancestors in a specific way. Moreover, people are responsible to help the poor from the same clan. All the acts are based on some necessary substantial things, such as pedigree, tomb and public wealth. The common members and servants must act in the way required by the family rules. There is almost only one great family in one village. People from another family are forbidden to settle down here, even an adult daughter or a son-in-

Part II　Huizhou Culture

law is required to move out. The servants live around the village to protect it. As a clan becomes bigger and bigger, some of its branches move to another place and build a new village. However, all the branches will keep contact with each other.

The patriarchal clan system, a combination of the blood relationship and geo-relationship, is hierarchical. It requires people in the same clan to honor their ancestors and hold filial piety. Besides, they insist on a bureaucrat-oriented attitude to make sure the position and privilege of their clan. Thus education, as a main road to officials, must be a vital content of the clan rules. In addition to education, they also pay huge attention to Confucian ethics, which acts as enlightenment education. The rich clans establish various education institutions for their members. Intelligent children must enjoy careful cultivation. For those clever but poor, the clan special funds or Huizhou Merchants will support them in learning. The fate of the members is related to the development of the clan. In such a society, a man can be successful only when his clan is honorable. In conclusion, a clan provides a good condition for its members to achieve success while the members study hard for glorifying their clan. Although Huizhou clan changes to some degree as the time goes, Huizhou Culture is identical to the orthodox culture in general, and thus can be seen as one of its good examples.

Huizhou is the hometown of Cheng-Zhu and the cradle of Neo-Confucianism of Cheng-Zhu. In return, this theory has far-reaching influence here. Zhu Xi greatly develops Neo-Confucianism from the traditional theory, which is more speculative. This new theory is a correction to the early Confucianism. Zhu Xi has been relegated before his death, however, the emperors in the later dynasties regard his thoughts as orthodox culture. Then Neo-Confucianism becomes the main stream of the development of the Chinese culture. In Huizhou, the theory is inherited generation by generation. After Zhu Xi, numerous distinguished men emerged one after another. (Zhao Jishi, the book *The Xin'an Neo-Confucianism*) The thoughts of Neo-Confucianism fertilize the local people, and also benefit other people in society, civilization, customs, etc. Therefore, this place is rarely affected by cults. Nurtured by Neo-Confucianism, the intellectuals here focus on learning and pursue moral standard more than material gains. People consider Huizhou an area where Confucianism is well-developed and call Huizhou "Southeast Zoulu" (Zoulu is another name of Shandong Province, Confucius' hometown and the cradle of the Chinese civilization.) During the Ming and Qing Dynasties, there are an increasing number of people who acquire position and fame through learning. It is even no surprising that there emerge several topmost scholars from one single family. The talents appear continuously in Huizhou. In She County, for example, there are many Zhuangyuan (the No. 1 Scholar) in the imperial examination such as Tang Gao, Jing Bang, Hong Ying and Hong Jun. For senior officials, there are Xu Guo, Cheng Guoxiang and so on. As for Confucians, there are Zhu Sheng, Tang Zhongshi, etc. In business, Tang Wenfeng and Yangning are excellent. In the field of politics, Tang Xiang and Wu Shi are excellent officials. In respect of military, Wong Hongzong and Wang Yingzhen can be representatives of outstanding leaders. Some as Jiang Chun and Bao Yanbo (two famous salt merchants) are even been favored by Emperor Qian Long in the Qing Dynasty. These people are only a small part, but it is enough to prove that Huizhou is rich for its talents. There emerge 28 Zhuangyuan and 17 prime ministers in the history of Huizhou, both taking up 24% of the total. The talented here are honored in the related field. Zhu Xi, Dai Zhen and Hu Shi are the most representatives in academic circle and they are monuments of the history of thought. The numerous talents contribute a lot to and hold an important position in the Chinese culture.

  The talents in Huizhou are far more than one type. There are high officials, wealthy traders, honorable scholars, gifted artists, skilled craftsmen and many others, with the total number of 5,399 in written records. These intelligent people show their talent in a variety of fields, involving politics, economy, philosophy, Confucianism, literature, art, science, crafts, architecture, medicine, etc. They make remarkable achievements for humans, such as

Xin'an Medicine, Three Wonders of Huizhou-style Architecture, Huizhou Three Carving Techniques, the "Scholar's Four Jewels", Huizhou Cuisine. Some scientific and technological inventions are not only advanced domestically, but also have a widespread and profound influence overseas. On the one hand, the remarkable achievements in Huizhou culture are a regional phenomenon. On the other hand, it is a result of the typical national culture. In some sense, Huizhou culture reflects the essence of the traditional Chinese culture.

Obviously, the success of Huizhou culture can be attributed to more than one single factor, including the local traditions, social structures, moral force and some others.

Among these factors, a significant one is the promotion of the culture quality of Huizhou people. Besides, Huizhou people always keep up with the times. During the two periods of social transformation respectively in the Song and Ming Dynasties, they adapt to the changes fast and get ahead both in imperial examination and business.

After the period of the Five Dynasties, the selection of talented people is not based on their family background any longer. It is a huge change for the Chinese bureaucratic system. A mediocre person can't get a high position or enjoy any privilege just because of his family background any more. As the imperial examination system is established, Huizhou natives choose to promote education in response.

The honorable clans in Huizhou are the privileged classes in the central plain originally. When they move to Huizhou, they lose their positions and are restricted by the poor local resources. The hard environment makes them hard-working and aggressive (a possible origin of the Camel Spirit as Hu Shi called). To adapt to the new environment, they transform their original culture creatively and succeed in imperial examination in the Song Dynasty. The huge success exerts a far-reaching impact on the governor-oriented values, a significant part of Huizhou culture.

It should be pointed out that the success in Huizhou politics in Song

Dynasty stems from two aspects, namely, the attention to education and the enterprising spirit. These two cultural genes are inherited in the regional history and result in the great development of Huizhou culture. They are not changed completely, nor are frozen. Instead, they transformed to be stronger and stronger and become part of the traditions of Huizhou.

From the Mid-Ming Dynasty, Huizhou residents choose to focus on business as a response to the new social and economic transformation. In fact, Huizhou merchants have come to take the first place in business. It is a remarkable achievement in economy after taking a superior position in politics in the Song Dynasty.

In the 16th Century (within the Mid-Ming Dynasty), mercantilism has swept the western world. Maritime trades become more and more common, meanwhile, an international marine trade circle has been formed gradually. During that time, the domestic commodity economy is booming in China. There are an increasing number of business chances. The traditional social economy is turning, which indicates the coexistence of challenges and opportunities.

The history of Huizhou marine merchants can be traced back to the Eastern Jin Dynasty. However, as a business group connected by clan relationship, it rises in the Mid-Ming Dynasty and booms during the period of the reign of the emperors Jiajing and Wanli in the Ming Dynasty. People from Huizhou go outside along rivers. A common route is starting from Xin'an River, first going east to Hangzhou Bay, then to the east coast and finally to the ocean. In fact, Huizhou maritime groups are engaged in smuggling trade at that time. The existence of Xin'an River offers them a chance to challenge the sea. During the period of the reign of Emperor Jia Jing of the Ming Dynasty, some merchants under the leadership of Xu Brothers and Wang Zhi from Huizhou and Deng Liao from Fujian, establish an international overseas trade market near Hangzhou Bay. Wang Zhi follows the western businessmen to build gigantic armed ships. With the ships, Huizhou marine merchants expand their business and lead the first trend of oversea trades in China.

The so-called marine merchants are a kind of professional merchants who transform the traditional economy to the market-oriented economy. (J. R. Hicks, *Theory of Economic History*) Huizhou merchants seize the opportunity from the marine trades in the Mid-Ming Dynasty, connect it with the business of tea, salt, lumber and pawn. They also build a commercial area. In addition, they promote the commercialization and urbanization especially in the middle and lower reaches of Yangtze River and the coastal area of the Beijing-Hangzhou Grand Canal, while building commercial colonies in Nanjing, Wuhu, Anqing, Wuhan, Suzhou, Hangzhou and so on. Without the developed business and overseas trade, it would be impossible to form big commercial cities. Huizhou merchants seize the commercial opportunity and enjoy the reputation that there is no town without Huizhou Merchants.

Some people consider the smuggling traders the Japanese Pirates under the reign of Emperor Jia Jing. Some scholars of Japanese pirates think that the forged Japanese pirates as Jiang Zhi ruin Jiangnan area. But scholars in social and commercial history of Jiangnan area maintain that thanks to the overseas trade, the economy of Jiangnan is growing at that time.

At present, there are two different voices for smuggling trade that Huizhou marine merchants are engaged in, based on the historical fact and the value judgment respectively. For the perspective of historical fact, people only focus on the truth. But the problem is that all the related records are official, so researchers must analyze if the records are true. And for the perspective of value judgment, scholars should not only judge the social and economic function of Huizhou marine merchants but also analyze their effects on the later generations or even on people nowadays.

No matter what scholars say, the fact is that Huizhou merchants are good at taking chances and have strong adaptability to changes. Besides, they never give up when they fail. It can be proved by the measures Wang Zhi's group takes after the crackdown on them. At that time, salt is a government monopoly. However, as it is a kind of daily necessities, the sale of salt is so huge that it is easy to make profits from its trade. Jin-merchants, a business group starting with salt deals, are a successful example. So it is no surprise that Huizhou merchants also show huge interests in it for commercial benefits. In the 5th year of the reign of Emperor Hong Zhi, Huizhou merchants take the advantage of revising the salt law and compete with Jin-merchants. After the smuggling trades are suppressed, a tremendous number of Huizhou merchants turn to the salt trade. It can be regarded as an excellent strategic shift for them.

If only judging from the perspective of marine trades, Huizhou merchants fail in the end, but generally, their efforts to develop "marine economy" ① is meaningful. After the reign of Emperor Wanli in the Ming Dynasty, Huizhou merchants gain advantage in salt business, and reach its peak in scale and capital. There are several reasons for their success. At first, they are good at connecting economic resources with human resources and social resources. Second, they seize the opportunity of the development of marine trade in the Mid-Ming Dynasty. Besides, they build a business network between land and ocean. Moreover, the distinguished ability of doing and expanding business is another key factor. Thus, Huizhou merchants control the marine economy and compete with Jin-merchants, a giant inland business group who make their fortune from the northwest frontier. Relatively speaking, Huizhou merchants are called "marine merchants" while Jin-merchants "inland merchants". In fact, however, both of them engage in multi-business.

The success of Huizhou merchants has a profound ideological and cultural origin. In political ethics, they esteem Neo-Confucianism of Cheng-Zhu, and stick to the official standard. However, in business ethics, the theory of Wang Yangming is the most popular one. His theory proposes that

---

① The so-called "marine economy", an economic form combining land farming with sea farming with the latter the priority, refers to the economic activities based on all the marine resources, including the related activities in coastal areas (e. g. inshore fishing, fish farming and salt manufacturing), marine trades and overseas colonial activity.

merchants are as important as the other classes, trying to break the traditional prejudice that officials are superior to businessmen. Huizhou merchants not only pursue success in business, but also promote the development of culture and cultivate talents. On the one hand, they improve their own cultural quality in this way. On the other hand, they create another bureaucratic group, transforming from doing business in Confucian way to cooperating with officials. In this way, Huizhou merchants keep their business prosperous for more than 300 years.

Opportunity, as a chance factor of success, is necessary sometimes. As mentioned above, Huizhou merchants' success depends on seizing two critical historical chances to a great degree. When they encounter setbacks, they never give up but take active measures to deal with them. A typical example is that when Huizhou marine businessmen are suppressed, they turn to develop salt trade and build the competitive advantage in the commercial fight with Jin-merchants.

It seems that scholars should make a further study of the historical position of Huizhou marine merchants and their role in the social economy of Jiangnan area in the Mid-Ming Dynasty, because the study of them is a key to making a breakthrough and a foundation for further achievements in the study of Huizhou Merchants.

The society of Huizhou is an immigrant society. The talents from the central plain move to this region and gradually accept the local aboriginals. From the Wei, Jin, Southern and Northern Dynasties to the Sui and Tang Dynasties, many honorable families move into Huizhou. During the Ming Dynasty, especially after the reign of Emperors Jiajing and Wanli, Huizhou inhabitants emigrate to do business. There is a saying that at the age of 13, a boy could still enjoy a carefree life at home, but when he turns to 17, he must suffer a wandering life to do business. Another saying is that when a boy grows to 13 years old, his parents should force him to go outside for doing trade. Many people from Huizhou wander outside and try their utmost to adapt to any hard condition. The emigrated people go back to their hometown regularly. The flowing population adds new energy to the society and stimulates the talents' creativity. In this way, the local residents and migrants can keep interaction and promote the advancement of the Huizhou culture.

A strong point of Huizhou is that people here attach great importance to education and knowledge, which is critical to people's quality. Today, they still pay great attention to the intelligence and have the advantage of human resources. In a traditional society, the development in an area often relies on its natural resources. However, people from Huizhou can share resources by trading because Huizhou is always an open society and the united Chinese Empire provides enough space for developing business. Huizhou merchants exchange production factors (including funds, labor forces and natural sources) to get natural sources from other places. It is more common during the age of marine merchants. Depended on trading, they have accumulated wealth, boosted the social economy of Jiangnan area and promoted its commercialization and urbanization, even leaving the saying "There is no town without Huizhou merchants". It is also common at present to draw the strong points of others to make up for one's own weakness in business as Huizhou merchants do. The Jews and Japanese all do well in this field. But it is more estimable for Huizhou merchants to master such a skill hundreds of years ago.

The social structure and function of Huizhou is another advantage in the advance of Huizhou society. Huizhou is a society in the control of gentries. Generally speaking, these gentries are more enlightened. Moreover, many Huizhou merchants are public-spirited in charity based on their powerful economic strength. Thus this place was a fairyland those days. Competition is fierce, However, people from Huizhou are affected by Neo-Confucianism of Cheng-Zhu and official-oriented values, so they are pushed to pursue scholarly honor. Besides, the Mercantilism stimulates the locals to engage in business in order to glorify their families. Theoretically, the patriarchal clan system always clashes with flourishing business. However, as a matter of fact, they usually complement each other. Huizhou is no exception. People in Huizhou combine being an official by taking an imperial examination with becoming rich by doing business successfully. The two sides unite to promote the social progress of Huizhou. Thanks to them, Huizhou develop itself in an all-around way history.

In conclusion, Huizhou has made an indelible contribution to Chinese culture which can be proved by both the historic records and the material relics. So when people review the glorious tradition of Chinese society, they can never pay no attention to Huizhou area. That's the reason why Huizhou Studies becomes popular in recent years. Nowadays, it is a historical mission to explore the historical and cultural background of Huizhou and carry forward the fine traditional culture of China.

Published in *Journal of Huangshan University*, Vol. 7, No. 2, 2005
Written by Ye Xian'en
Translated by Cheng Hongzhen

Part III
The Patriarchal Clan System in Huizhou

Chapter 8 Three Issues Related to the Patriarchal Clan System in Huizhou

Since the Song and Yuan dynasties, patriarchal clans in Huizhou were highly developed and typical, which has raised great interest and concern in the academic field home and abroad. In the last half century, many writings on the clan systems in Huizhou were published, thus making great achievements. There are, however, various opinions and many issues to be further discussed in the academic circle. That is why I am writing this article to share my opinions regarding three issues related and looking forward to advice from the experts.

I. The Issue Related to the Spirit Tablets "Not to Be Moved Out over a Hundred Generations" and "Not to Be Moved Out over Five Generations"

During the Song and Yuan periods, the clans established ancestral halls and held sacrificial rites every year. ①The descendants of the clan either built ancestral halls in the family or at tombs. In this way, they rested their

---

① *Domestic Codes in Mingzhou's Wu Family*, Xiuning.

Part III The Patriarchal Clan System in Huizhou

forefathers at peace and set sacrificial rites. During the Ming and Qing periods, especially after the mid of the Ming Dynasty, when people enjoyed looser sacrificial rites under prosperous clan commerce, there was a boom in building ancestral halls in Huizhou. Many magnificent and splendid ancestral halls were erected, and they appeared everywhere.

Like other places in China, the removal of ancestors' spirit tablets, that is, "not moved out over a hundred generations" or "moved out over five generations", remains an issue to be resolved.

Then, how about the rules about Huizhou ancestral halls during the Song and Yuan periods? It is recorded that the temple system was not established during the Song and Yuan periods,① but Zhu Xi's *Family Courtesy* exerted great influence nationwide (He was in Xin'an then, which was later Huizhou). People in Huizhou regarded *Family Courtesy* as the classic for clans, full of brilliance and wisdom. They obeyed rules in *Family Courtesy* and dared not to do anything against it. ②Therefore, the requirements and regulations regarding ancestral halls in Zhu Xi's *Family Courtesy* could basically represent those during the Song and Yuan periods.

In Zhu Xi's *Family Courtesy*, *Ancestral Halls*, it is recorded that if gentlemen decide to construct houses and buildings, it is necessary to build ancestral halls to the east of the main room, with four cabinets to worship ancestors' spirit tablets, saying: in the ancestral hall, four cabinets are close to the north, with one desk in it.

The orders were great-great-great-grandfather, great-great-great-grandfather in the west, great-great-grandfather, great-grandfather, grandfather and father. Cabinet I, II, III and the west Cabinet could be vacant if sacrificial rites were not properly offered. The rules and regulations set by Zhu Xi were not for ancestral halls for clans and their branches, but for domestic

---

① Chang Jianhua, *History of Patriarchal Clan Systems*, Shanghai People's Publishing House, 1998.

② Jiajing Period, Volume II of *Record of Huizhou—Custom*.

ancestral halls. This kind of ancestral halls were built to the east of the principal room, with four cabinets in it. Four generations' spirit tablets were enshrined and consecrated in them: great-great-grandfather, great-grandfather, grandfather and father, that is, four family members within five generations.

What about the regulations in "title change and removal rites" related to domestic ancestral halls?

According to *Family Courtesy*, *Funeral*, *Great Auspice*, records about removal of ancestral halls are: great-great-grandfather, great-grandfather, grandfather and father. On the first day of the month, wine and fruits were served in the ceremony. If there were no close relatives, then blessings on the board were used. If titles of the spirit tablets were changed or new titles were added, they were removed to the west. The western cabinet was emptied for the new owner. If there were close relatives, the spirit tablets would be moved out to the grave, unburied, after the blessing rites. If they were remote relatives with remaining relationship in the clan, they would be moved to the house of the eldest, who would worship it after blessing rites were held. In other cases, change of titles and removal were carried out as before. If there were no longer close relatives, then they were buried between two stairs after the blessing rites. The rest of change of titles and removal were alike. According to *Family Courtesy*, *General Rites*, *Ancestral Halls*, "The rite of title change and removal could be seen in the chapter of *Funeral Great Auspice*. When the great-great-great-grandfather no longer had any close relatives, their spirit tablets would be moved to the tomb. Sacrificial offerings will remain unchanged for a hundred generations. When the relatives of the second generation all died or the relatives of the great-great-grandfather all died, the spirit tablet of the great-great-great-grandfather would be moved out and buried. His tomb would be in the charge of his descendants by turns, which would not be changed over a hundred generations.

Then, why was the spirit tablet of great-great-great-grandfather moved to the tomb? According to Zhu Xi's explanations, emperors and dukes had temples, with spirit tablets hidden there. But now, people have no such temples to place them, so they have to be buried at the tomb. ①

Yang Fu said, with the passage of time and change of opinions, the ceremonial rites remained very important. It might be inadequate to express respect since in *Family Courtesy* it only worshipped ancestors with wine and fruits in ancestral halls. It is necessary to implement the ceremony at the previous night and gave the title to the spirit tablet. When the ceremony was over, the spirit tablet of the great-great-great-grandfather could be buried at the tomb, and the spirit tablet to be moved and the new one should be placed in temples respectively.

According to the historical literature, during the Song and Yuan periods, tomb ancestral halls were pervasive and popular. For some clans in Huizhou, they constructed tomb ancestral halls at the tombs of previous generations, such as Family Wang's in Fengtingli, Wuyuan, Family Wang's in Huiling, Wuyuan, Wang Jieran's in Wuyuan, Family Wu's in Xin'an, and Family Luo's Yanggan Tomb Ancestral Hall in Chengkan, Shexian County. ②

Zhu Xi's student asked him: now, since all common people have their forefathers, could they only worship ancestors over four generations while not enshrining those beyond? Zhu Xi said, the forefathers could only have tomb sacrificial offerings. Yang Fu said, when the relatives of the great-great-great-grandfather all died, his spirit tablet could be placed at the tomb. The tomb ancestral halls however need to be built to hold tomb sacrificial offerings. ③

From the aforementioned comments, our conclusions are: during the Song and Yuan periods, in domestic ancestral halls, whether for the great-great-great-grandfather or great-great-grandfather, their spirit tablets would

---

① *Zhu Xi's Family Courtesy*.
② Chang Janhua, Chapter 2: Ancestral Sacrificial Offering and Domestic Temples, Ancestral Halls. Table of Tomb Ancestral Sacrificial Offering in Yuan Dynasty, *Record of Patriarchal Clan*.
③ *Zhu Xi's Family Courtesy*.

be moved out when all of their relatives passed away. The difference lies in: the great-great-great-grandfather's spirit tablet would be moved to the tomb ancestral hall and continued to be worshipped, while the great-great-grandfather's would be buried between two stairs at the ancestral hall or at the tomb place. In the Mid-Ming Dynasty, the ancestral rules and folk ancestral worshipping systems in China underwent dramatic changes. In the 15th year of Jiajing Period (1536), Xia Yan, the Director of the Ministry of Civil Office in his "Advice to Encourage Subjects to Employ Rites" wrote: The Emperor has the desire to worship his ancestors, and nine temples were completed. Despite all of the difficulties over 2,000 years, the emperor had the temples constructed. Only meritorious statesmen could have their forefathers' spirit tablets in the temples. During Taizu and Taizong periods, there were worshipping in temples, but since Renzong Period, no offering in five temples, which might be due to inadequacy of the record. There were no definite regulations to forbid subjects to worship their ancestors. There were many filial children and grandchildren who wanted to worship their forefathers. It would be very fortunate if temples could be built to indicate emperor's status, and send his imperial edicts and implemented business there. Xia Yan's "Three Discussions" include: first, meritorious statesmen's use of temples; ancestral sacrificial offerings for subjects at the Winter Solstice; third, construction of domestic temples nationwide.① According to the record of historical literature, "The Emperor Agreed" and "The Emperor Followed The Practice" indicated that memorials to the throne were accepted by Emperor Jiajing. In the Ming Dynasty, officials with "Pin" (certain ranking of Chinese ancient officials) were allowed to establish domestic ancestral temples to worship their forefathers. For common subjects, however, they were only permitted to enshrine their ancestors in their main

---

① Xia Yan, *Advice in Guizhou from Xia Yan*, Volume 21.

room.① But since officials were allowed to establish domestic temples, subjects also followed their suit to enshrine theirs, which became a custom then.② It was recorded that Emperor Shizong of the Ming Dynasty adopted Great Scholar Xia Yan's advice and allowed ordinary people to establish ancestral temples, which made clan temples everywhere.③ It was recorded that since the 15th year of Jiajing Period (1536), there was a boom in Huizhou to establish ancestral halls. Many halls were built, and they were spread everywhere.④ Then, what about the regulations for worshipping spirit tablets in clan ancestral halls in Huizhou during the Ming and Qing periods? According to the record, regulations related in Family Xiang's ancestral halls in Guixi, Shexian County, in terms of the house, there were three cabinets, and the principal room was in the middle, with two rooms in the left and right. Rules for sacrificial offerings were as follows:

For five generations dating from parents, the spirit tablets were desirably placed in the middle for worshipping and would never be moved out for the benefit of their descendants. Honorable people, civil and military officials, people did excellently in the imperial exams, and people who are kind and virtuous, loyal and filial. The spirit tablets of those who were both honorable and successful would be paced at the left and right of the middle cabinet to glorify their ancestors and descendants, and never be moved out.

Money was raised to establish tomb ancestral halls to worship spirit tablets. Great efforts were made to pay tribute to spirit tablets and people

---

① *Continued General Literature Survey: Survey of Temples and Domestic Ancestral Halls for Ministers and Major Officials*, Volume 6.

② Chang Jianhua, *Record of Patriarchal Clan* for reference.

③ Xi Baogan, *Table of Loyal and Virtuous People in Foshan*, Volume 9, quoted by Ye Xian'en's "The Rural Society and Tanent-Servant System during Ming and Qing dynasties"; Anhui People's Publishing House, 1983.

④ Zhao Huafu's "Several Issues Related to Ancestral Halls in Huizhou", *Collection of Papers of International Academic Conference on Huizhou in* 1995, published by Anhui University Publishing House, 1997.

who were devoted to the compilation of family archives were rewarded. Spirit tablets of people with great contributions would be worshipped and never be removed.

Spirit tablets of people's parents, those untitled, civil and military scholars would be places at the tomb place, and be moved out over five generations. ①

These are regulations of "not moved out over one hundred generations" and "moved out over five generations" for the spirit tablets of ancestral halls in Huizhou over the Ming and Qing periods. The regulations show that during the Ming and Qing periods, the removal of spirit tablets in ancestral halls were not only quite different from that in the Zhou Dynasty, but also greatly distinct from that over the Song and Yuan periods. One major difference and change is: over the Ming and Qing periods, besides the spirit tablets of great-great-great-grandfather that would not be removed over a hundred generations, those of other people within five generations including parents, virtuous and successful people, honorable and meritorious people would never be removed either.

As it is known to all that China is vast in territory, and that the ancestral halls in the whole country varied a lot. However, one thing was in common everywhere: the spirit tablet of the original ancestor was placed in the central part of the cabinet, and would never be removed during the Ming and Qing periods.

What were regulations about "removal over five generations" of ancestral halls over the Ming and Qing periods? According to the record of literature and research on the spot, during the Ming and Qing periods, in Huizhou, when parents died, their descendants would establish spirit tablets for the deceased, which were also named as "God tablet" "grain tablet"

---

① *Historical Studies in Anhui Province*, Issue 2; *Family Xu's Family Tree of Chengdong Ancient Shexian County*, Volume 7; Xu Chengyao, *Casual Talks of Affairs in Shexian County*, Volume 18.

"wooden tablet" "soul position" "god position" and "board position", etc. At first, the spirit tablets were placed in the chamber, and were later sent to ancestral halls on the worshipping day according to the regulations, which is called "sending tablets" or "entering tablets". In order to standardize sizes and make them look tidy and beautiful, most of spirit tablets were made at the same criteria. Descendants of the deceased would report to the ancestral halls and they would help fill them. It is regulated in almost all ancestral halls that money should be paid to have spirit tablets entered. For most of ancestral halls, "sending tablets" ceremony was held annually, and it was usually set on the day before winter worshipping. According to domestic rules, except those deprived of the right to enter ancestral halls, other members in the clan enjoyed equal rights and everybody's spirit tablet was entitled to enter the ancestral hall and be worshipped by the descendants. This kind of right was holy and inviolable.

Then, which people's spirit tablets were not allowed to enter ancestral halls? Regulations of the ancestral hall of Family Zhou in Chengxi, Jixi County made it very clear in its *Rules of Ancestral Halls*: those who died young or unmarried girls, incestuous, adulterous or disobedient males and females.

And those who sold their wives or daughters to others as concubines would never be allowed to enter the ancestral halls. Those who had the same surname yet did not belong to the clan, adopted sons, or those who became family members after marriage would never be allowed either.① Most of regulations related to ancestral halls in Huizhou are almost the same. Regulations of the ancestral hall of Family Zhou in Chengxi, Jixi County made in *Rules of Ancestral Halls* are representative and typical.

In one ancestral hall, many spirit tablets of ancestors were enshrined, and there were many generations: four or five generations at least, eight or nine generations or even more. Then, how to implement the regulations of

---

① Xu Chengyao, *Casual Talks of Affairs in Shexian County*, Volume 18.

moving them out over five generations? Based on the research, except the spirit tablet which would not be removed over a hundred generations, other spirit tablets could only be worshipped over four generations (sons, grandsons, great-grandsons, and great-great-grandsons) according to the ancestral regulations. When the great-great-grandson died, there were no longer relatives. Till the appearance of great-great-great-grandson, that is, the fifth generation, the spirit tablet would be moved out from the ancestral cabinet or buried underground, or placed in the chamber of the ancestral hall.

So, despite many generations of spirit tablets of the worshipped ancestors, for each great-great-grandson in the clan, their forefathers were all great-great-grandparents, great-grandparents, grandparents and parents. For ordinary ancestors in the ancestral hall, every spirit tablet conformed to the stipulations and principles of "moved out every five generations" or "removed when there are no more relatives". In *Family Courtesy*, Zhu Xi said: when there are no more relatives for the great-great-grandparents, the spirit tablets would be moved out to get buried. During the Ming and Qing periods, though regulations about "removed over five generations" stipulated in Huizhou ancestral halls and cabinets, and those set in *Family Courtesy* are different to a certain extent, they are basically the same in principle.

II. Categories of Ancestral Sacrificial Offering in Huizhou

There are many kinds of ancestral worshipping in Huizhou, such as Spring Rites, Festival of Hungry Ghosts (Zhongyuan), Autumn Rites, Winter Rites, Yearly Burning (Shaonian), anniversary of forefathers, etc. In terms of worshipping seasons, there were chiefly Spring Rites, Autumn Rites and Winter Rites; in terms of worshipping places, there were ancestral hall enshrining, tomb enshrining and domestic enshrining.

According to *Record of Shexian County—Customs* after the foundation of People's Republic of China, worshipping ceremonies were firstly held in spring and autumn, then in solstices. In *Survey of Customs and Rites in Shexian County*, worshipping rites all followed Lord Wengong's *Family*

Courtesy, all places are basically the same. For domestic sacrificial ceremonies, they were chiefly held in spring and autumn. If they were held in the solstice day, then that violated conventions. ①

In *Family Courtesy*, Zhu Xi said, besides sacrificial rites in traditional seasons, one family once had sacrificial offering in winter solstice, beginning of spring, the third month of. Then they felt very upset because they thought offerings in winter solstice and beginning of spring went against regulations. So they stopping worshipping at those times, but held worshipping activities in the third month of autumn.

It is also recorded: the humane primogenitor's worshipping was held in winter solstice while the ancestors' was held in the beginning of spring. But according to the record of genealogy in Huizhou, most of clans held worshipping rites in spring and autumn, and in winter as well. For instance, according to *Regulations of Family Cheng in Xin'an*, for worshipping in spring and autumn, it is set at the dawn of the fifteenth of the middle month. In *Domestic Rules of Family Xu*, a clan in Chengdong, Shexian County, it is recorded that: the root of people could be traced back to ancestors, and they would be worshipped in spring and autumn. Worshipping activities could provide people with the opportunity to express their filial thoughts. ②

According to the regulations in *Clan Rules* of Family Wang in Zefu, worshipping rites at winter solstice and the beginning of spring in Family Courtesy could never be lost. ③ The regulations of *Clan Rules* from Family Wang in Wukou, Wuyuan are: worshipping rites at winter solstice and the beginning of spring in Family Courtesy could not be lost. ④

---

① Family Zhou, *Genealogical Tree of Chengxi Jixi County*, Volume of Ancestral Offering.
② Family Xiang, *Genealogical Tree in Guixi, Shexian County*, Volume 22.
③ *Family Huang's Family Tree in Tandu Xiaoli, Ancestral Tombs*, in Shexian County, Volume 5.
④ Xu Chengyao, *Casual Talks of Affairs in Shexian County*, Volume 18.

According to the Offering Affairs, *Rules of Family Bao in the Tangyue, Shexian County*, except worshipping rites in spring and autumn, Festival of Hungry Ghosts and Yearly Burning, winter offering would be held at the solstice day. Money should be paid in advance to people in charge to buy pigs and sheep in preparation for worshipping items. ①

What is stipulated in *Family Hu Longjing School in Mingjing* related to sacrificial offering affairs going like this: in terms of worshipping rites at spring equinox and winter solstice, a thorough cleaning of ancestral temples by servants in charge is necessary three days in advance, such as washing of enshrining wares and wiping of desks and tables. The head of the ancestral hall should be in charge of the rite. ②

According to *The regulations of Family Wu*, *Domestic Rules in Mingzhou*, Xiuning, rules are: at winter solstice, the sacrificial offering was only for Lord Zurong's parents instead of others. It was held solemnly in his privilege. Worshipping rites at the beginning of spring conformed to *Family Zheng's Domestic Rules* and people were very discreet in making decisions. According to our survey, at the period of People's Republic of China, most of worshipping activities in Huizhou were held twice a year, that is, in spring and winter. *Family Shao's Genealogical Tree in Huayang, Jixi. Clan Rules*, revised in the 2nd year of Xuantong Period (1910), recorded that sacrificial activities could not be held too frequently, otherwise, people would feel bored and show no respect; sacrificial activities could not be held too infrequently either, otherwise, people would become lazy and forget about their forefathers... On the first day of the year, people in my clan worship God and ancestors, sweep graves at Tomb Sweeping Day, hold sacrificial offering at the hall at the Festival of Hungry Ghosts. We also worship honorable people at the front hall, and the tradition has lasted a long time. As to the worshipping of ancestors at the winter solstice, it is a

---

① *Family Xu's Family Tree of Chengdong Ancient Shexian County*, Volume 7.
② *Family Shao's Genealogical Tree in Huayang, in Jixi*, Volume 18.

custom through all the ages. If there were no such ceremonies, then how could filial and kind descendants feel at ease?

In the 3rd year of Xuantong Period (1911), according to the revised *Family Hu Family Tree in Mingjing, Shangchuan. Twenty-Four New Made Ancestral Rules*, all worshipping rites should be held at the spring equinox in spring and the winter solstice in winter. Animals are offered to worship great-great-father, great-grandfather, grandfather and deceased father, while delicious food is provided to honor collateral relatives. All ceremonies are held carefully according to the requirement of Zhu Xi's *Family Courtesy*, so, at the end of the Qing Dynasty, these clans still employed spring and winter worshipping rites as their chief sacrificial activities.

In Huizhou, all worshipping activities for ancestors, whether Spring Rites, Festival of Hungry Ghosts, Autumn Rites, Winter Rites, Yearly Burning or anniversaries of the birth or death of ancestors, will all be held at the ancestral halls, that is why such activities are also termed as hall sacrificial offering. In *Jiyuan Record—A Miscellany of Hometown*, Zhao Jishi wrote: In Xin'an, people with the same surname lived together, without the mixture of other surnames. Its folk custom was very ancient and traditional. People were very courteous to each other, and each surname was unified under the ancestral hall. In winter, a thousand people all gathered to worship ancestors according to Wengong's *Family Courtesy*, and carried out the ceremony in a very polite and proper way. In *Family Huang's Family Tree in Xin'an—Record of Xixi Hall*, it was recorded that: Nowadays, every family must have a temple, in which there are spirit tablets. There are sacrificial rites there.

In *Family Huang Tandu Clan in Shexian County—A Brief Record of Tandu Huang Family's Special Ancestral Hall*, it is said that sacrificial offering rites are of chief importance in terms of requiting and following ancestors. Ancestral temples are constructed; spirit tablets are displayed, with bamboo and wooden containers placed beside; bells and drums are in preparation for the rites; people bow and kneel down to worship their ancestors in a very pious way. Whether in the rainy spring or frosty autumn, worshipping rites are held regularly, and people will be devoted to them in all their lifetime. The spirit tablets will be enshrined and kept over a hundred generations, which is regarded as a rewarding deed. ①

Domestic Rules of Family Shao in Huayang, Jixi County made ancestral rules as follows: according to *Family Courtesy*, gentlemen will build ancestral temples first if they want to establish a family. The purpose of constructing ancestral temples is to rest spirit tablets of the forefathers at peace. If ancestral halls are not built or maintained, then the coming-of-age ceremony, marriages, funerals, sacrificial rites or other kinds of ceremonies will have no way or place to be held. ②

In *Family Xu's Domestic Rules* of Clan Xu in Chengdong, Shexian County, the construction of ancestral halls is to rest forefathers at peace, hold sacrificial rites and thus unifying members in the clan. ③

In *Family Wang's Family Tree—Clan Rules*, the establishment of ancestral halls is to memorize ancestors and honor ceremony and decorum. On the first day of January according to the lunar calendar, juniors and seniors are gathered for mutual Spring Festival congratulations. Rites are held at the beginning of spring, winter solstice according to *Family Courtesy* to enshrine ancestors and will be continued forever.

At Tomb Sweeping Day, many clans in Huizhou would hold sacrificial ceremonies at the tomb place, which was termed as "tomb sacrificial ceremony", ("marking" "marked hanging" "money hanging" "paper hanging" "additional titling", etc.) According to the record of Survey Related to Customs in Shexian County, "tomb sacrificial ceremony" is the most solemn and grand activity, which is also named as "money hanging" "paper hanging". If it is held at Tomb Sweeping Day, it is called "marking"

---

① *Family Huang Tandu Clan in Shexian County—Sacrificial Rites*, Volume 6.
② *Family Shao's Genealogical Tree in Huayang*, in *Jixi*, Volume 18.
③ Family Xu's Family Tree of Chengdong Ancient Shexian County, *Volume 7*.

or "additional titling", etc. For clan ancestors, their spirit tablets will then be worshipped in the whole clan, while branch ancestors will be worshipped by their own descendants. Even clans of a small number of people will hold tomb sacrificial ceremonies. So, since the Han, Jin, Tang, Song dynasties up to now, all big clans have a long family tree and their ancestral tombs are all well preserved, and never got lost or abandoned. ①

In *Family Xu's Domestic Rules* by Family Xu Clan in Chengdong, Shexian County, it is recorded that in ancient times, tomb sacrificial activity was not a custom. The reason why it would not be abolished and is regarded so important for centuries is that ancestors' spirit was embedded there. ② According to Family Wang's Family Tree in Wukou, Wuyuan, the field is used to build tomb ancestral halls for worshipping. Descendants of all branches in the clan collected rents by turns, and prepared sacrificial items within five days at Tomb Sweeping Day. Representatives, junior or senior would be selected to gather at ancestral tombs to have worshipping ceremonies. Different in opinions from Xu's family, *Chapter of Clan Rules* in Volume 11 of *Family Cheng's Family Tree in Xiyan Town Shexian County* held that tomb ancestral sacrificial offering was the ancient custom. It was mentioned in Mencius' sacrificial rite. Every year, people old and young in the clan would go to the tomb of the humane primogenitor to sweep it and worship him according to Wengong's *Family Courtesy*. In the 20th year of Wangli Period (1592), at Tomb Sweeping Day, all members of Family Huang in Huizhou would arrive at the ancestral tomb at Huangdun, Shexian County to hold worshipping ceremonies. So, over 50 officials and men of letters, along with servants and carts, would hold grand and solemn sacrificial rites. It was so glorious and splendid that it attracted many spectators. ③

---

① Xu Chengyao, *Casual Talks of Affairs in Shexian County*, Volume 18.
② *Family Xu's Family Tree of Chengdong Ancient Shexian County*, Volume 7.
③ *Family Huang's Family Tree in Tandu Xiaoli, Ancestral Tombs, in Shexian County*, Volume 5.

According to clans in Huizhou, the ancestral temples are the harbor of their ancestors, and the tombs are the place where their spirits and bodies are hidden. Even if descendants cannot see their forefathers, they can see the places where they depend and live as if they saw ancestors themselves. Sacrificial offering and tomb worshipping activities both belong to major rites and should be dealt with respect and discretion. ①

Apart from ancestral and tomb sacrificial rites, there were domestic sacrificial rites in Huizhou as well.

In *Family Courtesy*, Zhu Xi wrote: Gentle will establish ancestral halls first if they want to build houses. Four cabinets were set at the east of the principle room to worship spirit tablets of deceased ancestors.

The ancestral hall at the east to worship great-great-grandfather, great-grandfather, grandfather and father is the domestic one. Sacrificial activities held there are actually domestic rites. During the Song and Yuan periods, most of clans in Huizhou didn't build ancestral halls. So, it was only a rare phenomenon. ②

Therefore, for clan juniors, the sacrificial activities were held in ancestral halls or in the house. There is no doubt that the sacrificial activities in the house are also regarded as domestic sacrificial rites. In the middle of the Ming Dynasty, after the construction of ancestral halls, the chief worshipping form is to combine ancestors to hold sacrificial activities. The spirit tablets enshrined in the ancestral hall include: the progenitor, deceased ancestors, the great-great-grandfather, great-grandfather, grandfather and father. The progenitor would be worshipped by all clans; deceased ancestors would be honored by all clans or their own clan; the great-great-grandfather, great-grandfather, grandfather and father would be worshipped by sons, grandsons, great-grandsons and great-great-grandsons. In terms of people to be worshipped

---

① *Family Wang's Family Tree of Xuanren*, Xiuning County Clan Rules.

② Zhao Huafu, "Several Issues Related to Ancestral Halls in Huizhou", *Collection of Papers of International Academic Conference on Huizhou* in 1995, published by Anhui University Publishing House, 1997.

and families engaged in sacrificial activities, even though the sacrificial rites for the great-great-grandfather, great-grandfather, grandfather and father were held at the ancestral hall or at the tomb place, they could still be termed as domestic sacrificial activities.

In the historical literature of Huizhou, clan ancestral halls are also termed as domestic ancestral halls (or domestic temples). "Zongpu" (clan family tree) is also named as "Jiapu" (family tree, or "Zupu" "Jiacheng"). Therefore, what we must point out is that the domestic sacrificial activities mentioned in the literature is either about all clans' sacrificial offering or one clan's (or a branch, a school, a door's) sacrificial rites, or domestic sacrificial activities.

In order to guarantee the smooth holding of sacrificial activities, clans in Huizhou would establish all kinds of corresponding sacrificial organization, which they termed as "Hui" (association) such as Progenitor Association, Dunben Ancestral Association, Tomb Sweeping Day Association, Winter Solstice Association, Winter Sacrificial Association, Lord Chang Association, Lord Yczhao Association, Ye Winter Solstice Association; Lord Mao Association; Lord Yi Association; Lord Huang Association; Lord Ding Association; Lord Yun Association; Lord Zhong Association; Lord Five Three Association, etc.[①] Some of these associations held sacrificial rites in spring, some in winter; some sacrificial activities were held at ancestral halls; some were held at tomb places. Some association include spring and winter sacrificial rites, and ancestral hall and tomb sacrificial activities as well. Members of the clan organized sacrificial ceremonies and donated money to buy fields and collect grain, so the sacrificial rites could be long preserved. Hu Tengpu in Yixian county in "Tomb Sweeping Association" said that in Anhui, people of the same clan lived together, and had ancestral halls for ancient primogenitors. Following generations from primogenitors were recorded in the family tree. The branch members in most cases had branch ancestral halls. Ancestral

---

① Zhang Youyi, *A Study on Land Relationship in Huizhou during Ming and Qing Periods*, Chinese Social Science Publishing House, 1984.

halls belonged to associations. Those who have not established ancestral halls also pool money to set associations. People with much money could make money by selling grain and wheat every year, while people with little money could loan money for sacrificial activities. ①

In order to prove these associations are not sacrificial activities, two examples are quoted as follows. Example 1, in *Family Dong's Family Tree—Preface of Tomb Sweeping for Lord Zhu Linlin*, it is written: Though Winter Solstice and Mutual Congratulations (two were associations here) were established early respectively, ancestral halls were established for branch members at Tomb Sweeping Day to save money for tomb sweeping. At that time, people old and young all gathered at the tomb place, and their admiration for the spirit of ancestors was witnessed by white clouds and pine trees. People were very courteous to each other, and the ceremony was extremely grand. However, only the lord himself had no one special ancestral hall, and it truly made people feel upset. So, his descendants all tried to express their fidelity and benevolence by establishing Tomb Sweeping Association. Fortunately, with unanimous efforts and ancestors' blessings, people donated money willingly and made it possible. There were altogether 59 members, which were divided into 7 groups. They also discussed the articles about the association, and promise to observe them forever. Year after year, the 11th day before Tomb Sweeping Day, every person was tidily dressed and participated in the sacrificial ceremony in the ancestral hall, then they went to the tomb place together, sweeping it and worshipping ancestors to express their deep and fonder feelings. At Year Gengzi, money was spent on the dry field of the mulberry forest numbered 1329, 1330, 1331, 1332 from a person whose surname was Fang in Zaokui at a size of three "mu" five "fen" nine "mao" five "si". The land was managed by the notary. If there were no justice or discretion, then did it make any sense to memorize the ancestors? What is recorded in *Preface of*

---

① *Miscellaneous Essays of Hu Teng*.

Part III The Patriarchal Clan System in Huizhou

Tomb Sweeping for Lord Zhu Linlin is the spring season sacrificial rite and Tomb Sweeping sacrificial association established for their ancestor Dong Lin by his descendants Family Dong, a branch clan of Zhulin school in Youshan, Wuyuan County.

The second example is that in Wuyuan, according to Family Dong's Family Tree. Preface of Winter Sacrificial Rite of Lord Yubao of Zhulin clan. Lord Lin was regarded as the earliest ancestor of the Zhulin clan since the parting of two schools of Lin and Pei, with following Lord Yubao to the tenth generation. Sacrificial rites were held both in spring and autumn for all ancestors. Why only Lord Yubao was not worshipped as other ancestors? His descendants were over two hundred members and there were no reasons for that. Fortunately, relatives as Benjing, Benyao, Benming and Runrun, Changqiu, etc. who were diligent and tolerant, volunteered to establish associations. They set Winter Sacrifice and named it Worshipping Rite. There were 125 members in total, each donating some money for six years. Prosperity was guaranteed due to their concerted efforts. Descendants could gather at the ancestral hall one day before the winter solstice and expressed their piety. This should be completed with many people's hard work.

In *Preface of Winter Solstice Worshipping Rite for Lord Yubao of Zhulin Clan*, it is recorded that the winter solstice sacrificial rite association was set by Family Dong of Zhulin school in Youshan Wuyuan county. In the 56th year of Qianlong Period (1791), the Benshi Hall of Family Hu's ancestral hall at Xidi Mingjing, Yixian County was set, and it was organized by Dunben sacrificial association. The sculpture of Dunben sacrificial association, now erected at the entrance of Xidi village, records that Lord Wanzhao, etc. 37 ancestors in total, would be set spirit tablets. So each family was supposed to pay 20 *liang* of money, 740 *liang* in total. There were 40 fields, altogether 16,172,667 *mu*, which was all used to establish the sacrificial association, which was set for all sacrificial activities in Benshi Hall, including spring, autumn, winter and tomb sacrificial rites, etc.

Ⅲ. Purpose of Female Ancestral Construction and Worshipping of Spirit Tablets in Huizhou

During the Ming and Qing periods, there were ancestral halls everywhere in Huizhou, and cities and countryside were adjoined. A couple of clans not only established ancestral halls, branch ancestral halls, domestic ancestral halls, but female ancestral halls as well. According to the literature and field trips, Family Luo, Family Huang of Tandu, Family Bao of Tangyue in Shexian County, and Family Huang of Huang village in Xiuning county all established female ancestral halls. In *Family Huang Tandu Clan in Shexian County—A Brief Record of Tandu Huang Family's Special Ancestral Hall*: during Kangxi Period in the Qing Dynasty, Family Huang of Tandu prepared wooden materials to establish a special ancestral hall for the mother, with five columns in the hall, three doors in the front, and rooms and ancestral hall doors in the back. The hall stands 3 *zhang* and 5 feet, with a depth of 27 *zhang* and a width of 6 *zhang* and 4 feet. The building was finely constructed as a whole.

It had almost everything in an ancestral hall. 30,000 *liang* silver was spent at its completion. During Jiaqing Period, Bao Qiyun, the son of the rich salt merchant of the Bao Family of Tangyue built Qingyi. In terms of its size, refinement of construction, high quality of materials, beauty of decorations, it has surpassed Dunben ancestral hall (colloquially named as male ancestral hall) of the Bao's Clan in many respects. So, why some clans desired to build female ancestral halls?

The Pacifying Spirit Rule of *Family Luo's Family Tree—Eight Principles of Clan Rites* by Family Luo in Chengkan explained the reasons and purposes of constructing female ancestral hall for their clan. It said that if the male and female were in different rooms in their lifetime, and their souls would feel ill at ease when their spirit tablets were put in the same hall after death. It was necessary to have one special hall to separate their spirit tablets. Those who died in chastity would be put at the left and those who died with titles were put at the right. Therefore, a female ancestral hall was set at the right of Mr. Luo Dongshu's ancestral hall of Luo's clan in Chengkan, Shexian County. Also, if the male and female were in different rooms in their lifetime, and their souls would feel ill at ease when their spirit tablets were put in the same hall after death. It was necessary to have one special hall to separate their spirit tablets. The left side for people who died in chastity and the right side for people who had titles indicating that the female ancestral halls were not established merely for virtuous and virgin females. In *Family Huang Tandu Clan in Shexian County—A Brief Record of Tandu Huang Family's Special Ancestral Hall*, the purposes and reasons for constructing female ancestral halls for Huang's clan were also clearly explored. It said that our village was in a remote area where husbands either went to other places to pursue study or did business in other places. They would be away from home for many years or decades of years, and females helped to raise children and deal with everything at home. As to the growth of a child, from infantry to adulthood, it was chiefly under the cultivation of the mother, the mother would send the child to school to receive education. What a major role mother played in the family! The child's success was because of Mother's care in his childhood and advice in his adulthood.

  The establishment of ancestral halls in my hometown was in honor of ancestors, who were generally termed as progenitors. It is understandable for their respect for them and trace for their own root. However, most of worshipping rites were not for mothers. The spirit tablets were ancestors' instead of mothers'. It was very unfair for mothers who played the role both as a mother and as a father by raising children from an infant to an adult, cultivating them and making them receive education. It made descendants feel very upset when their mothers were not properly dealt with. When people held sacrificial activities in the past, they looked around but could not find their mothers' spirit tablets, and then felt very upset. In order to make up for this, Huang's clan in Tandu prepared materials and constructed the grand female ancestral hall specially for women in Family Huang. It went beyond doubt that it was set for females' spirit tablets to make their souls peaceful instead of only for those of chastity and virginity.

During the Jiaqing Period in the Qing Dynasty, Bao Zhidao and Bao Shufang, father and son who were of rich salt merchants of the Bao Family of Tangyue spent a large amount of money rebuilding Lord Siwan Ancestral Hall (also termed as Dunben Hall, or colloquially male ancestral hall). This ancestral only worshipped males instead of females. Bao Qiyun, the rich salt merchant established Qingyi female ancestral hall to honor females only and set their souls at peace. Since it is "only for females" to "prosper sacrificial rites", not an ancestral hall for heroic females. In related historic literature, especially in the record of *Branch Genealogical Tree about Xuanzhong Hall of Family Bao of Tangyue*, it was not mentioned that the female ancestral hall was constructed to specially worship spirit tablets of virtuous females.

Most of domestic rules in Huizhou stipulated that except people deprived of the right to enter the ancestral hall out of some special reasons, generally speaking, the spirit tablets of women could all enter the ancestral hall. That was the rule of the ancestral hall. According to the record of *Rules of Worshipping Spirit Tablets* of Family Xiang's Ancestral Hall in Guixi, Shexian County, there are three rooms, the middle one is the principle one while the right and the left are rooms for spirit tablets of the previous generations in order, which reflects the system of the ancestral hall. The spirit tablets of five generations following the humane primogenitor would be placed at the central part and never be removed to benefit their descendants and boom the clan. The spirit tablets of parents will be put in the chamber in order and removed over five generations. ①

According to *Domestic Rules of Family Wu of Mingzhou* in Xiuning County, in the picture of winter solstice sacrificial rite, the spirit tablet of paternal progenitor is in the left, while that of maternal progenitor is in the

---

① *Family Xiang's Family Tree in Guixi—Sacrificial Rites*, *Shexian County*, Volume 22.

Part Ⅲ　The Patriarchal Clan System in Huizhou

right. In the picture of the beginning of spring sacrificial rite, the spirit tablet of paternal ancestor is in the left, while that of maternal ancestor is in the right. According to *Family Hu Family Tree in Mingjing, Shangchuan— Twenty-four New Made Ancestral Rules*, it is regulated in the preface that fist, the spirit tablet of great-great-grandfather, great-grandfather, grandfather and father should be accompanied by that of their principle wife, along with that of the woman they married later whether they had children or not. If their principal wives had no children while their concubines had, then their spirit tablets could also enter the ancestral hall. If the principal wives had children, then the money for spirit tablets should be doubled. If the concubines bore children who died young, then their spirit tablets would not be allowed to enter it; second, as to the branch relatives, the wife of the great-great-granduncle, the wife of the great-granduncle, the wife of the granduncle, the wife of the uncle, the wife of the brother, the wife of the nephew, and adults who have no children, then the spirit tablets of males are all placed in the east while those of the females in the west according to the order of generations. They would be removed every four generations.

The spirit tablets of adolescents under 15 were not allowed to enter the ancestral hall. According to the regulations in Zhu Xi's *Family Courtesy*, generally speaking, women's spirit tablets could all enter the ancestral hall. The record in Volume 1 of *General Rules—Ancestral Hall*, the spirit tablets of those without descendants would be put along with those of the ancestors. The spirit tablets of granduncle will be put along with that of the great-great-grandfather; those of the uncle will be put along with that of the great-grandfather. Those of the wives of the brothers will be put along with that of the grandfather. Those of sons and nephews will be put along with that of the father. They all were put toward the west and in the central place of the cabinet. It is also recorded that at the first and fifteenth day of the lunar month, sacrificial activity is held. The note is: the husband washed his hands and dried them, lifting and opening the cabinet and putting male ancestral spirit tablets in front of it; the wife washed her hands and dried them, placing female ancestral spirit tablets in the east. Worshipping for the male spirit tablets went first. It also records that: announcement is given if necessary. Its note is: the great-grandson is filial in worshipping his great-great-father and great-great-mother. The grandson is filial in worshipping his grandfather and grandmother. The son is filial in worshipping his father and mother.

Volume 5 of the book *Sacrificial Rite—Earliest Ancestors* records that worshipping gods. The note records that at the winter solstice, a filial grandson knelt before the fireplace in the ancestral hall to worship his great-great-grandfather and great-great-grandmother. *Sacrificial Rite—Ancestors* records that containers were displayed and positions were arranged a day earlier. The note reads: the spirit tablet of the grandfather is at the west of hall, while that of the grandmother is at the east of the hall.

Sacrificial Rite—Anniversary of Death records that: spirit tablets.

Note: The spirit tablet of the man and that of his wife were put in the same cabinet, which was painted in black. Spirit tablets of husband and wife were allowed to enter the ancestral hall.

Female ancestral halls were not constructed only for virtuous women. Except for some deprived of the right to enter the ancestral hall due to special reasons, women in general could all enter the ancestral hall. This has embodied the principle and spirit in ancestral regulations of *Family Courtesy* in Huizhou.

Published in *Anhui History Studies*, No. 2, 2003
Written by Zhao Huafu
Translated by Zhou Qing

Chapter 9 Genealogical Tree in the Ming and Qing Dynasties in Huizhou and Its Social Customs

There are various social customs in Huizhou, which is always the focus of scholars, and plays an important role in helping people realize the social customs in Huizhou. The formation of these social customs is definitely the result of multiple factors. The genealogy of the Ming and Qing dynasties in Huizhou however could not be undervalued.

I. Profound Significance of Genealogy

About the social customs in Huizhou, Zhao Jishi once said: "In Xin'an, people with the same surname lived together, without the mixture of other surnames. Its folk custom was very ancient and traditional. People were very courteous to each other, and each surname was unified under the ancestral hall. In winter, a thousand people all gathered to worship ancestors according to Wengong's *Family Courtesy*, and carried out the ceremony in a very polite and proper way. In Xin'an, there were many kinds of social customs, which surpassed in the respect many other places. The tombs of a thousand years would never be touched, and a clan of a thousand members would never live in a scattered way. Genealogy of a thousand years is kept in good order."[①]

The relationship between social customs in Huizhou and its genealogy in the Ming and Qing dynasties has already been stressed. The very existence of "Genealogy of a thousand years" has made it possible that "people of different surnames lived together as a clan in Xin'an". It also made it a reality that "the tombs of a thousand years would never be touched, and a clan of a thousand members would never live in a scattered way". Therefore, the scene "there are many more customs than other places" appeared. The

---

① Zhao Jishi, *Jiyuan Record*, *Pan-Leaf Record*, *Miscellaneous Records in the Past*, Volume 11, Huangshan Bookstore, 2008.

reasons for the special social customs in Huizhou are multiple, which was progressively formed in history. Its exploration and discussion are the chief concern of scholar at different times. In the 43 rd year of Wangli Period in the Ming Dynasty, Hong Youzhu, the magistrate of Huizhou Perfect once said, during my official period, people enjoyed rich resources and the official work was relaxing. While standing at a high place to appreciate the beautiful scenery, I couldn't help thinking a lot. White clouds are floating over Huangshan Mountain. People admire Zhu Xi in their minds. [1] In this magistrate's eyes, the social customs in Huizhou is correlated with Zhu Xi's influence. About its formation, no more discussion is carried out here due to much exploration by experts in this field. This article chiefly probes into the influence of genealogy in Huizhou during the Ming and Qing Dynasties over local social customs.

About the function of genealogy on social customs, *Preface of Continued Genealogy in Family Wu* recorded in *Family Wu's Genealogy in Shangshan* in Xiuning County said that, "It is natural for each clan has a genealogy. Emperors of three dynasties and feudal officials established clan laws to unify its members. In this way, they knew whether the relationship was close or remote. The order of generations was clear, and it was a very important custom. The court historian had the genealogy, and those who were filial, friendly and harmonious would be credited while the impious, unfriendly and inharmonious ones would be sentenced. So, celebration was for good things while condolence for sad things. People would help each other in need and poverty. Gratitude and rites remain for remote generations. That is why the justice remains with the passage of time. The branch of the clan boomed and the clan itself was solid. It was a custom prevalent there. Later, the rules were not popular in the country. The laws were loose and education was degrading. The customs have changed, so the

---

[1] *Family Hong's Family Tree in Jiangcun—Preface of Genealogy of Prefecture Lord Xunzai* in Xiuning County, the 8th year of Yongzheng Period.

noble refused to deal with the humble. The rich would not talk with the poor. The conflicts mostly arose from people with different surnames, and people took revenge against each other. Alas! It was truly a pity! Gentlemen in the large clan expressed their disappointment about the degradation of the customs."① From the above dissertation, the author of the genealogy thought the genealogy in the Ming and Qing dynasties were closely related to social customs. For clans, they "celebrated good things and expressed condolence for sad things. People would help each other in need and poverty. Gratitude and rites remain for remote generations. That is why the justice remains with the passage of time. The branch of the clan boomed and the clan itself was solid". So, it could play a role in keeping the clan in order and making the society stable and peaceful. If the family tree with Family Wu was aimed at one surname and one clan, then, Shu Kongzhao in the Wanli Period explored the relationship between genealogy and clans, local officials, the world and court. He said that, "So, the function of genealogy is to unite people and advocate piety and benevolence. It genealogy is compiled for this, and then it will play a positive role. It will make good politics at court, promoting good customs in the society. It will make the clan prosperous in the local place, and Family Shu is a well-known clan. In all, it is very beneficial to people! People once said, people of different families could become brothers if they had shared ideals and thoughts, while even biological siblings could become enemies due to discord. After genealogy was compiled, people come together for celebration or condolence, helping each other in need, encouraging each other in life. The noble would not bully the humble; the rich would not humiliate the poor. The strong would not beat the weak. The junior would not challenge the senior. The compilation of

---

① *Family Wu's Genealogy in Shangshan—Preface of Continued Genealogy in Family Wu* in Xiuning County, the 13th year of Tongzhi Period.

genealogy was truly beneficial. "①

In Shu Kongzhao's opinion, to social customs, genealogy of the Ming and Qing dynasties was not only about a whole clan, instead, it "will make good politics at court, promote good customs in the society. It will make the clan prosperous in the local place, and Family Shu is a well-known clan. In all, it is very beneficial to people!" It played a very positive role in making the society and nation to set customs. Of course, all this began from the clan and got realized by "gathering for celebration and condolence, helping each other in need, encouraging each other in life. The noble would not bully the humble; the rich would not humiliate the poor. The strong would not beat the weak. The junior would not challenge the senior." These aspects could be referred to as away, and a reflection of social customs as well. As to the impact of genealogy on social customs, *Preface of Wu Gengmei* recorded in *Family Hu's Family Tree in Liuchuan*, Jixi said, "Today, the wealthy and successful members in the clan gathered to discuss about genealogy. People were devoted to compile it to fasten ties. The information provided in the genealogy is also the literature for national history. The country collected data related to clans. People of the same clan helped each other and gradually formed the custom. They also built ancestral halls based on that. The compilation of genealogy made people clear about their origin and family relationship, and would help each other in the same clan and work industriously for its prosperity. Therefore, genealogy plays a positive role in both management of the clan and rule of the nation."② The emphasis on the befit of genealogy on the clan, society and the nation is not merely about "the custom", but "the employment of genealogy" and "harmony of family and stability of the nation". In all, genealogy plays a positive role in the

---

① *Family Shu's Family Tree in Huayang—Preface of Shu Kong* in Jixi County, the 9th year of Tongzhi Period.

② *Family Hu's Family Tree in Liuchuan—Preface of Wu Gengmei* in Jixi County, in the 35th year of the People's Republic of China.

formation fine customs. In *Family Hong's Family Tree in Jiangcun Village—Preface by Hongchang* in Xiuning County, "since the residence of our progenitor of Family Hong in Jinangcun village, members in our clan were well preserved in genealogy despite a length of many dynasties. Since I was born late, I failed to get the opportunity to know the former format. Today, the boom and development of the entire country has spurred our clan to perfect our genealogy."① So, Hongchang didn't regard the compilation and repair of Family Hong's genealogy as the business of his own clan, but one cultural embodiment of the booming country. From this perspective, we can see that Hongchang expressed his strong sense of commitment and view this as a beneficial thing to both his clan and the whole nation.

Hu Duqing in the 45th year of the Wanli Period of the Ming Dynasty (1617), in his *Preface of Family Li in Pengtian, Lanhu* probed into social customs in terms of ethics and patriarchal notions: "Genealogy is to honor our ancestors and make our descendants worship them. It is not merely a means. It discloses the origin of the clan and the reason of its development. estors, we'll show respect and love to them spontaneously. That is why the custom is kept from my great-grandfather to my grandfather, and to my uncles and brothers. We all belong to the same clan. So, this notion could be widened to infinity. People of the same clan should respect each other and treat each other in the equal way. Also, they should love each other, show benevolence and respect to each other, which is the embodiment of benevolence and piety. The harmonious relationship in the folk will gradually form fine customs, which will make the whole country peaceful and rational. That is very root of courtesy and rite."② The preface illustrates the relationship between the "same clan concept" and benevolence and piety derived from the

---

① *Family Hong's Family Tree in Jiangcun Village—Preface of Hongchang* in Xiuning County.

② *Family Li's Family Tree in Santian—Preface of Family Tree in Pengtian, Lanhu,Wuyuan*, in Wangli Period.

"same clan concept" in genealogy. It concludes that "when piety and benevolence are possible in the folk, the fine custom is established, which has constructed the very root of courtesy and rite. " The employment of the "same clan concept" in disclosing the relationship between genealogy and social customs made it dialectical and profound in theory.

From what is mirrored in these family trees, they had something in common. That is, the major influence the genealogy has exerted on the social customs is not merely related to the atmosphere of a clan, but also to that of the whole region or the entire country.

Of course, while genealogy in Huizhou in the Ming and Qing dynasties is playing a positive role in the society, some thoughts advocated in it could also exert some negative influence. For instance, in the 9th year of the Xuande Period in the Ming Dynasty (1434), Tian You in writing the preface of *Family Hong's Genealogy in Jiangcun Village* mentioned: "Since we moved from Huangshi to Jiangcun, whose ancestors called Banxian, due to genealogy. We spent many years tracing our origin because every generation was clearly recorded, and everything was true. In the East Jin Dynasty, people didn't care much about the rating of the family, but since the Sui and Tang dynasties, people paid attention to that. Families with higher social status were proud and luxurious, which would make people rival with each other. Is that very terrible when it gradually develops into vicious competition?"[①] The disadvantages mentioned by Tian You are related to those clans living in the south of the Yangtze River, including Huizhou areas. It was very universal there to use genealogy to "improve social statues" and "boast one's family background". The consequence is that people "became proud and luxurious" and "rivaled with each other". The vicious rivalry took place very frequently in Huizhou. For instance, Family Cheng's genealogy criticized *Cheng Minzheng's Unified Clan Genealogy of Family Cheng in Xin'an*. But the real purpose is to show dissatisfaction to

---

① *Family Hong's Genealogy—Preface of Re-carved Genealogy* in Xiuning County.

his "unification of the clan", which is typical of a rivalry in the clan. What is written above is the general impression of the relationship between genealogy and social customs in Huizhou by some scholars and compilers of genealogy in the Ming and Qing dynasties. The following will focus on some social customs closely related to the genealogy in Huizhou in the Ming and Qing dynasties.

II. Genealogy in Huizhou in the Ming and Qing Dynasties and the "Benevolence and Tolerance" in Huizhou

Among many kinds of social customs in Huizhou, "benevolence and tolerance" are what scholars compliment and universally acknowledge. Cheng Guangxian in the preface of *Record of Distinguished Clans* in Xin'an has made a conclusion very explicitly. He said, "The record of distinguished clans is to narrate people's virtue. The boom of Xin'an originated from its benevolent and tolerant social atmosphere. In Xin'an and Ziyang, people are taught to be benevolent and tolerant. That notion of education has made people responsible. This kind of concept has been spread to the whole nation. People love each other, respect each other. Sages and men of virtue in Xin'an all follow such rules and customs. Despite various geographical conditions, people's pursuit of virtues is similar. Humanity and kindness are the very root of human nature. Historians of the court also collected some customs from the folk. Gradually, people in other places of the country also follow the customs. The nation is peaceful and harmonious." Confucius said: "The benevolence of one family will make the whole nation benevolent; the tolerance of one family will make the whole nation tolerant." This is the essence of Confucian instruction, and in Zhu Xi's lifetime, he also advocated this principle. In this preface, Cheng Guangxian made it very clear that benevolence and concession were advocated by Zhu Xi, which constitutes the essential part of Confucianism. Huizhou, as the "Ziyang, hometown of Confucianism", promoted the theory of Zhu Xi by "educating people with benevolence and tolerance". That is, "people born in the hometown of

Confucian, Ziyang all bear this responsibility. " Just under this strong sense of responsibility and the influence of Zhu Xi's theory, benevolence and concession have become one of the most important customs. From Cheng Guangxian's perspective, benevolence and concession were not merely prevalent in Huizhou, and they also made it a place which shouldered the mission of guiding social customs. That is, "benevolence and concession were common in Xin'an, and it set a positive example for the whole nation in terms of customs. " Confucius said: "The benevolence of one family will make the whole nation benevolent; the tolerance of one family will make the whole nation tolerant. " So, "the customs were not merely limited to Xin'an, the quintessence was gradually spread to different places, which made the whole nation peaceful. " Therefore, in Cheng Guangxian's opinion, there is a process from "benevolence and tolerance" of Zhu Xi, to the atmosphere of "benevolence and tolerance", to "a peaceful world. In this process, "benevolence and tolerance" is the starting point and the core of everything. Then how "benevolence and tolerance" is represented? It is actually the gist of *Record of Distinguished Clans in Xin'an*, in which it was advocated and highly recommended. Cheng Guangxian's contribution is not just the generalization of social customs in Huizhou, more importantly, he thought what *Record of Distinguished Clans in Xin'an* commended is also "benevolence and tolerance". It is universally acknowledged that *Record of Distinguished Clans in Xin'an* is the general assembling of genealogy of all families and clans, which was in effect the task of propagating and succeeding "benevolence and tolerance. " In other words, genealogy plays a very important role in the formation of "benevolence and tolerance" in Huizhou. Just as the compiler of *Record of Distinguished Clans in Xin'an* has once said, "The cultural relics of rites in Xin'an are displayed, and this can also reflect the customs in the country. " If *Record of Distinguished Clans in Xin'an* was compiled in the form of local clan genealogy, and generalized the social customs of "benevolence and tolerance" in Huizhou, then *Family Wu's Genealogy in Linxi*, Shexian County summarized the same social customs in Family Wu.

In Chongzhen Period, Bi Maoliang in *Preface of Family Wu's Genealogy in Linxi* said, Family Wu's genealogy "is well unified and organized in a good order, which is regarded as one of the best genealogies. Confucius emphasized concession and courtesy. It is a very important custom and should be regarded as priority in making domestic rules and compiling genealogies. ①

Here, Bi Maoliang concluded that "concession" is the fine tradition of Wu's family, and he also realized that the relationship between genealogy and courtesy, that is: "Courtesy plays an important role. With genealogy, people's ranking and status are clear. With the right order of ranking, people could behave in a courteous way. And they will be more tolerant and make more concessions." So, "benevolence and concession" could be advocated based on the compilation of genealogy.

Ⅲ. Social Customs Related to Genealogy in Huizhou in the Ming and Qing Dynasties and Its Emphasis on Genetic Connection

As Zhao Jishi has once said, in Huizhou, "genealogy of a thousand years is kept in good order". From the development of genealogy in Huizhou in the Ming and Qing dynasties, the genealogy in Huizhou at this period has facilitated the formation of social customs of stressing blood lineage and the purity of kinship due to its continued efforts in keeping the genealogy complete and blood relationship pure. Its formation and maintenance was made possible through genealogy. In order to keep the purity of kinship, it is essential to deal with stepsons. As to the clan, the biggest risk of having stepsons is that they might lead to a chaotic situation of the blood relationship. That is why most clans tried hard to guard against that. For instance, it is regulated in *Branch Genealogy of Lord Fuqi in Xiaojiang— Common Rules* in Wuyuan, "People who have no biological children and raise children with different surnames should be recorded in case it could

---

① *Family Wu's Genealogy in Linxi—Preface of Family Wu's Genealogy in Linxi*, in Shexian County, carved in the 14th year of the Chongzhen Period.

cause confusion of clans; people in the clan with different surnames should be recorded and prudent in marriage; people who have their sons-in-law as sons should be recorded and ethics and customs should be respected."① For stepsons with different surnames and sons-in-law as sons, it has made clear explanation, which could guarantee the purity of the clan blood relationship. In *Family Zhan's Genealogy in Qingyuan—Common Rules*, "Stepsons should be noted along with their biological fathers, and their foster fathers could be further illustrated. For people from other clans with different surnames to serve as stepsons in the clan, it should be recorded that they came to look for a certain foster father. If people in the clan want to serve as stepsons in other clans, it should be clearly recorded and never be hidden. Therefore, it could cause no chaos for descendants in their marriages. Everything should be noted down as it is."② Therefore, the corresponding rules in Zhan's family in Qingyuan are a little loose. Their stepsons could be recorded in the genealogy and their children who served as stepsons in other clans should also be clearly noted, and they have already made explanation about the purpose for them to do so, that is, "it would no longer cause chaos for their descendants in their marriage." That is fairly reasonable. Also, from the practice of "recording everything according to the fact" has more or less followed the tradition of "telling the fact". As to why it is necessary to make clear stipulation of about stepsons, there is detailed illustration in Huizhou genealogy. There are basically two reasons. First, "succession of the custom of kinships" is the foundation of stipulation for stepsons. For the purpose of succession, it is explained in *Family Zhang's Genealogy in the Southern Xiuning County, Xin'an. Common Rules* in the Jiajing Period of the Ming Dynasty: "The role of stepsons is to honor ancestors and beckon

---

① *Branch Genealogy of Lord Fuqi in Xiaojiang—Common Rules in Wuyuan*, the 2nd year of the Xuantong Period.

② *Family Zhan's Genealogy in Qingyuan—Common Rules*, in Wuyuan, the 50th year of the Qianlong Period.

descendants. It is fair for those who had no their own descendants to have children from others to make their family further prosper. It is necessary to adopt children with definite origins in the same clan to keep the ethical order in the clan. "① This helped explain how to adopt children, and provided very important theoretical foundations for adopting children in the same clan, which clung to the traditional ethics and patriarchal clan systems. It is obvious that "the succession of customs of kinships and empathy" is the most rational foundation. Stipulations in Family Zhang's genealogy in Lingnan have illustrated reasons related to ethics about stepsons in a more reasonable way. But further theories should be constructed related to whether the adoption is affected by material factors. As to the explanation of this question, Family Zhang in Xingyuan responded as follows. Second, succession of family business is the stipulated material foundation. According to *Family Zhang's Genealogy in Xingyuan—Common Rules in Wuyuan*, "The phenomenon of adopting children is very common, which has caused much chaos and confusion." The adoptive parents might be uncles or granduncle, so the ranking and titles are confusing, which is a pervasive phenomenon. If the adopted children are from their own clan, then they are named as "successors", which means they will succeed the family business. If the adopted children have different surnames, then their complete names should be recorded and labeled as "adopted children". If the adopted children have no surnames or complete names, then they should be marked as "found children". In case it might cause confusion later, further indication would be made to differentiate them. Children in the clan who later become adopted children of other clans and have different surnames, then they are not allowed to become heirs. ②

---

① *Family Zhang's Genealogy in Xiuning, Xin'an—Common Rules*, quoted from (Japanese) *Duoheqiu Wulang's Research of Genealogy*, Japanese Literature Library, 1960.

② *Family Zhang's Genealogy in Xingyuan—Common Rules*, in *Wuyan*, the Qianlong Period.

Conclusions can be drawn based on the above-mentioned regulations: first, "succession" was chaotic at that time, so the compiler thought it was very common; second, the compiler revealed the very reason for the regulations, that is, to inherit family business. People in the same clan could make properties employed and succeeded in the clan. Members in the clan who later became adopted children of other clans might cause the outflow of assets. People with different surnames who inherited properties in the clan should also be marked, so the disputes related to properties might be avoided in the future. The illustration of this issue has disclosed the core reason of keeping blood relationship pure, and that is the shared reason why every clan would make stipulations for adopted children in compiling genealogy. Since rational explanations have been made in both ethics and material factors, the stipulations about adopted children in genealogy became comprehensible. Besides, in the Ming and Qing dynasties, genealogies in Huizhou made definite stipulations for "making sons-in-law sons" and "adopting sons". *Family Zhan's Genealogy in Qingyuan—Common Rules in Wuyuan* stipulated that, "it is a violation of making sons-in-law sons or adopting sons, which should not be recorded."[①] The purpose is to emphasize the purity of the clan blood relationship. Since sons-in-law and adopted sons haven't any blood relationship with other members, they might pose threat to others in terms of possessions once their positions get established in the clan. So, they definitely cannot be recorded in the genealogy. The second way to keep kinship pure is to record migrated branches. Many migrations might make many branches lost relationship, or loose relationship, which ultimately led to the alienation of family members in the clan. What's more, other clans, especially those with the same surname but different ancestors, might take advantage of this alienation and disturbed the clan order. As what is stipulated in *Family Zhu's Genealogy*

---

① *Family Zhan's Genealogy in Qingyuan—Common Rules*, in *Wuyuan*, the 50th year of the Qianlong.

in Yicheng—Common Rules in Shexian County, "Families in the clan and branches should make clear records when they migrate to other provinces or counties. This will help further checking. If the clan migrated to other places, detailed information should be provided. All details should be kept for future use."① Therefore, Family Zhu tried hard to make information related to its branches very accurate.

As to branches which migrated elsewhere, there are some recorded regulations. According to rules in *Family Xu's Genealogy in Shaokeng—Common Rules*, "People who migrated to other places must note down complete names of the place, and the original migration place set by the grandfather and the place later settled down by the grandson. Then it would be easy for relatives in the clan to visit them."② A clear record of the migration for the branches will help keep the clan relationship pure. Another way to achieve this is to keep a correct record of those who have no children. Then it could avoid misunderstanding and would not be taken advantage of by others. In *Family Ge's Genealogy in Quantang—Common Rules* in Jixi, it is regulated that, "Those who have no children should be marked as "no successors". Those whose children died should be marked as "children died young", and those whose kids died before 15 years old should be marked as "children died early". Those who has been adopted but hasn't been decided as heirs should be marked as "would-be heirs". Then confusion could be avoided." "Those who have no heirs should be recorded very clearly; otherwise, there would be no literature after several generations."③ In general, in the Ming and Qing dynasties, much importance was attached to the blood relationship in genealogies in Huizhou, which has played an essential

---

① *Family Zhu's Genealogy in Yicheng—Common Rules*, in Shexian County, the 2nd year of the Xuantong Period.

② *Family Xu's Genealogy in Shaokeng—Examples of Old Genealogy*, Shexian County, Minguo Period.

③ *Family Ge's Genealogy in Quantang—Common Examples in Jixi County*, the 3rd year of the Xuantong Period.

part in shaping the social custom of cherishing blood ties in Huizhou.

Ⅳ. Huizhou Genealogies in the Ming and Qing Dynasties and Social Customs of Cherishing Marriages in Huizhou

From recorded Genealogies in the Ming and Qing dynasties, they played a very important role in strengthening marriage ties. In Record of Renowned Clans in Xin'an, Wang Feng said: "Based on history, from the times of Emperor Huang to now, names of the clan were kept and families were paid high tribute to. This ancient custom has always been kept in Xin'an. Tight marriage relationships, distinct and clear genealogies are all well preserved customs." Obviously, in Wang Feng's opinion, "tight marriage relationships" is a very important social custom in Huizhou. In *Family Huang's Genealogy in Xiaoli—Tandu* in Shexian County, its *Domestic Rules* said that, "Marriages are the root of humanity. It is vital to choose the virtuous people who respect customs and rites, and who are kind and obedient of domestic rules."① From that, we can see that in Huang's clan, they emphasize "distinguish the good from the bad". In *Family Shao's Genealogy in Shaoyang—Newly Added Ancestral Rules* in Jixi, it is regulated that: "In terms of marriages, it is necessary to make people match each other. It is forbidden to marry those violent and immoral people. Otherwise, ancestors will be humiliated. People who violate such rules will not be allowed to enter the ancestral halls."② It can be seen that in Shao's clan stressed "well-matched marriages", and the punitive measures were made to "forbid them to enter ancestral halls". In some genealogies, there are more rigid rules for marriages and more detailed reasons for that. For instance, in *Family Zhan's Genealogy in Qingyuan—Common Rules* in Wuyuan, it is recorded that: "There are definite rules and laws for marriages. If people disobey

---

① *Family Huang's Domestic Rules in Xiaoli, Tandu of Family Huang's Genealogy of Xiaoli, Tandu* in Shexian County, Volume 4, the 9th year of the Yongzheng Period.

② *Family Shao's Genealogy—Additional Ancestral Rules* in Jixi County, the 36th year of PRC.

them and marry those inferior to them, they will be eliminated from the genealogy and never get the opportunity to get re-entered."① In this case, apart from the use of laws, social customs are also emphasized. Punitive measures are also specific and various. In the Ming and Qing dynasties, there is a close relationship between the custom of valuing marriages and genealogies in Huizhou area. On the one hand, it is the continued tradition since the Wei and Jin dynasties, and there is a connection between them. On the other hand, the "well-matched marriages" in Huizhou marriage customs is not a random rule, instead, it is based on comprehensive factors, among which, genealogies play a vital role. For instance, according to *Record of Renowned Clans*, the history of "renowned clans" is actually the recorded history of each clan; therefore, genealogies have become an important index to decide whether clans could be labeled as "renowned ones". It is common in the Huizhou genealogies of the Ming and Qing dynasties, many clans supported each other by using the marital relationship to seek mutual development. For instance, in the 32nd year of the Kangxi Period (1693), Zhu Qun, the descendant of Zhu Xi of the 16th generation said in illustrating the relationship between Family Chen and Family Zhu in Huizhou: "There are very few renowned clans in Xin'an can surpass it. Lord Yuantan migrated to Wuyuan as the 28th generation of the Minister in the Tang Dynasty. My grandmother, Mrs. Chen gave birth to Lord Xiang of the Qingyuan School. The marital tie and connection of Cheng and Zhu will continue and promote the development of neo-Confucianism."② From what Zhu Kun has said, we know Family Zhu and Family Cheng had marital relationships for generations. The following example can also direct reflect the social custom in Huizhou. In the 6th year of the Xianfeng Period (1856), it is recorded in *Unified Contract* established by the Wang's clan that,

---

① *Family Zhan's Genealogy in Qingyuan—Common Rules in Wuyuan*.
② *Family Chen's Unified Genealogy in Xin'an—Preface of Zhukun*, the 2ed year of the Kangxi Period.

"*Family Wang's General Genealogy* said that, adopted sons and people with different surnames can't disturb the order of the genealogy. Marriages should be properly matched. Rigid rules should never be disobeyed...As to ill-matched marriages, Shengji once disobeyed domestic rules and married a Tang family and caused death, which made many people died, which is a lesson for us to draw from. From then on, villages made contracts to forbid "ill-matched" marriages. But several clan members including Jiyang paid no attention to the lesson, and still got married to Family Zhang and Family Tang. So according to other members' decision in the clan, Jiyang etc. would not be included in the genealogy, which is a fair treatment. It is necessary to make corresponding articles of association in advance lest other unexpected trouble or disputes arise later. Everybody should fight bravely against violent behavior and should never retreat."[①] From that we can see the Wang's clan held a determined attitude as to forbid "ill-matched" marriages.

The formation of the special social customs in Huizhou area is not restricted by a certain period of time or a single reason, however, the role played by the genealogies should never be undervalued. It is easier for us to understand the interactive relationship between genealogies and the local society, knowing local social customs better in Huizhou in the Ming and Qing dynasties with a more thorough knowledge of the function of the genealogies.

Published in *Anhui History Studies*, No. 6, 2011

Writen by Zhou Xiaoguang & Xu Bin

Translated by Zhou Qing

---

① *Unified Contract*, collected by the Library of Anhui Normal University.

Part IV
Huizhou Files

Chapter 10　A Review of the Research into Huizhou Files from the Late-1980s to the 1990s

　　The past decade(the late-1980s to the 1990s) has seen great achievements into the research into Huizhou files. Each stage of the achievements is indispensable to the progress of the research into the whole historical context—Ming and Qing history. The research into Huizhou files is by no means a local history research, instead, it is based on a comprehensive research into the files in different places all over China in Ming and Qing, thus bringing the research a universal sense. Since the middle of 1980s, the collection and sorting of Huizhou flies began to draw great attention from scholars. Anhui Museum and The History Institute of Chinese Social Sciences undertook the collection, sorting and publishing work. The Chinese Social Sciences Press published *Huizhou Economic Files in Ming and Qing* (the 1st series in 1988, the 2nd series in 1990). Huashan Art and Literature Press published multi-volume series *Huizhou Contracts and Files in One Thousand Years* (photocopy, 40 volumes, 1991). All these publications have promoted the research enormously. Even in Japan, there is a Huizhou

Files Institute in Tokyo University Oriental Institute. In 1996, Peking University Press published *A Corpus and Interpretation of Contracts in Chinese History*, which was based on the collected Huizhou files in Peking University library. There is no doubt the publishing and sorting work has promoted the research profoundly. Meanwhile the discovery of new materials and the making of new points have enriched and enlarged not only the research into Huizhou Studies but also into the history of Ming and Qing.

This essay aims to review the achievements in the past decade and give a brief introduction to the academic trends of Huizhou files research.

Ⅰ. Huizhou Files and the Research into Chinese Social and Economic History

The research into Huizhou files began in the field of class-relation exploration. At the beginning of 1980s, land-relationship and tenancy forms became the focus of research, leading to a further economic analysis of the files. Materials like the tenancy contracts, grain-rent contracts, property certificates and so on caught researchers' attention. The researchers have attempted to explore issues like, the position of tenant farmers, land rent rate, rent form, grain output and so on by using micro-analysis. They hold that the traditional macro-analysis of jumping to a general conclusion by only a few cases is not convincing at all. "More ridiculous is that a hasty conclusion is drawn to suggest that 'progresses' and 'changes' were made merely from a comparison between a few cases in different places in different dynasties."[1] Since the late 1980s, some researchers tried to conduct economic analysis by means of exploring the economic and social history. That means to analyze the genuine state of the society by investigating the land price, land sale, land management, per *mu* yield of grain and so on (*mu*, a measurement of land in China, 1 *mu* = 666.67 square meters). In

---

[1] Zhang Youyi, Page 3, *The Preface of the Research into Land Tenure in Huizhu, in Ming and Qing*, Chinese Social Sciences Press, 1984.

Ming and Qing more and more land were possessed by individuals and land sale became more popular. Zhou Shaoquan explored the frequency of land sale and tried to analyze the reasons of more frequent redistribution of land possession by studying the incomplete statistics of land contracts in Ming kept in Anhui Museum. The conclusion drawn was that the deep-rooted notion of people at that time was "the most significant issue in one's life was to have one's own land". Those who had a few pieces of land took it as the source and basis of their living. Those who had official titles took land as their means of retreat while holding positions in government office was to fulfill their political ambition. Those shopkeepers and traders took land as the safest treasure, free from flood and fire, robbery and theft, so they held that trade was the way to increase wealth while land was the way to keep wealth.① Peng Chao conducted a statistical analysis of the land price and land rent based on the files in Ming and Qing kept in Anhui Museum. Peng's research suggested the notion that the land price was determined by land rent was poorly supported and in effect, the land price was influenced by many other factors expect for land rent. Peng's conclusion was that in every dynasty land price was in the tendency of the so-called "two-end low, intermediate high" while the land rent was not the same case.②

About the land management: as there were limited land resources and abundant forestry in Huizhou, timber production had always been the vital part of local economy. The local people held that "the produce from the land was immediate but not abundant while the produce from the forestry was time-consuming but abundant. Forestry was rewarding and more profitable than land renting, which may not been seen in a short period of time but

---

① Zhou Shaoquan, *On the Trend of Land Sale in Huizhou in Ming—and the Relation between Huizhou Merchants and Land Sale*, Chinese Economic History Research, 1990, Vol. 4.

② *The Land Price and Land Rent in Huizhou, Ming and Qing*, Chinese Economic History Research, 1988, Vol. 2.

could be recognized over years." ① Huizhou locals were intensively concerned with forestry and over years they had accumulated a lot of experience of planting, managing and maintaining woods, for instance, the measures against deforestation, fires and so on. Many official bans against deforestation and other notices of forestry maintenance were issued in Huizhou in Ming and Qing (see Zhang Xuehui *A Preliminary Study of Forestry Management in Huizhou History*, *Chinese History Research*, 1987, vol. 1). Huizhou locals ran the forestry mainly in "Lifen" way, which was distinct from "Zhufen". "Lifen" meant distributing the produce according to the labor one contributed to forestry and the proportion of the profit allocation was also determined by specific labors. This distribution method first arose in Emperor Hongwu years and became a usual practice in Emperor Tianshun years in Ming. "Lifen" practice led to the separation of possession and occupancy right which brought about the "Tianpi Right". ②

Per *mu* yield of grain was always a major concern in economy history, however, the records in ancient documents were not accurate. In order to get the exploitation rate of land rent, per *mu* yield of grain should be estimated as it represented the agricultural development in specific regions. In 1992, *The Measurement of Per Mu Yield of Grain in Huizhou in Ming and Qing* by Zhou Shaoquan was published in *Research into the Ming History*, Vol. 2. In 1993, *On the Per Mu Yield of Grain in Huizhou in Qing* by Jiang Taixin and Su Jinyu was published in *The Research into Chinese Economic History*, Vol. 3. Both essays attempted to calculate the per *mu* yield of grain by means of the first-hand contracts and files. The first essay, by extensive collection and careful sorting, managed to identify the proportion of rent rate and its yield of grain and then made the attempt to estimate the per *mu* yield

---

① Zhou Shaoquan, Zhao Yaguang, *Doushangong Family Files* (the collated and annotated version), Huangshan Press, 1993.

② Chen Keyun, "*Lifen*" in Forestry Management in Huizhou in Ming and Qing, *Chinese History Research*, 1987, Vol. 1.

of grain at that time. The second essay also explored the per *mu* yield of grain by means of land rent rate and further pointed out the decline tendency of yield of grain in Huizhou in Qing. In effect, a good harvest was more influenced by mild weather rather than the relation between the landowner and tenants.

Next let's move to the economic situation of the various classes in the countryside. The research used to focus on the relation between the farmers (usually with little land or no land at all) and the landowners while deeper analysis of the economic status of the two parties was rare. The following essays attempted to explore the life and economic situation of farmers and landowners respectively. They are *The Analysis of the Life of Hu Clan in Qimen at the End of Ming*, *The Oriental Journal* (Japan), Vol. 67, Mar. 1995, by Zhou Shaoquan, and *The Analysis of Economic Situation of Masses and Landowners in Ming and Qing*, *Chinese Social Sciences*, 1996, Vol. 4. There were very few case studies of farmers' life mainly because the relevant materials were rare. Zhou's essay, by using the 36 contracts and files from 1487 to 1637, tried to illustrate the Hu clan's origin, their economic situation and their reducing to tenant farmers. The essay managed to outline the general status of a farmer clan's daily life and activities in comparatively peaceful time (compared with the period of class-conflicting tension). This essay, by making use of the contracts and files, has attempted, for the first time, to draw the family tree of Hu clan in order to clarify the member relation within the clan. Luan Chengxian's essay has tried to analyze the family structure and economic status of a wealthy landowner during the turning years (for over 120 years) of Ming and Qing by using the official files about land and population in the 800,000 words *Yellow Volumes* (official household registration). On the basis of this case study, the essay has tried to explore the economic status of the landowners in feudal society and categorized them into three kinds, namely, living together and sharing all the property, living together and dividing up the property, living apart and dividing up the property. The main features of the second kind included the even division principle, the economically independent branches within the same clan, the multi-layer and multi-branch property possession system.

Yulin Volumes (land registration) and *Yellow Volumes* are the basis of the tax system in Ming and should be intensively concerned in the research into the economic history in Ming. Thus *On Goods of Ming History* put it: "*Yulin Volumes* were the basis of land policy while *Yellow Volumes* were the basis of tax." Before the 1980s the research into *Yulin Volumes* was insufficient while the discovery of the original version of *Yulin Volumes* in Huizhou has promoted the research enormously. In 1988 *The Textural Criticism of Yulin Volumes in Longfeng Years of Emperor Zhu Yuanzhang Reign* by Luan Chengxian was published in *Chinese History Research*, Vol. 4. The essay, with well-based analysis, has identified one *Yulin Volume* as produced in 1364, Song (the nation title by the rebellion farmers at the end of Yuan Dynasty) and thus put forward a new notion of the beginning years of the production of *Yulin Volumes* in Ming. The author published *The Textual Criticism of Yunlin Volume in the 9th Year of Emperor Hongzhi Reign* [1] and *The Textual Criticism of Yulin Volumes in Qimen County*. [2] These two essays gave a detailed analysis of the production of *Yulin Volumes*, its form, its contents and the land files within. The second essay made contribution to the identification of the production of *Yulin Volumes* as in Longfeng Years. The research into *Yellow Volumes* was based on the official documents and used to limit to the volumes themselves. What's more, there even existed some faults in the research into *Yellow Volumes* mainly because of lack of first-hand documents. Fortunately the original versions of *Yellow Volumes* and other first-hand files were found, which promoted the research beyond the system issue and made it possible to explore the key issues in social and economic life at that period of history.

---

[1] *Research into the Ming History*, the 1st series, 1991, Huangshan Press.
[2] *Chinese History Research*, 1994, Vol. 2.

Part IV Huizhou Files

By using *Yellow Volume* versions of Huizhou files, The Yellow Volumes Research in Ming (by Chinese Social Sciences Press) by Luan Chengxian will be published this year and it is the latest achievement of research into Yellow-Volume-System and social and economic history in Ming and Qing. By making full use of the million-words *Yellow-Volume* files and absorbing the achievements home and abroad, this 360,000-word long writing aims to explore the Yellow-Volume System and some major issues of social economic history in Ming and Qing. This book has made several original points, for instance, it has corrected the 40-year-long misunderstanding of the photos of the original version of *Yellow Volumes*. Also it has challenged the records of "Jiashouhu" in Ming history, holding that "Jiashou" was, in fact, a title instead of the "head" of "Jia". Another concern of the writing was the household registration in *Yellow Volumes*, especially the registration of women. The author held that there existed changes in different periods of history, for instance, after the Mid-Ming, women and children were not registered in the *Yellow Volumes* at all. Also, new exploration of other major issues was conducted, for example, the land possession of various classes, land distribution patterns, land sales, rural economic structure, economic status of wealthy landowners, the relation between nation, landowners and farmers.

  The essays on class-relation were not numerous while disagreement still existed. With the discovery of new files and the progress in this field, the research was further developed. Some case studies were indeed revealing, for instance, the carrying Out of the imperial decree to free the slaves in the 5th year of Emperor Yongzheng Reign was clarified with the discovery of lawsuit files of Wang, the master, and Hu, the slave, in Ershiduoqu village, Xiuning County in Emperor Qianlong Years.

  The essay by Chen Keyun was published in *The Criticism on Qing History* in 1995, namely *The Carrying out of the Imperial Decree to Free the Slave in the 5th Year of Emperor Yongzheng Reign in Huizhou—Based on the Case Study of Lawsuit of Wang and Hu in Xiuning County in the*

30*th Year of Emperor Qianlong Reign*. This essay was based on the lawsuit from the winter in the 30th year to April the 33th year during Qianlong reign and described vividly the shock caused by the issue and implement of the imperial decree, which involved numerous documents and comments from officials of all ranks.

The constructive point was the author managed to illustrate the imperial decree, on the one hand, helped to relieve the exploitation of the master to his slaves, on the other hand, it also intensified the conflict between the two parties. The final result proved, more often than not, it would be extremely tough for the slaves to completely get rid of the slave system. In the implement process the attitudes and activities of all parties involved were displayed, among them were government officials of various ranks, local institutes, masters and slaves, especially the county head and his changing attitudes. *The Rural Society and the Farmers in " Huyi Lawsuit " in Xiuning County during Emperor Kangxi Reign in Qing* by Zhou Shaoquan was collected in *The Essays of the International Conference of Huizhou Studies in 1995* (Anhui University Press, 1997). This essay held that from the Mid-Ming to the beginning of Qing both the "lijia" (one way of government administration) and local regulations were practiced and in the rural society clan power and economic capability worked together to determine the global strength of a clan. Meanwhile the servants and slaves were accordingly classified into different grades, namely, the head servants and the inferior slaves. To sum up, the rural society from the end of Ming to the beginning of Qing was hierarchy composed of various and complicated classes. Our last concern was the issue of "Huodian" (one kind of servants). In 1997, Liu Chongri in his essay claimed that though "Huodian" suggested the tendency of being reduced to slaves at the end of Ming and this tendency was consistent with the changes of tenancy system. "Huodian" has significant difference from other servants and they were free to leave or even marry into and live with the master's family. In other words, they were not closely subordinated to their masters. ①

II. The Research into Huizhou Files and Huizhou Merchants

As to the research into Huizhou merchants, *The Huizhou Merchants in Ming* by Fu Yiling (see *The Merchants and Commercial Capital in Ming and Qing*, People's Press, June 1956,) and *The Research into Xin'an Merchants* by Japanese Fujii Hirosi (for the Chinese version see *The News Report of Anhui History Research*, 1959, Vol. 9,10) had systematic analysis of the relevant research. *The Collected Materials of Huizhou Merchants in Ming and Qing* (Huangshan Press, 1985) was a continuous effort in this field. The approach of exploring Huizhou merchants by the use of contracts and files began from 1980s. Yang Guozhen in his *Research into Land Contracts and Files in Ming and Qing* (People's Press, 1988) attempted an exploration of the relation between medium and small businessmen and land by making use of Huizhou files. *The research into Huizhou Merchants* (Anhui People's Press, 1995) was a new starting point, as it was both a summary of the previous achievements and a new effort in this area. The most noteworthy was the chapter "*The Case Studies of Huizhou Merchants*". There was three case studies based on Huizhou files, namely, *The Business Practice of Huizhou Merchants in Huzhou Files in Ming and Qing* by Zhou Shaoquan, *The Research into a Few Fork Contracts of Dividing up the Family Property* by Zhang Haipeng and *An Research into Jiang Clan, the Tea Merchant in She County* by Jiang Yi. The first essay explored the business practice in the commercial files, namely, by stock and by contract. Also it illustrated the possible transformation of different practices and their difference in terms of capital possession, management right, profit division, compensation for losses and so on. The essay employed *The Principle of Arithmetic* by the famous mathematician Cheng Dawei (happened to be a

---

① Liu Chongri, Reflection on the Origin and Character of "Huo Dian, *Research into Ming History*, the 5th series, Huangshan Press.

Huizhou local) to prove and analyze the way of profit division among commercial partners. The second case study made a comparison between the dividing up family property in two merchants' families, describing various commercial notions of the two Huizhou merchants. The first case was about Wang Zhengke, a Xiuning merchant who gave up farming for business, he started to buy lands after accumulating some wealth. In this way he managed to be both a businessman and a landowner. When he retired from business he went back to his hometown and divided his property evenly to his three sons. The second case was about the famous Hu Kaiwen Ink Store. Its founder Hu Tianzhu and his son Hu Yude penned two agreements of dividing up the property during Emperor Jiaqing and Emperor Daoguang reign respectively. A most distinctive feature of the agreements was that the division of property went together with cooperation in business in the same store. However if another store was to be founded it was not entitled to use the same name of the original store. This agreement ensured the prosperity of the ink store for more than 170 years from Emperor Jiqing reign to 1950s. The third case was a tea merchant whose three generations ran tea business for over 80 years. With the help of hundreds of account books and thousands of business letters the author analyzed the changing management patterns and business philosophy in the transition period from a traditional tea merchant to a modern one. There was also a lot of information of tea production, tea transportation and tea sales, which was enormously helpful to the relevant history research. *A Case Study of Huizhou Pawn Businessman—Cheng Xuyu in Xiuning in the 2nd Year of Emperor Congzhen Reign* by Luan Chengxian was published in *Huizhou Social Sciences*, 1996, Vol. 3. This essay explored the dividing-up-property files of the family and their family tree to investigate the identity of the Cheng businessman in Shuaidong, Xiuning, his industry, his capital form and so on. The author pointed out both learning to be scholars and doing business, for Huizhou men in Ming and Qing, were ways to the outside world and make achievements. However Huizhou men always stuck to the traditional notion, taking business as secondary to learning Confucius Classics and farming. In addition, their business practice was greatly influenced by their feudalism philosophy.

Another significant topic of Huizhou merchants was Huizhou merchants and their social network. The Japanese scholar Usui Sachiko conducted a detailed research and she held the basic feature of feudal economics was to buy at a cheap price and sell at a high price. The purchasing, transportation and selling of goods needed capital, information and the cooperation of traders and storekeepers. In this way, the elementary commercial network was established. The network of Huizhou merchants was based on blood relation and region relation. Compared with other businessmen groups, the secret of the powerful network of Huizhou men lay in their tradition: they usually conducted business with their clan members and their region relation was their blood relation in a larger sense. In other words, the relation was based on members within the clan and marriage with other clans. The common ancestors, to the Huizhou merchants, were the key to identify themselves with other clan members. Huizhou merchants' network was an efficient coordination of personal relations and it was further transformed into capital investment, employment relation and compilation of family tree. Particularly, the compilation of family tree and popularity of building ancestral halls were directly connected with the establishment and expansion of the network. What's more, the identification of the merchants helped to expand and empower the network. On the other hand, the author held the merchants' power was seriously weakened because of the government exploitation, the widespread illegal salt sale, especially the immigration of the local merchants to other places. All these brought about great changes to the traditional network in terms of its form and function. With the autonomy activism at the end of Qing, the political function of the network was reinforced. ①

---

① *Anhui History Studies*, 1991, Vol. 4.

Ⅲ. The Research into Huizhou Files, Clan and Clan System

Huizhou emphasized its clan and clan system, which made a popular research subject in itself. In the 1980s Ju Mi's essay *The Land Possession and Patriarchal System in South Anhui from 1600 to 1800* was published in *The Research into Chinese Social economic History*, 1982, vol. 3. Ye Xian'en's essay was *The Rural Society and Slave System in Huizhou in Ming and Qing*. All these essays attempted to analyze the clan system in Huizhou. Since the 1990s it has become popular to conduct research into clan system with the help of historical files. Some essays attempted to probe further into the clan property and temple property. These included *The Research into the Clan Property of Cheng Clan Renshan Family in Qimen Huizhou in Ming and Qing* by Zhou Shaoquan in 1991[①], and *Temple and Land Relation in Huizhou in Qing—Focusing on Bao Clan and Xu Clan in Shexian County, Huizhou Region* by Liu Mao.[②] The first essay analyzed the origin, internal structure, management pattern, management system, profit division and function of the clan property of Cheng clan. It pointed out the clan land possession, though with a seemingly collective form, was in effect, private. As it was stable and fixed, multi-layered and multi-branched, the clan land possession became the main force to maintain the clan system when the system later fell into decline. The second essay, by making use of the files and family tree materials, explored the temple property of Bao clan and Xu clan in Shexian County, who were closely related with the salt merchants in Huai River region. The essay made detailed analysis of the temple property: its origin, structure, tenancy, land rent division and so on. Some scholars explored the transfer of clan property to temple property and analyzed the double effect of "poor village, rich temple" in rural Huizhou.[③]

---

    ① *Genealogy*, the 2nd series, Culture and Art Press, 1991.
    ② *Research into Chinese Economic History*, 1991, Vol. 1.
    ③ Chen Keyun, *The Development of Clan Property in Huizhou in Ming and Qing*, *Anhui University Academic Journal* 1996, Vol. 2.

An Exploration of the Clan Property in Huizhou in Ming and Qing—with the Example of Cheng Clan in Qimen, by Yan Jun was published in *Research into Ming History*, the 5th series, Huangshan Press, 1997. This essay tried to explore the management, profit division of the Cheng clan in a new approach. The author held: " The clan property was the basic element of economy in Huizhou in Ming and Qing... the clan property of Cheng in Shanhe Qimen was the clan economy in microcosm. Except for Cheng, there were more wealthy clans who possessed over thousand *mu* of land, like Hong and Zhang in Qimen County, Bao, Xu and Jiang in Shexian County. The impact of clan property was enormous to Huizhou society and the clan property based on forestry not only maintained the clan power but also ensured the prosperity of Huizhou merchants in terms of capital source and clan support.

According to Li Wenzhi, the clan system in Ming and Qing had evolved into the basic social institution to maintain the feudal administration. In Huizhou, with the powerful clan system, to farmers, clan heads were more awesome than government officials. Li quoted Fu Yan, the county head of Shexian County in Emperor Congzhen years in Ming, "In Huizhou, seniors in the clan were greatly respected and every clan had its clan head and respectful seniors." (see *The Form and Municipality Function of Clan System in Ming—on the Ultimate Source of the Development and Variation of Clan System Being the Feudal Ownership*, The Research into Chinese Economic History, 1988, Vol. 1) *The Reinforcement of Rural Governing of the Clan System in Huizhou in Ming and Qing* by Chen Keyun was published in *Chinese History Research*, 1995, Vol. 3). The essay held that since the middle of Ming the clan system had reinforced the rural administration in Huizhou, infiltrating into all aspects of social life. The author believed that in the feudal society farmers were far away from the government while clan system was there all the time. Consequently farmers were more concerned with the clan regulations and it was not a rare case for them to take clan rules over government laws.

Recently the topic of "the integration of members of the same clan" became popular in the clan research. Japanese scholar Nakajima Yoshiaki in Waseda University held that there existed various social institutions by blood link or by region link in Huizhou in Ming. While the competition of land and other precious sources became more ferocious and the lawsuits were more serious, the integration of members of the same clan was more widespread (see *Huizhou in Ming—The Clan Conflict and the Integration of Members of the Same Clan*, Social Economic History, Japan, 1996, Vol. 62, No. 4). In 1997, Professor Park Won in Korea University published two essays, namely, *The Enlargement of Clan Institution in Huizhou in Ming—Exemplified by Fang Clan in Liushan* (History Research, 1997, Vol. 1), and *The Transformation of Zhengyin Temple and Clan Institutions in Huizhou in Ming and Qing* (outline) (International Conference of the Ming History in Changchun, Aug., 1997). The essays illustrated the transformation of Zhengyin Temple from a clan temple to an ancestral hall then to a grand ancestral temple. From the analysis of the lawsuit caused by the theft of the temple monk and the "Treaty of Ten Parties", the evolvement of the clan system from the Beisong Dynasty was clearly illustrated. In his essays, the author emphasized that, "The most distinctive feature of clan system was the enlargement of the integration of members of the same clan and the reinforcement of regional social relation. The enlarged and reinforced clan institutions became the basis of clan power, which was widespread in rural society in Qing." The main reason of the reinforcement of clan system was the decline of Jiali System (a form of government administration) and the weakened government power since the Mid-Ming. The confusion and chaos caused by the decline of government administration promoted the union of clan to deal with the social unrest in rural areas.

Ⅳ. The Research into Huizhou Files and Social System in Rural Areas in Ming and Qing

The reason that Huizhou files became the focus of research into rural society in Ming and Qing was that files discovered were enormously significant to the insight into rural society at that time. In his essay *The Status Quo and the Subject on Rural Social System Studies in Ming and Qing* (International Conference on Huizhou Studies, Huangshan, 1994), Professor Yamamoto Eishi in Keio University put it: "The research into rural society in Ming and Qing must take it as a strategy to make flexible use of the Huizhou files and other contracts." The author emphasized, compared with the rural society in Edo Times in Japan, the fact that the rural society in Ming and Qing was not fully revealed was mainly because the historical files were not fully investigated. The files were priceless to the research into the mechanism and function of all agencies like village associations, Hui (a kind of fork organization), and "Lijia" System (a basic official administration in Ming). Village association, according to Chen Keyun, was a fork association organized by region relation or blood relation for a common purpose, for instance, to defend one's hometown, to promote virtues and punish evils, to protect forestry, to deal with corvee and tax. As it was non-official, it was more agreeable with the villagers emotionally and psychologically. The village association, to some extent, bridged the gap in basic rural administration in feudalism society. Village association and "Jiabao" (household registration usually with military purpose), though having some connection, were distinct as the former played an edification function. Village association involved more in dealing with corvee and tax and tried to help to develop the rural collective economy. [1]

"Hui", a kind of fork association mainly played the role of ancestor memorials and public services. The memorial and religious belief system that "Hui" tried to establish were both associated with ancestor worship and a more general god worship. "Hui", distinct from clan ancestor memorial and tomb ceremony, had its own ceremony, namely "Huiji" and it got its financial

---

[1] Chen Keyun, *On the Village Association in Huizhou in Ming and Qing*, *Chinese History Research*, 1990, Vol. 4.

source from its members' land donation, which was taken as the property of "Hui". This meant the land rent was the economic source of all ceremonies and memorials. There were two kinds of sacrifices of the memorials, namely "Pork Sacrifice" and "Vegetable Sacrifice". The widespread and increasing number of "Hui", together with the donated land of the members, brought about the separation of religious life which generated impact to the traditional religious associations. ① The organization of "Hui" was mainly in two ways, one was based on groups with specific common interest, for instance, the region-related group and the blood-related group, the other was open to anyone who was willing to join. In this way, "Hui" was another important force in the rural society as other organizations like village association, "Baojia" and "Lijia". ②

"Lijia" System, "Respectful Seniors" and "Liangzhang" System made the core of rural administration founded in Ming. The Respectful Seniors System was founded at the beginning of Ming, according to Nakajima Yoshiaki, because of the corruption of "Xuli" class (official workers) in Ming. As a result, the local clans, especially those wealthy and prestigious clans, had to maintain the social order with their own capability. The Respectful Seniors in Ming included both wealthy clans with the traditional virtues and well cultivated scholars strongly influenced by Zhuzi, the prestigious Confucius scholar in Song. ③ However, there were debates about the existence of Lijia Registration, Lizhang, Liangzhang, and Respectful Seniors System after Emperor Jiaqing years in Ming. Zhou Shaoquan, with abundant related materials in Huizhou files, in his *Lizhang and Respectful Seniors at the End of Ming and the Beginning of Qing in Huizhou Files*, held that the Bianshen (official registration system) was

---

① Liu Miao, "*Hui*" and "*Huiji*" *in Huizhou in Qing*, Jianghuai Forum, 1995, Vol. 4.

② Shibuya Yuuko, "*Hui*" *in Huizhou Historical Files*, History Research, Japan, Sep. 1997, Vol. 67.

③ *The Renowned Clans in Huizhou and the Respectful Seniors in Ming*, The Oriental Studies, the 90th series, July 1995.

going on till Emperor Jianqing years and Emperor Daoguang years in Qing, consequently, Lizhang, Painian which were established at the beginning of Ming, existed in Huizhou until the middle of Qing. ①

V. The Research into Huizhou Files and Chinese Law History

The Japanese scholars had long noted the importance of files in the research into law history. As the Japanese professor Terada Hiroaki in Northeast University put it, "Foreign scholars were greatly interested in ancient Chinese civil contracts of land sale, especially from Song to Ming and Qing...as the land sale contracts were accurate record of property arrangement by people by their will at that period of time. Their notions of land sale, land rent and land possession were precisely reflected in the land contracts. There lay the significance of investigation of land contracts in Qing in regard to the research into ancient Chinese civil laws. ② Huizhou files were the first-hand materials which were helpful to the law history research in various ways, for instance, land sale, contract system, dividing up the clan property, civil lawsuits, lawsuit system and so on. The large quantity and various categories make the files worthy of study in themselves, which should have been noted more. For instance, Qiyue and Hetong were taken as one concept with the same meaning "contract" in modern Chinese law while in the ancient times they were distinct from each other, as some were taken as Qi while others as Yue, still others as Hetong. In 1993, Zhou Shaoquan published *The Similarity and Difference between Qiyue and Hetong in Huizhou in Ming and Qing* in *Chinese History Research*. The essay illustrated ten types of Qiyue and four types of Hetong to explore the situations involved and the different rights involved. To sum up, Qiyue was

---

① *Chinese History Studies*, 1998, Vol. 1.

② *The Collection of and Research into Land Contracts in Qing* by Japanese Scholars, *The Essays of International Conference of Chinese Law History Research*, 1990, Shanxi Press.

a one-way contract, one party made and signed the contract while the other party held the contract. By comparison, Hetong was made and signed by all parties involved and each was entitled to holding the contract. Also, the author pointed out though they fit different situations their difference was not absolute and they were, in effect, both distinct from and related to each other.

 The research into law history with the help with Huizhou files began with land contracts. In 1987, Zhou Shaoquan published *The Exploration of Qiwei in Land and House Sale* in *Chinese History Research*. By making use of the straight materials the essay analyzed the formation, development, form and content of the title deed—Qiwei which began from Yuan to the end of Qing for 600 years. The essay further pointed out that the Qiwei was not only a certificate, more important, it was an official legal guarantee of the private ownership of the land or house sold. *The Exploration of the System of Land Sale Title Deed* by Zhang Xuehui was published in *Pingjiang Journal*, 1989, Vol. 4, Book I. The essay gave a comprehensive illustration of the origin and evolvement of title deed and held that title deed was an important component of the national tax system and a legal guarantee of land ownership. In other words, title deed both ensured the national tax and avoided conflict of people as well. Wang Yuqua, by the analysis of red land certificate and Yellow Volumes, pointed out, "Title deed was to ensure the land tax, what's more, its original purpose was to maintain the quantity of tax." The white land certificate was to guarantee the interest of the two parties of the sale while the red land certificate with an official stamp was to ensure the interest of the government. ① Chen Gaohua published *The Process of land Sale and Contracts in Yuan* in *Chinese History Research*, 1988, Vol. 4. This essay explored the process of land sale and contract form in Yuan Dynasty by making use of land sale files and Qiwei at that time. By

---

 ① The Red Land Certificate and the Yellow Volumes in Ming, in *Research into Chinese Economic History*, 1991, Vol. 1.

comparison with the files in other places the essay tried to illustrate the general features of land sale in Yuan and also distinguished the difference between pawn and sale. In the same year, Yang Guozhen published *The Research into Land Certification in Ming and Qing* by The People Press. The book attempted to explore vertical structure and horizontal structure within the ownership mechanism. As the author held the making use of files to explore the Chinese ownership mechanism could avoid copying foreign or the ready concept to simplify or fossilize the complex internal structure and various forms within the mechanism. The author analyzed the national, clan and individual interest existing side by side. Also the author explored the evolvement from Yongdian to "one land two owners" and pointed out the difference between Yongdian Right and Tianmian Right, the former reflecting the separation between land ownership and land right the latter reflecting the division of land ownership. Consequently the former belonged to the change in tenancy system while the latter belonged to the change in ownership system. What's more, it was not true to history to generalize Yongdian Right and "one land with two owners" by using Yongdian System.

The land Diandang (land pawn) was rather complex in ancient China. Modern legal concepts could not give an accurate distinguish between Dian and Dang to understand the genuine implication of the two in that particular period of time. So the most sensible way was to conduct the research on the basis of first-hand historical files. Zheng Limin analyzed the historical land pawn agreements in Ming and Qing kept in Anhui Museum and Huangshan Museum. After careful investigation he held that the pawn happened mainly because the borrower was badly in need of money and he usually had the intention of redeem his property. Superficially the borrower collateralized his land to get the money he needed. It was mutually beneficial on the basis of credit of the two parties involved. In effect it was a temporary transfer of land right and it followed the way of land sale. The biggest difference between Dian and Dang was that Dian did not have to pay interest while Dang had to. In addition, the borrower could not rent the land after Dian while he could after Dang. Also the author made comparison between land pawn and land sale, emphasizing the difference and connection of "Dian" and "Huomai". ①

The large quantity of agreements of clan-property-division and wills in Huizhou files were enormously enlightening to the research into issues like dividing up the family property and inheritance. Japanese scholar Usui Sachiko published *On the Division of Family Property in Huizhou*, in *Modern China*, No. 25, Oct. 1995). The essay gave detailed analysis of the 248 files of family property division and other relevant files kept in The History Institute of Chinese Academy of Social Sciences and Peking University. The analysis covered many aspects, for instance, the concept of family in traditional Chinese society, the profession of the families involved, the choice of file-maker, the reasons of the division, the content and method of the division, the management of common property and so on. The author held that in China family division referred to the division of house and family property instead of setting up a new family. The administration of property division rested on the clan seniors, however they were not entitled to making the division proportion at their own will. Meanwhile theoretically speaking widows were also entitled to inheritance. The author held, at least in Huizhou, "family division" was conducted flexibly in specific situations, which was not only a conceptual behavior. For inherit issue, Usui Sachiko penned the essay *On the Inheritance of Clans in Huizhou*.② The essay classified the inheritance relation into four categories, namely, Inheritance Files, Son-in-law by Adoption Files, Selling-oneself Files and other files and gave detailed interpretation respectively. Moreover, the author held the genuine purpose of adopted sons was not to carry on the family line but to inherit the family property. In effect, "inheritance" was, to a large extent, a

---

① *Chinese History Research*, 1991, Vol. 3.

② *The Collected Essays of International Conference of Huizhou Studies in* 1995, Anhui University Press, 1997.

guarantee of obligation and of the rights of the one who undertook the obligation.

Huizhou locals tended to resort to law when in conflict and no wonder they left a large quantity of legal files. The files were in various forms, for instance, arrest papers, letters, bail bonds, copies of lawsuit, litigation requests, court opinions and so on. All these enlightened the research into legal system and those beyond the system. *The Exploration of Resorting to Law of Huizhou Locals in Ming and Qing* by Bian Li[1] held that the key reason of the locals' resorting to law was the increasing gap between the rich and the poor caused by increased number of businessmen and the changes in social customs. The lawsuits mainly covered issues like, land and hill ownership. Meanwhile, with the preference of resorting to legal devices, the Huizhou locals gradually strengthened their notion of legal contracts in their social activities. Another focus of the research was the position of Lizhang and Respectful Seniors in the legal system in Ming and Qing. *On the Legal Procedure in Ming with the Example of the Family Record of Wu in Mingzhou* by Nakajima Yoshiaki was collected in *The Collected Essays of International Conference of Huizhou Studies in 1995* (Anhui University Press 1997). The essay investigated the series of legal files in the Family Record of Wu and analyzed the general features of trial procedure in Ming. Also the essay illustrated the procedure difference between Ming and Qing and focused on the significance of seniors and Lizhang in the legal procedure, including the investigation, conciliation, summons from the court and so on. In 1997 Zhou Shaoquan delivered *The Legal Files in Huizhou in Ming and Qing and the Local Ruling in Ming* (outline) at the International Conference of Ming History Studies in Changchun. The essay generalized the features of legal files in Huizhou and illustrated the local ruling of "lawful citizens governing lawful citizens" policy founded at the very beginning of Ming by its first emperor Zhu Yuanzhang and the changes of the local ruling. The

---

[1] *Jianghuai Forum*, 1993, Vol. 5.

essay made use of the original version of legal files to explore the changing position of Lizhang and Respectful Seniors in the local ruling system, especially the downfall of the two in the local trial at the end of Ming. Furthermore, the essay pointed out though there existed the difference of law, courtesy and emotion in legal cases, all cases were ruled by both reason and ration. There was no other independent legal system or principle nor the so-called "the Third Area" in it.

The past decade has seen fruitful achievements in the relevant research and this essay tried to get the most important and influential ones with detailed analysis. The essay attempted to interpret the ideas from the author's original perspective, reasonably, misunderstanding and mistakes are unavoidable. Any suggestion and correction from scholars is sincerely and warmly welcome.

Published in *Trends of Chinese History Studies*, No. 2, 1998

Written by A Feng
Translated by Li Qiao

Chapter 11 Huizhou Historical Files and Huizhou Studies

I. Forewords

Huizhou Studies (or Hui Studies) appeared in the 1980s. Immediately after its appearance some articles attempted to explore its relation to and distinction from Xin'an Confucius, whose abbreviation is also Huizhou Studies. Meanwhile other articles tried to distinguish this new discipline with Huizhou Regional Studies. Fortunately, now agreement has been reached on this point and there is no more debate over that kind of stuff. Also, there used to be a great disagreement as to the name for the new discipline—Huizhou Studies or Hui Studies. Now this disagreement also seems to come to an end. However, there existed disagreements about the research objects, research range and historical span as well. Some hold that Huizhou Studies should be the studies of Huizhou history, namely "a complex discipline focusing on Huizhou history". [1] Others think that Huizhou Studies should be "the studies of Huizhou history and culture", [2] namely "regional studies of Huizhou history and culture". [3] Still others believe that Huizhou Studies should be a "general culture" of Huizhou in a given historical period, which should focus on "the process of the formation, prosperity and decline of Huizhou culture with its distinct character in the later part of Chinese feudal society. Huizhou Studies is the research into the

---

[1] Foreword to *Journal of Hui Studies*, *The Opening Issue of Journal of Hui Studies* Oct, 1994.

[2] Zhen Jiaqi, The *Object of Hui Studies and the Task of Hui Association*, The opening issue of *Journal of Hui Studies*.

[3] *The Speech of Wang Deqi*, the Standing Member of Shexian County Party Committee, The opening issue of *Journal of Hui Studies*.

formation, booming and decline of the conflicts in that specific period in history". ① Others strongly object to this "period limit", as they firmly believe it would be incomplete to exclude the history before the Song Dynasty and the history after the Opium War in Qing, which is indispensable to the origin and later variations of Huizhou culture.

Rather, they hold that "the Huizhou culture from the Nansong Dynasty to the end of Qing should be the main content or the key focus of Huizhou Studies instead of the only and all content". ② As to the research range, some limit it to the "one region and its six counties". As to the research content, some believe that it could be generalized as "Huizhou in its history" or "Huizhou's history". As to the accurate region concept, there are frequent changes in regional zones, for instance, Chun'an, Wuyuan and Jixi all used to be part of Huizhou region. If this is the so called "first region", there should be still "the second region", covering much larger areas, which includes Hangzhou, Jingdezhen, Nanjing, Shanghai and Yangzhou, to name just a few. These people take "Xin'an River" as "the cradle of Huizhou Studies"③ and they believe it is too narrowly restricted if Huizhou Studies limits itself within the six counties of Huizhou region. Others hold that "Huizhou culture should not be confined to the culture within Huizhou region, rather, it should include all the culture elements created or heavily influenced by Huizhou people even if they later immigrated to other places. The key point is to enormously identify with Huizhou and its culture". ④

---

① On the Object of Hui Studies and its Profound Meaning, *The Essays of Hui Studies* (Vol. 1), Zhao Huafu, complied by *The Social Science Association of Huangshan and* the Editorial Office of *Huizhou Social Science*.

② Liu Boshan, The Basic Concepts and the Research Value of Huizhou Culture, *The Collected Essays of the 10th Anniversary of Huizhou Institute in Hangzhou*, compiled by Huizhou Institute, Aug. 1997.

③ Speech of Chairman Wu Cunxin at the Annual Meeting, *Hui Studies Newsletter* Vol. 15, 16.

④ Liu Boshan, The Basic Concepts and the Research Value of Huizhou Culture, *The Collected Essays of the 10th Anniversary of Huizhou Institute in Hangzhou*, compiled by Huizhou Institute, Aug. 1997.

As to Huizhou Studies, we put forward the idea that the discovery of Huizhou historical files has brought about the Huizhou Studies—"the new discipline which aims to research into the history and culture of Huizhou and is getting more and more attention from scholars home and abroad". [1] Therefore, there is an umbilical link between Huizhou Studies and its historical files.

This essay attempts to explore the position and role that Huizhou Studies holds in Chinese academic development in terms of the Huizhou historical files and Huizhou Studies.

II. The Reasons Why Huizhou Studies Has Come into Being an Eye-catching New Discipline

1. The discoveries of large quantity of new materials have brought about the new disciplines.

It has been more than 100 years since the discovery of oracle bone inscriptions in the late 1898. In the following year, 1899, inscribed wooden slip in Han Dynasty and Jin Dynasty was discovered in Xinjiang Province, in Dunhuang county and Juyan county, Gansu Province. [2] These three great discoveries have given birth to three new disciplines, namely, Oracle Bone Inscriptions Studies, Wooden Slip and Silk Book Studies and Dunhuang Studies. After one century's efforts, these disciplines have gained worldwide attention and fame. As the history studies has suggested that the discovery of large quantity of new historical materials may directly lead to new disciplines. The well-known scholar Wang Guowei put it well when he said, "New disciplines are usually the result and fruit of new discoveries, which has been proved throughout history."[3]

---

[1] *Foreword to The Contracts and Files in Huizhou in a Thousand Years*, Huashan Culture and Art Press, 1991.

[2] Li Xueqin, *The Elementary Stage of Ancient Chinese Characters*, China Classics Press, 1995.

[3] Wang Guowei, *The Newly-found Academics in the Past Two or Three Decades*.

It is also the case for Huizhou Studies, the great discovery of Huizhou historical files directly leading to Huizhou Studies. Years ago when the director of the Museum of Anhui Province, Mr. Liu Hehui put forward this view, he was severely criticized. The critics firmly held that Huizhou Studies was not the equivalent to Huizhou historical file studies. It was true that the two were not the same. However if there were not the discovery of historical files, should there be any Huizhou Studies? Some believe that the richness and achievements of Huizhou culture has made Huizhou the focus of history studies, the multitude of scholars who are interested in Huizhou culture have made the discipline of Huizhou Studies. But is it the whole story? A comparison between Huizhou, Suzhou and Hangzhou may make some sense. The latter two cities have been enjoying the most splendid culture progress, especially in Ming and Qing, Suzhou was at the peak of its economic prosperity, together with its abundant resources and advanced civilization, Suzhou was nothing less than Huizhou. There are as many as scholars who have devoted themselves to the research into Suzhou culture as those into Huizhou culture. Nevertheless, with all the above mentioned facts, there is no discipline like Su Studies at all.

Another case in point is Dunhuang Studies. Dunhuang Grottoes are the treasure created by ancient Chinese, but before its historical files were found there were few people going there, let along the discipline of Dunhuang Studies. Since the discovery of and research into the files, Dunhuang Studies has come into being and was highly developed. A large number of researchers and tourists have been attracted not only by Dunhuang Grottoes but by the well-known Dunhuang Studies as well.

Consequently we hold that the direct and vital reason of the formation of Huizhou Studies is nothing but the finding of its historical files. Of course, that does not mean Huizhou Studies is historical files themselves, instead, it means with the intensive research into historical files, more efforts are required for the research into the splendid history and culture of Huizhou. The historical files are the most cherished and straight materials of the research into Huizhou Studies. In other words, the historical files and Huizhou Studies should never be separated with or opposed to each other.

2. The characteristics of Huizhou historical files.

The year 1957 saw another piece of striking news in Chinese history in the newspapers. That was the finding of Huizhou historical files.

The huge number, the vast categories, long historical span and high academic value have caught enormous attention from scholars home and abroad.

Although no one can give an exact number of the files, the generally estimated number is 100,000 pieces. It was put forward in April 1988, in my essay "The Origin, Collection, Sorting and Research of Huizhou Historical Files" at The Huizhou Historical Files Conference at Anhui University. It was based on my interview in Jixi County. On Nov. 28's afternoon, I interviewed Mr. Yu Tingguang, head of Bureau of Cultural Relics in Jixi County. Mr. Yu had been working in Tunxi Book Store since 1952 and he was appointed to take in charge of a branch store of ancient books which was set up in September 1956. Huizhou historical files were mainly collected by the branch store and were then sold to places all over China via China Book Store in Beijing and Ancient Book Store in Shanghai. Mr. Yu also said: "The ancient contracts were mainly collected in Qimen county. In the scrap yards there were full of these old contracts, which were kept in gunny bags and even in bamboo baskets. We collected about tens of thousands of them in 1957. In total we had over 100, 000 old contracts."[①]

That was why I said in my report: "According to the head of Tunxi Ancient Book Store, they have collected over 100, 000 old contracts. Together with those spread to other places, there should be more." At that time this number was approximate but appropriate. But now it turned out to be far from the reality. There were mainly the following reasons involved. One was that many relevant institutions had not sorted their files and

---

① Zhou Shaoquan, The Origin, Collection and Sorting of Huizhou Historical Files, Japan: *The Research into the Ming History*, Vol. 20.

underestimated the number. For instance, Huizhou Museum (now Huangshan Museum) was estimated to have 10,000 pieces, now it turned out to have more than 30,000 pieces. The second reason was some institutions with collections were unknown and were not included. For instance, the reference room of History Department of Nanjing University and Tianjin Library which had a rich collection of Huizhou historical files were not included. Last year I found 31 pieces of Huizhou ancient contracts from the Nansong Dynasty (1256) to the Ming Dynasty (1639). Recently it was said there were some 900 pieces of Huizhou historical files in Harvard University, among them over 700 letters about Fang Yongbin, the well-known scholar and businessman in Yansi Town of Huizhou at the end of Ming. The third reason was that some institutions had a larger number of collections than that was previously estimated. For instance, Chinese Academy of Social Sciences was formerly estimated to have 10,000 pieces of collection, in fact it has about 14,000 to 15,000 pieces. What's more, there are more and more files being spread to the outside world from different places in Huizhou region.

For instance, South China Research Center (located in Guangzhou) bought some Huizhou folk files in Huangshan in 1996.[1] Japanese visiting scholars in Chinese History Institute also bought some Huizhou files in Huangshan.[2] In addition, there are countless files kept by the local folks.

In 1997, on my way to visiting Huizhou ancient performing stages I happened to find some 100 pieces of files dating from the middle Qing to the Republic of China (1912 — 1949) bought by Bureau of Cultural Relics of Qimen. Even on the roads of Tunxi county, there were historical files being

---

[1] *For the Interpretation of a Title Deed*, News Report of South China Research Center, Vol. 10.

[2] Professor Yamamoto in Keio University and Mr. Nakajima Raaki in Waseda University bought 10 pieces of Huizhou files and presented them to the History Institute.

sold. Some believed "there was still large quantity of files within this region". ① Some said "there might be about 100,000 pieces undiscovered". ② The exact number of Huizhou files is surely much bigger than previously estimated, but there are difficulties in getting an accurate number. One difficulty involved is the approach to count and to calculate. For instance, the number of *Yulin Volumes* (land registration books) from 1647 to the Republic of China (1912—1949) kept in Xiuning county was over 80,000. The counting approach was based upon the following principle: "As many of the *Yulin Volumes* and other land registration books have been incomplete or partially damaged, thus, as long as there is independent academic value in terms of land allotment and field system, one single page is taken as a piece."③ The principle of counting by taking the files' independent content has also met with challenge. For instance, as to the copy books and the renting books, should one whole book be counted as one piece or each contract in the book is taken as one piece? As there were no fixed criteria even in the same book, different methods of counting have been used for different collection agencies and different kinds of files. All these have brought great chaos and confusion to the counting work. In *The Total Archives Catalogue of Huizhou Historical Files* compiled by Mr. Yan Guifu, the author claimed, "To our knowledge, there are over 130,000 pieces of the historical files in store. It is based on the following statistics: over 90,000 pieces in the Archives in Anhui Province, 30,000 in Huang Shan Museum, 4,453 in the History Department of Nanjing University and

---

① Yan Guifu, *The total Archives Catalogue of Huizhou Historical Files*, Huangshan Publishing House, 1996.

② Liu Boshan, *the Basic Concepts and the Value of Huizhou Culture*, *The Collected Works of the 10th Anniversary of Hangzhou Huizhou Studies Association*, compiled by Hangzhou Huizhou Studies Association.

③ Liu Boshan, *the Basic Concepts and the Value of Huizhou Culture*, *The Collected Works of the 10th Anniversary of Hangzhou Huizhou Studies Association*, compiled by Hangzhou Huizhou Studies Association.

some in other institutes.① The 4,453 files kept in Nanjing University are in form of volumes while those in Huangshan Museum are in form of both volumes and pages. For those in Xiuning Archive, 80,000 of them are in form of pages and 4,158 are in form of volumes. There are other archives mentioned in *The Total Archives Catalogue of Huizhou Historical Files* which are kept in other institutes, but it's hard to decide how many of them are identified as historical files. The above mentioned 30,000 pieces in Huangshan Museum were bought after 1970s and those in Xiuning Archive were found in later years. Both of them were not included in the 100,000 pieces which Mr. Yu Tingguang estimated to have been sold by Tunxi Ancient Book Store. Considering all these factors, we may not exaggerate to say it's virtually impossible to give an exact number of the files since there is no accurate number of both files outside Huizhou and those undiscovered yet. If a vague number is required it may be over 200,000, taking all the following sources: libraries, museums, archives, colleges and institutes, in both volumes and pages.

There are many kinds of Huizhou historical files, as being illustrated by many articles. Approaches to distinguish different kinds of files vary in terms of collection, sorting and researchers. Some archive researchers take all the files as archives, including ancient books, steles, brick-carvings, wood-carvings and bamboo-carvings. These files are sorted as education files, culture and art files, patriarchal clan and economy file and government files. Huizhou historical files are sorted as education files, patriarchal clan and economy files and government files.②

In my book *The Classification of Huizhou Historical Files*, the files are classified as eight categories, namely, (1) land files, (2) taxes files, (3) business

---

① Yan Guifu, *The Total Archives Catalogue of Huizhou Historical Files*, Huangshan Publishing House.

② Wang Guojian, The Category and Employment of Huizhou Historical Files, *Huizhou Social Science*, 1991, Vol. 1.

files, (4) clan files, (5) examination and education files, (6) social files, (7) class-relation and class-conflict files, (8) government files. ①

The would-be-published *The Category of Huizhou Historical Files* compiled by History Institute of Chinese Academy of Social Sciences has divided the files into nine categories, namely, (1) land and property files, (2) taxes files, (3) business files, (4) clan files, (5) government files, (6) education and examination files, (7) institutions files, (8) social relations files, and (9) other files. The nine categories can be further divided into 122 sub-categories and the first five categories which cover 82 sub-categories can be divided into 152 branches.

This may well illustrate the complexity of the category of the files. The files also cover enormously, which has two layers of meanings. The first layer of meaning, though the three categories, namely, the land and property files, taxes files and business files occupy the most, yet other files are various, covering virtually all aspects of social life of the locals. For this reason, some take the files as new materials of research into the history and economy of Huizhou. The fact is that the files have meant far more than that and they have covered all social life and daily life from big issues like municipal administration, to customs and other trivial affairs like birth, sickness, death and marriage. The second layer of meaning is that the files have covered those travelling to other places for government issues or for business tasks. Although most of the files were made within Huizhou, but still part of them were not. In other words, Huizhou files should not be confined merely to Huizhou region. The range of the research into the files should be enlarged to gain wider horizon. As early as in the 1920s and 1930s the term "general Huizhou" was put forward, thus there is no reason we should confine the research within Huizhou region, especially after considering the development of science and technology and advancement in

---

① Zhou Shaoquan, *The Category of Huizhou Files*, *Huizhou Social Science*, 1992, Vol. 2.

modern transportation and communication.

The long history span of Huizhou historical files is obvious if we compare with other files discovered in other places in China during the same historical period. As is known, there are quite a few historical files found in many places in China, for instance, the land files in Hong Kong in Qing, the land files in Zhujiang Delta Region, the Minbei files in Fujian province in Ming and Qing, the Danxin files in Tai Wan in Qing, the land files in Yanzhou and Lanxi *Yulin Volumes*, Zhejiang province in Ming and Qing, the files in Ba County, Sichuan Province in Qing, the files in Ziliujing Sichuan Province in Ming and Qing, the files in Guizhou Province in Qing, Dingwu (Na clan of Li nationality) Yunnan Province in Qing, the business files and Taihu files in Jiangsu Province in Qing, other files besides Huizhou files in Anhui Province (for instance, Nanling files in Ningguo county), Huolu land files in Hebei Province in Qing, Baodi files in Shuntian (now Beijing region) in Qing and the land files in north-east China and Neimonggu province in Qing. Those were but only a small part of the files discovered, more examples and details could be found in *Chinese Precious Historical Files in Ming and Qing* written by Mr. Qin Guojing. With the comparison with other files we may safely draw the conclusion that Huizhou files enjoy the longest historical span. To our knowledge, the earliest file is *The Selling-hill Contract in Wugong, Qimen County*, in 1215,[①] now kept in Beijing Library while the latest is a contract in 1949, with the time span over 730 years.

The academic value of Huizhou files is closely related to their characteristics, namely, thought-provoking, continuous, specific, genuine and typical.

---

① Zhang Chuanxi, *A Corpus and Interpretation of Contracts in Chinese History*, Peking University Press, 1995. This contract is a copy instead of the original version. The earliest original version of Huizhou Files is the one in 1242, in the Southern Song Dynasty, see *The Land-sale Contract of Li Sicong and Others in Xiuning County*, *The Chapter of Song, Yuan and Ming of Hui Zhou Files in One Thousand Years*, Vol.1, Huashan Art and Literature Press, 1991, compiled by Wang Yuxin and Zhou Shaoquan.

Part IV Huizhou Files

Being thought-provoking means arousing our attention and confirming our cognition. For instance, some historical terms may not be much illustrated in previous ancient works, but they are clearly explained in Huizhou files, which consequently catch our attention and enhance our knowledge. A case in point is Qiben (tax certificate) and Qiwei (the attachment to the certificate issued by government) which appear in both *Laws in Yuan Dynasty* and *Laws in the Ming Dynasty*. But no detailed information is given about the function and form of Qiben. Fortunately, we know not only the appearance of Qiben but also the relation between Qiben and Qiwei when we read these Huizhou files, the files of Qimen county in the 28th year of Emperor Hongwu reign in Ming① and the Qiwei of the same land trade on that day. When we read the Qiben in Yuan Dynasty in *The Unearthed Files of Heicheng* (the Chinese version),② by comparison with that of Huizhou's we have a clear idea about the changes of Qiben in the two successive dynasties—Yuan and Ming. As for Qiwei, it was mentioned in previous historical works but the original version was never seen. By seeing the Qiwei from Emperor Hongwu years in Ming to the end of Qing, together with the analysis and reference to other relevant materials we have come to understand the history of Chinese land trade system in Ming and Qing. As for being continuous, it means Huizhou files have lasted for several hundreds of years.

Although there are historical files in many parts in China, they cover only a period of history with no related information before or after, which is vital to getting the whole picture. The continuity of Huizhou files is obvious in the case of the lawsuits in Ming and Qing Dynasty. There are Danxin files in Tai Wan, Taihu files in Jiangsu province, Baxian files in Sichuan province, Nanling files in Anhui Province and Baodi files in Shuntian region (now Beijing region). Although all the files are large in quantity and rich in

---

① The original version is kept in the Library of Anhui Normal University.
② Li Yiyou, *The Unearthed Files in Heicheng*, Science Press, 1991.

content, but they cover only part of Qing (some only in Emperor Tongzhi and Emperor Guangxu years), thus making it impossible compare the changes of lawsuits in the regions in Qing and Ming. Although there are some lawsuit files in Ming in the incomplete files of Liaodong kept in Liaoning Archive, but they have only officials' remarks and government documents with no plaints of litigants or defendants. In this case it would be difficult to work out the original meaning of the files. The earliest lawsuit files were in 1427 (the 2nd year of Emperor Xuande reign in Ming) and the latest were in 1924. Except for those kept by government there are files kept by local forks as well. For instance, there is "Chaozhao" (the copy by county clerk and with an official sign) of *The Lawsuit of Wang, Li and Hu Clan in Qukou, Xiuning in the 32nd Year of Emperor Kangxi Reign, Qing* (now kept in the History Institute of Chinese Academy of Social Sciences). There is *The Unfair Lawsuit Case of Pan Clan During Emperor Tianqi and Emperor Congzhen Years* copied by clan members (now kept by the History Department of Nanjing University). There was *The Yanggan Yard Lawsuit Case* copied by the clan involved (the Luo clan in Chenkan, Shexian County in Emperor Jiajing years, Qing). There were lawsuits compiled by clan members as family files, for instance, *The Family Files of Lu Clan in Dabu* (now kept in Huangshan Museum), the last volume of which was about lawsuits. There was local lawsuit report like *Gaojian, Qimen Lawsuit Report in Emperor Daoguang Years* (now kept in the History Institute of Chinese Academy of Social Sciences). Except for those, there were single pieces of lawsuit report as well. In addition, there are abundant different kinds of files. For instance, the sentence reports of county magistrates of Huizhou in Ming and Qing. For instance, the 9th volume (*Sentence Reports*) of *A Journal of Shexian County* in Emperor Congzheng years in Ming by its county magistrate Fuyan (now kept in Anhui Provincial Library) and *Haiyang Journal* in Emperor Kangxi years in Qing by Liao, the county magistrate of Xiuning, (now kept in the History Institute of Chinese Academy of Social Sciences). There are also materials used to teach people how to write official forms for filing a lawsuit, like the so called "Secrets and Skills of Writing Official Forms for Filing a Lawsuit", (the book *Er Bi Ken Qi*, for example, now kept in Wuyuan Library in Jiangxi province, is one of them). Other files include the record of sharing the legal fare by clan members. These lawsuit materials are rich in content and cover a long history, which has been priceless to the research into the changes and practices of lawsuit issues in Ming and Qing. Meanwhile, they act as the "reference standards". In other words, by comparing them with the lawsuit files in other regions, we may get a clear view about the status of the local lawsuit issues in the Chinese lawsuit history in Ming and Qing.

Huizhou files are more specific and concrete, compared with the general description in documentation. Documentation, though rich in content and covering widely, is nothing but the society in the eyes of upper class and the scholar-bureaucrats. They may cover widely but not exactly, they may be described lively and vividly but not truly and sincerely. However the truth is that the history research is revealing only if it is based on facts and objects. Take the research into Chinese farmers and peasants as an example as they have been occupying the biggest part in Chinese society, especially in ancient China. But the research into farmers' life is rather insufficient. Chinese history authorities used to mainly focus on wars farmers got involved in and the reasons that may cause the wars and other background information. Although some aspects of farmers' life are covered, yet the big concern is the situation in time of class conflicts rather than the daily life in peaceful time. Consequently more empirical study is called for. The reason of lack of empirical study is simple and obvious: in the old times farmers did not have the written genealogy and family trees as the wealthy landlords did. Nor did they have the clan documents like ancestral hall records, testaments of real-estate sale and rent records. As a result it's hard to trace the evolution process of farmers' clans over long period of time. To explore farmers' life merely on the few words from the scholar-bureaucrats is far from being effective. By uncovering the mask of scholar-bureaucrats' records the Huizhou files give genuine and detailed materials and they make it possible to reveal the farmers' true life in the old times. In the single-piece Huizhou files and testaments of real-estate sale, there are 36 pages about the nine generations of a Hu clan in Wudushu (now Hongcun village), Qimen county. Reading these files in order, we can easily find out how this Hu clan was reduced to poverty. They started as being tenants by renting lands from landlords and they were further exploited by rent in kind, labor rent and usurious loan. Their hard-earned lands were again taken by the landlords' usurious loan, leading to their being servants of the landlords at last. The final tragedy was they were not able to live in the same house passed over by their ancestors and buried in the same graveyard with their ancestors after death. These files are able to offer genuine and details through the evolution process.

Compared with other historical materials, being genuine is the most striking characteristic of historical file. They are documents created at the genuine time in history rather than those compiled in later time for certain purposes. As a result, they are the most reliable proof of history. They are the true records of genuine events in history, for instance, the original versions of land sale contracts, rent contracts, receipts for a loan, indentures to sell oneself, to name just a few. In addition, other files, like lawsuit files, notices of government and villages and village contracts signed by all male village members, are all genuine and historical records without artificial make-up.

Huizhou files are typical and case studies may help to reveal specific type of people. Take the case study of landlords, we can find out some landlords were "the gentry" households whose members were scholars or high-rank government officials, others were wealthy land owners but with no scholars or government official titles, still others accumulated their wealth through commercial profits. Intensive case study can be done by taking one or two from these different types of landlord clans. The research may cover the following aspects: successive generations, family education, land accumulation, land management, founding of Ancestral Hall, clan-estate management, relation with local government and other clans, commercial activities, wealth accumulation and so on. These may help to investigate the different features of different types of landlords and common points of the same type of landlords. For instance, Cheng clan in Shanhe, Qimen county was outstanding for the 5 Jinshi (presented scholar title) in their clan in Ming. The Cheng clan had all kinds of detailed and written files, for example, written pedigree, written clan regulations, the fete ceremony records, rent contracts, lawsuits records and so on. In addition, the village annals *Heshanxiangzhi* mainly focused on this Cheng clan, providing rich reference materials for the research into this case study. Another case study was about Zhu Xueyuan, the head of the Sanjia Li (110 households making one "Li" in Ming) Xiuning county. There were so many relevant materials for research. For instance, there were five *Yellow Volumes* (census and land register) in Emperor Wangli years, and other register files in Emperor Tianqi years, and Emperor Congzhen years in Ming and Emperor Shunzhi years, Emperor Kangxi years in Qing. The files have covered about 120 years (from 1581 to 1701), lasting for two dynasties, Ming and Qing. These materials are precious and helpful to the research into both Zhu household and his neighborhood. The abundant materials of Wu clan in South Xixi, She county and Cheng clan in Shuaikou, Xiuning county are the most typical files for research into the businessman-landlords and the businessman-landlords-gentry.

  The above-mentioned advantages and features of Huizhou files have attracted so many scholars' devotion to the research that a new discipline was created, namely the Huizhou Studies which focuses on the Huizhou files and the social status that they reflected and the new discipline also aims to explore the laws of the later period of Chinese feudal society. It is well predicted that Huizhou Studies is to bring revolutionary changes to the research into Chinese history, especially in Ming and Qing. However, Chinese scholars are not as sensitive to Huizhou files and Huizhou Studies as those foreign scholars are. Maybe it's just like what the old Chinese poem says: "I see not the true face of Lushan mountain just because I am in the mountain." In 1985, the American scholar Joseph P. McDermott who taught in Japanese International Christianity University published *Huizhou Original Files—the Key to the Research into the Later Part of Imperial China*. In this paper the author held that Huizhou files were critical to the exploration of the social history and economic history in the later part of Chinese feudal society. ① In 1994, famous Japanese scholar Professor Tsurumi Naohiro published *The Files in One Thousand Years and Contracts Sorted and Kept in the History Institute of Chinese Academy of Social Sciences* in *Japanese Academic Journal* (Vol. 76. No. 1, 2). The Japanese scholar held that the publication of the book was memorable achievement of the research into Chinese middle-age history and modern history and it was nothing less than Yin Dynasty ruins and Dunhuang files which have bought enormous progress to the ancient Chinese history research. It will surely bring revolutionary transition to the research into Chinese middle-age history and modern history. The publication of the large quantity of materials is priceless to the research into Chinese history, as the materials are first-hand and complete, covering over 700 years, from the Song Dynasty to the Republic of China. ②

The specialist in Huizhou Studies, Professor Usui Sachiko has drawn the conclusion in her *Huizhou Files and Huizhou Studies*: "The most striking feature of Huizhou Studies is its abundant files. It is the large quantity of files that has made it possible to conduct a comprehensive study beyond the individual subjects previously." The individual subjects include land possession, commercial, clans, regional society, nation power, local administration system, social status, classes, ideology, culture and so on. These materials are helpful to correct the faults that individual subjects may produce. What's more, the materials are continuous to the Republic of

---

① For the Chinese version, see *The News Report of Hui Studies*, 1990, Vol. 1.
② For the Chinese version, see *The Trends of Chinese History Research*, 1995, Vol. 4.

China and they provide vital clues to the exploration of the features and changes of pre-modern society and modern society in China. ①

III. The Academic Position of Huizhou Files and Huizhou Studies

Tsurumi Naohiro's point is knowledgeable and intelligent when he commented on Huizhou files as "surely bring a huge transition to the research into Chinese middle-age history and modern history". Taking the one-century history studies into consideration, Huizhou files and Huizhou Studies provide us with great opportunity and possibility to the comprehensive exploration of genuine social status in China.

In Qing, the study of Confucian Classics was booming while the study on history was on decline. According to famous scholar Chen Yinke, "It is the boom of the study of Confucian Classics that has led to the decline of the study on history." At that time Chinese scholars limited their learning to book knowledge while books were mainly confined to Confucian Classics. At that time if a scholar was accomplished in one of the Confucian Classics in three years he was seen as a specialist in the Classics. As a result fame in the academic circle and the consequent wealth and position was sure to come. Thus more and more talented men who could have done great achievements in history textual criticisms have turned to the Confucian Classics study. The popularity of Confucian Classics Study has been lasting until the beginning of 20th century, which made some scholars sticking to the Classics for all their life.

The turning point of Chinese traditional academy to modern academy is based on the great discoveries in history and culture areas at the end of Qing Dynasty, especially on the discovery of inscriptions on bones or tortoise shells of the Shang Dynasty and the discovery of Dunhuang historical files. Many scholars were greatly excited by the newly discovered materials, as

---

① *The Basic Issues of Ming and Qing History*, Jigu Academy, Japan, 1997, compiled by Mori Masao.

the famous scholar Wang Guowei put it in *History with New Discovery*: "Our generation is fortunate to have both record materials and unearthed materials. We have the unearthed materials to supplement the history records and to prove which records are reliable. In this way we come to know some of the history records, though somewhat vulgar, they reveal the facts. This double-prove approach benefits the research from today on." These discoveries help scholars to loosen the bonds of the confusion of the Confucius Classics, offering more materials for the development and progress of history research. Most scholars were enthusiastic about the studies of the inscriptions on bones or tortoise shells in Yin ruins, the unearthed relics in Beimang Mountain, the Dunhuang files and the inscribed wooden slip in Xinjiang. The academic circle sincerely believed in ancient relics and unearthed files so much so that they chose to ignore the books written after Sui and Tang Dynasty. Therefore, at the beginning of 20th century, "more historians in China were devoted to the research into ancient history" as the famous scholar Chen Yinke mentioned in his writings. ① Those who specialized in Ming and Qing focused their attention to official history and ignored the literary sketches as they only took official history as trustworthy. To them, sketches, novels and unofficial histories were arbitrary and thus unreliable. This situation changed in the 1950s and 1960s when the discussion about "the capitalism infancy" was put forward, with the rapid progress in economy history studies, scholars began to be interested in collected works, sketches, novels and local chronicles. In recent years, with the enthusiasm in social history in Ming and Qing, local chronicles and family archives are drawing more and more attention from scholars.

As is known, the policies and official laws issued by the governments in any dynasty were far from how they were carried out in effect. It was also true for the economic policies, there was always big gap between the laws and how they were put into effect in real life. Therefore the research into

---

① Chen Yinke, *Jingmingguan Drafts*, the 2nd Edition.

political and economic policies should be based not only on government decrees and official laws but also on how they were carried out in reality. For the past 50 years, great achievements have been made as history researchers enlarged their horizon by searching for straight materials, besides collected works, they have found useful materials in the local chronicles and literary sketches. In this way, the researchers have tried to reduce the gap between the policies issued by government and how they were put into effect.

Literary sketches are the records and description of the true events happened in history, interesting and vivid as they were, they were but the impression and reflection of the authors, not the events in themselves. What's more, the descriptions of the events were, sometimes, copied from other versions, usually lacking originality and even conflicting with each other sometimes.

Local chronicles, with abundant materials, are usually more detailed and concrete than the brief words in the official history. However, as the history-geography expert Tan Qixiang put it, "Local chronicles should be duly employed while old materials are not always trustworthy."[1] Professor Yamamoto gave his point in *The Status Quo and Subject of the Research into Social System in Ming and Qing*. He held that though the local chronicles were compiled by the local administration, in effect, they were penned by the lower-class intellectuals. These intellectuals may provide rich materials and give vivid descriptions of the events they were concerned. However, generally speaking, the writings were superficial and one-dimensioned, short of originality and strongly-prejudiced. As the writers were not concerned with common farmers' daily life and social activities, therefore, there were not so many descriptions and the limited descriptions were

---

[1] *Jianghai Journal*, 1982, 2.

but less interesting and fragmented pieces. ①

Now researchers have come to pay more attention to the village chronicles and genealogy files which are more detailed and concrete than provincial or county chronicles. The genealogy files which concern only one family clan are even more specific. As early as the beginning of 20th century, the prestigious scholar Liang Qichao put it well when he said: "It should be a worthy course to take all the genealogy files as the materials of research into various subjects."② Since the Reform and Opening Up the Chinese genealogy research has suggested there exists both significant academic value and rich history in genealogy files which are to be further explored. At the same time, as Mr. Chen Zhiping pointed out, "The genealogy files, without any social restrains, are private and unavoidably subjective and arbitrary." As a result, the employment of the materials should be done with careful selection. It is true that we cannot reproduce history but to approach it as near as possible is significant. More attention now is drawn to historical files. History research aims to understand the present better by learning from the past. History makes people wise and knowledgeable and better equipped for the present and the future. Since we study history for the better understanding of today, we should try to reproduce history as faithfully as possible. The history we study must be the genuine history rather the imaginary or made-up history. As to explore genuine history is our most significant calling, historical files are the most straight and valuable materials to help us draw the true picture of history.

Modern science research tends to put relevant things together and conduct isolated and stationary studies to create many new disciplines. For the past centuries, great achievements have been made about these disciplines. However the research was done separately within the discipline itself,

---

① Yamamoto, *The current Research and Subject of the Social System in Ming and Qing*, 1994, the First International Conference on Hui Studies.

② Liang Qichao, *The Academic History in the Past Three Hundred Years*.

ignoring the relations with other social or natural elements. In fact no phenomenon exists isolated and any phenomenon is fully understood on condition that it should be replaced to its original nature position with all the relevant factors around. With the development of sciences scholars come to realize the disadvantages of this isolated research, the situation that "difference in discipline means worlds apart" must be challenged. Consequently, nowadays, interdisciplinary subjects become popular. Recently a new trend arose that specialists in different fields came together to conduct "non-discipline" research (research beyond the boundary of disciplines). It is revealed there is a Santa Fe Institute in America, making the formerly unknown small town famous. This Institute was founded in 1984 for no definite discipline research and its most striking feature is the new term it created—Complexity Science. Specialists of economics, physics, biology science, artificial intelligence and so on gather together to share their views with all parties involved benefiting each other a lot. They hold that science research has come to the stage from being comprehensive to being separated and back to new integration.① This integration is to "replace" the man-made disciplines to their original natural position.

Huizhou files have created the possibility to do history research in its true nature. We should always keep in mind that Huizhou files are comprehensive reflection of history. It is unwise to take parts of them to do separate and one-dimension research and then try to replace it in its original position when faults arise.

As Chinese famous history scholar Chen Yinke put it in *The Survival of Dunhuang Files after the Disaster*: "Academic research in specific times has its individual materials and topics. Taking specific materials for specific research is the trend and feature of each arena. Scholars who conform to and pursue the trend are to make achievements while those who cannot are

---

① Hung Aihe, *Why Should the Clock Move Clockwise? —The Legend of Santa Fe*, Chinese Youth Press, 1997, Vol. 10.

marginalized. This has been acknowledged through history and those who have divorced themselves from the masses and from reality and act blindly are not expected to achieve anything. " What is the new material and what is the new topic in modern academic research? Can Huizhou historical files—the fifth great discovery in China, or rather all the historical files, be taken as the new material of modern research? Can we take the files for deeper and further exploration of genuine society in history? If the answers to both questions are positive, Huizhou Studies is surely becoming one of the main streams in modern academic research.

Published in *History Studies*, No. 1, 2000
Written by Zhou Shaoguan
Translated by Li Qiao

Part V
Huizhou Merchants

Chapter 12 A Discussion on Some Issues in the Research of Huizhou Merchants

Till now, the research on Huizhou merchants, starting from *The Textual Research on Huizhou Merchants in the Ming Dynasty*① published by Mr. Fu Yiling in 1947, has got a history of 67 years. Over the past 60 years, especially ever since the 1980s, the research on Huizhou merchants has achieved innumerable great achievements, including tens of published writings and more than 100 related papers. As to the comprehensive works on Huizhou merchants, in addition to *Research on Xin'an Merchants*②

---

① Fu Yiling, *The Textual Research on Huizhou Merchants in the Ming Dynasty*—one of the manuscripts on the history of China's commercial capital group, was published in No. 2 of The Research Report of The Institute of Fujian Province *in June* 1947, *and later included in* Merchants and Commercial Capital in Ming and Qing, *and was re-named as* Huizhou Merchants in the Ming Dynasty, *published by People's Publishing House in* 1956. Quoted in Collected Papers about Studies on Huizhou Merchants, *edited by Jianghuai Forum*, *published by Anhui People's Publishing House*, 1985.

② Fujii, Research on *Xin'an Merchants*, originally published in *Journal of Oriental*, No. 1-4, Vol. 36, in June/September/December 1953 and March 1954; Quoted in *Collected Papers about Studies on Huizhou Merchants*, edited by Jianghuai Forum.

published by Japanese Fujii in the 1950s, there are also *Research on Huizhou Merchants*① co-authored by Zhang Haipeng and Wang Tingyuan, *Huizhou Merchants*② co-authored by Wang Tingyuan and Wang Shihua, and *Research on Modern Huizhou Merchants*③ by Feng Jianhui, etc.

Through the research, the academic circle has basically made it clear about the development thread of Huizhou merchants, and has formed roughly consistent opinion about the main industries, main regions, main methods, and capital accumulation of the operations of Huizhou merchants, as well as the characteristics of Huizhou merchants. However, as to several key issues like the reasons of the emergence and development of Huizhou merchants, the fading and modern transformation of Huizhou merchants, and the summaries and compacts of the spirit of Huizhou merchants, etc., there is still no agreement in the academic circle. So, in this paper, we will focus on these issues to view our opinions.

I. Reasons on the Emergence and Development of Huizhou Merchants

Huizhou, located in mountains at the junction of Anhui, Jiangxi and Zhejiang, has "gradually developed into an independent administrative region... showing the geographical features of nature shed and watershed".④ In Ming and Qing, such a relatively closed administrative region at the government level has developed Huizhou merchants-a regional merchant school, the members of which almost traveled everywhere, played an extremely important role in the business circle, and won a certain social status. In that time, there are nine merchants out of ten families.

As for the understanding of the reasons of the emergence and development

---

① Anhui People's Publishing House, 1995.
② Anhui People's Publishing House, 2005.
③ Hefei University of Technology Press, 2009.
④ Yoshinobu Shiba, *Regional Development in Song Dynasty*, collected in *A Collection of the Studies on the Social and Economic History of Huizhou*, translated by Liu Miaoji, Huangshan Press, 1988.

of Huizhou merchants, there is a gradually deepening process.

The chorography of merchants in Ming and Qing as well as other related documents regard the narrow geography and dense population life forces as the only reason or fundamental reason. *Customs*, Volume 2 of *Record of Huizhou Prefecture* in the Jiajing period (1507—1567) goes, "Half of the mountains in Huizhou are uninhabited, few people have farmland and so engage in trading to earn money"; *The Trading*, Volume 10 of the Shexian County in the Wanli period (1573—1620) goes: "In the county, the population is nearly as much as that of a big county in Han Dynasty, but the outputs of cereals and grains fail to support one percent of the population, so how is it impossible for local people to go outside for making a living... To live on, everyone needs food." And there is similar record in the county annals of *The Customs of the Record of Huizhou Prefecture* in the Kangxi period (1654—1722), and *The Customs of Record of Huizhou Prefecture* in the Daoguang period (1821—1850) and the records of other counties in Ming and Qing. Wang Shizhen in the Ming Dynasty said, "Xin'an is located near a remote mountain stream, where there is little farmland and there are many people. For generations, it is free from wars, so it is becoming increasingly prosperous, but the farmland is too barren to be cultivated...so there is such a custom in Huizhou that thirty percent of the population stay at home, but seventy percent make a living in the outside world."① And Gui Youguang in the Ming Dynasty period said, "Sheshan County has little farmland on which to produce enough food for people, so there are many merchants here."② Tang Shunzhi said, "The land of Xin'an is hard and sterile, and the food storage is insufficient, people depend on doing business to live on, so they strive

---

① Wang Shizhen, *Fifty Narrations for Mr. Cheng*, Volume 61 of *Four Volumes of Yanzhou Mountainous People*, Wang Oratory Edition in the fifth year of Wanli period in the Ming Dynasty.

② Gui Youguang, *Epitaph of Li Jun, General Zhaoyong, Chengshan Military Command, Profile of Mr. Zhenchuan*, Volume 18, The Four Series Books.

to be merchants. "① Gu Yanwu in the early Qing Dynasty quoted the *Anhui Topology* in the Ming Dynasty in his book *On the Advantages and Disadvantages of Kingdoms*, "Huizhou has little farmland. In addition, more babies are born, and there is more infertile land due to more farmhouses and graveyards... so people are gradually becoming poor and have no farmland to produce food, and so Huizhou people choose to become merchants, the phenomenon of which is really caused by current situations."② Even in the eighth year of the Republic of China (1912—1949), Wu Rifa also said in *Origins of Huizhou Merchants*, "Huizhou is located among mountain ranges, which are rocky with few farmlands...Due to the dense population here, the cereals produced are insufficient to support local inhabitants, so there has formed a custom of doing business here...Merchants leave their homeland and dear families to travel outside for making a living, few of them have permanent residences in the outside world, all of which is due to the hard times."③ Japanese scholar Fujii said, "Topology author thinks that the land of Huizhou is too barren for farming. Meanwhile, the growth of population is the fundamental reason for the growth of Huizhou merchants. This saying is obviously incorrect."④

Since the late 1940s, scholars started to explore the reasons for the emergence and development of Huizhou merchants from the perspective of "social factors". As Fu Yiling stated, "We certainly admit that 'too little land for too many people' is a reason for the phenomenon that there are a lot of

---

① Tang Shunzhi, *Profile of Cheng Shaojun*, Volume 15 of *Collected Works of Jingzhou in the Tang Dynasty*, The Four Series Books.

② Gu Yanwu, Volume 32 *Jiangnan Twenty*, of *On the Advantages and Disadvantages of Kingdoms*, The Four Series Books.

③ Quoted in *Selected Works on Huizhou Merchants in Ming and Qing*, Huangshan Press, 1985.

④ Fujii, *Investigation of Salt Merchants in the Ming Dynasty—Studies on Frontier Merchants, Local Merchants, and Waterway Merchants*, originally recorded in No. 5-7 of Volume 54 of *Shigaku Zasshi*, published in May, June, and July in 1943; quoted in *A Collection of the Studies on the Social and Economic History of Huizhou*, translated by Liu Miaoji.

merchants in Huizhou, however, we will not take it as the only one reason. Instead, we think that it is mainly due to social factors."① And the "social factors", according to the analyses of scholars, can be generally divided into the following aspects: first, there are geographical advantages for Huizhou people to engage in business, "Geographically speaking, Huizhou is located in the center of Jiangsu and Zhejiang, the important economic centers in the southeast, the traffic of which is very convenient"②; second, "Huizhou has abundant products, especially local specialties, so it can trade freely with other places, which provides materialistic premises for commercial capital activities"③; third, Huizhou merchants have experiences of doing business, "In the past, in order to sell their handicraft works, Huizhou people got many business experiences. Now, so many advantageous conditions are more likely to seduce Huizhou people to engage in business activities"④; fourth, it is related to the innovations on salt laws in the middle of Ming Dynasty, "With the circulation of silver, the salt transportation and silver collection system established in the middle of Ming Dynasty should be indispensible premise for Xin'an merchants to lead China's business circle"⑤; fifth, the

---

① Fu Yiling, *The Textual Research on Huizhou Merchants in the Ming Dynasty—One of the manuscripts on the history of China's Commercial Capital Group*, was published in No. 2 of *The Research Report of The Institute of Fujian Province* in June 1947, and later included in *Merchants and Commercial Capital in Ming and Qing*, and was re-named as *Huizhou Merchants in the Ming Dynasty*, published by People's Publishing House in 1956. Quoted in *Collected Papers about Studies on Huizhou Merchants*, published by Anhui People's Publishing House, 1985.

② Fu Yiling, *Huizhou Merchants in the Ming Dynasty*, quoted in *Collected Papers about Studies on Huizhou Merchants*, edited by Jianghuai Forum.

③ Chen Ye, *On Formations and Characteristics of Huizhou Commercial Capital*, Communications of Historical Research in Anhui, No. 5, 1958.

④ Fu Yiling, *Huizhou Merchants in the Ming Dynasty*, quoted in *Collected Papers about Studies on Huizhou Merchants*, edited by Jianghuai Forum.

⑤ Fujii, *Research on Xin'an Merchants*, originally published in Journal of Oriental, No. 1-4, Vol. 36, in June/September/December 1953 and March 1954; Quoted in *Collected Papers about Studies on Huizhou Merchants*, edited by *Jianghuai Forum*.

cooperation between officials and merchants, "One of the important reasons for Xin'an merchants to dominate China's business circle lies in the emerging diligent scholars and incorruptible officials who travel in the outside world and protect and induce Huizhou merchants wherever they go"①.

After the 1980s, some scholars started to analyze the reasons for the emergence and development of Huizhou merchants from the perspectives of culture and concept. Mr. Tang Lixing thinks, "The emergence of Huizhou merchants benefits from clan forces. And the further development of Huizhou merchants in competition is indispensible to the support of the clan forces."② Mr. Wang Tingyuan thinks Huizhou merchants stick to the righteousness and benefit outlook of Confucius, which "plays an active role in promoting the development of Huizhou merchants" "the active role of the righteousness and benefit outlook of Confucius on the development of Huizhou merchants, is first reflected in the fact that it promotes the reputation of Huizhou merchants, which help them to obtain advantageous positions in competitions... Second, the righteousness and benefit outlook of Confucius solidifies the interior solidarity of Huizhou merchants, which is beneficial to the development of Huizhou merchants... Third, the righteousness and benefit outlook of Confucius promotes the combination between Huizhou merchants and feudal influence."③ Mr. Luan Chengxian thinks: "the cultural fusion promoted by mass immigration activities and unique mountainous geographical environment give birth to the characteristic Huizhou culture", "the human capital formed by the above cultural factors, namely the qualities of Huizhou merchants, is undoubtedly a kind of advantage,

---

① Fujii, *Investigation of Salt Merchants in the Ming Dynasty—Studies on Frontier Merchants, Local Merchants, and Waterway Merchants*, originally recorded in No. 5-7 of Volume 54 of Shigaku Zasshi, published in May, June, and July 1943; quoted in *A Collection of the Studies on the Social and Economic History of Huizhou*, translated by Liu Miaoji.

② Tang Lixing: *On Huizhou Merchants and Feudal Clan Forces*, Historical Research, 1986: No. 4.

③ Wang Tingyuan, *On the Righteousness and Benefit Outlook of Huizhou Merchants*, Journal of Anhui Normal University, 1998: No. 4.

which helps Huizhou merchants to behave better in business operations. So we should not say that the advantageous human capital formed by characteristic Huizhou culture is an important reason of the emergence and success of Huizhou merchants, or plays an important role in the emergence process of Huizhou merchants."[1]

In the above, we make a brief summary of the studies on the emergence and development of Huizhou merchants in the academic circle in three stages. Indeed, the reasons of the emergence and development of Huizhou merchants are multi-level, multi-dimensional, and diversified, so it is unilateral and unscientific to focus on one aspect and neglect the others. We think, the emergence and development of Huizhou merchants is the result of the comprehensive interactions between natural and geographical factors, social and economic factors, and cultural and psychological factors.

As to the natural and geographical factors, there are two important points: first, the contradictory aggravation of people and land is the direct motivation for Huizhou people to engage in business. In Ming and Qing, Huizhou encountered serious survival crisis, the Huizhou with lots of mountains and few fertile farmlands was incapable of supporting the increasingly growing population due to social stableness. So, engaging in business and striving to develop in the outside world have become important choices for Huizhou people to make a living and seek for development[2]. Second, the advantageous geographical position provides conveniences for Huizhou people to engage in business. Southern Jiangsu, eastern Zhejiang, northern Jiangxi and southern Anhui which are adjacent to Huizhou are economically developed areas. The lofty mountains and high ranges hold back the land transportation of Huizhou people, but the multiple water

---

[1] Luan Chengxian, *Economic and Cultural Interactions—an Important Enlightenment of the Rise and Fall of Huizhou Merchants*, Journal of Anhui Normal University, 2005: No. 4.

[2] Li Linqi, *Changes in Traditional Culture and the Minds of Huizhou Merchants*, published in Academic Monthly, No. 10, 1999; Li Linqi, *Huizhou Merchants and Huizhou Education in Ming and Qing*, Hubei Education Publishing House, 2003.

systems within the territory such as Xinanjiang Water System, Yangtze Water System, Le'anjiang Water System, Shuiyangjiang Water System, and Qingyijiang Water System are all suitable for waterway transportation, which provide great conveniences for Huizhou people to communicate with the outside world. From the Song Dynasty, by the water transportation, Huizhou has changed their specialties and handcrafts with neighboring Zhejiang, Jiangxi, and the south of the Yangtze River for grains[①].

As to the social and economic factors, there are three key points: First, after the middle of Ming Dynasty, the further expansion of social division of labor, the development of commodity economy in the south of the Yangtze River, and the implementation of the tax and carve system in ancient China provided very good social conditions for Huizhou merchants to engage in business. After the middle of Ming Dynasty, the division between agriculture and handicraft, the division between regions and industries in the handicraft field, and the division of agricultural regions were all much expanded. In the south of the Yangtze River, there emerged more towns and cities which gradually became prosperous. In addition, the commodity economy enjoyed rapid development, and the tax and corve system in ancient China were put into force in the Zhengtong period (1436—1449), and then "was introduced to the rest of the country". All of these significantly promoted the circulation of commodities and the booming of markets, and thus provided businessmen and Huizhou merchants with extensive activity space and very good business conditions[②].

Second, the innovation in the salt law in the middle and late Ming Dynasty has become an accelerator for the development of Huizhou merchants. Mr. Zhang Haipeng thinks that, "Huizhou merchants flooded into Huaidong and Huaixi in two groups, which was closely related to the political situations and innovations on the salt law of the feudal country in

---

① Li Linqi, *Huizhou Merchants and Huizhou Education in Ming and Qing*.
② Wang Shihua, *Rich Huizhou Merchants*, Zhejiang People's Publishing House, 1997.

the middle and late Ming Dynasty."① In the fifth year of Hongzhi period (1492), Ye Qi, Ministry of Revenue changed "make tax payments in rice to benefit salt traders" into "change for salt tickets by silver to benefit salt traders", so Huizhou merchants take advantage of geographical advantages to swarm into Yangzhou, Yizheng, and Huaian in groups to engage in salt business. In the forty-fifth year of the Wanli period (1617), Li Ruhua, Ministry of Revenue, Yuan Shizhen and Long Yuqi, salt administrative secretary, took the lead to implement "group salt transportation system", namely combine previously dispersed salt transporters into merchant group to transport salt. "The implementation of the group salt transportation system again absorbed multiple merchants to gather in Huaidong and Huaixi, the biggest salt site in the country, especially Huizhou merchants."② The implementation of "change for salt tickets by silver to benefit salt traders" and the "group salt transportation system" not only caused Huizhou merchants to occupy the advantages of salt operation in Huaidong and Huaixi, but also obtain the hereditary privileges that dominated the salt transportation and selling in Huaidong and Huaixi, and thus resulted in the phenomenon that Huizhou merchants "dominate China's business circles". Third, after the middle of Ming Dynasty, Huizhou "behaved best in imperial examinations", and a big group of Huizhou scholars were recruited to the imperial court, who became the political statesmen and benefit protectors of Huizhou merchants. The Huizhou scholars taking certain positions in central government and local governments planned and arranged for all town fellows to make sure that they would do well in business③, In the implementation of policies and negotiations of issues, they also tried to protect the interests of Huizou merchants. With the protection and care of these officials, it is

---

① Zhang Haipeng, Wang Tingyuan, *Studies on Huizhou Merchants*.
② Ibid.
③ *Revision of Xu's Genealogy at Eastern Shexian County—Xu's Mr. Hezu Visits Mr. Pengyuan*, Qianlong Edition, Qing Dynasty.

natural that Huizhou merchants did better than other merchant groups in business trading①.

As to cultural and psychological factors, there are also three key points: First, transform traditional values, eliminate the psychological pressure and thought barriers for Huizhou people to engage in business. After the middle of Ming Dynasty, Huizhou people began to change the traditional values that scholars were superior to merchants and the values that agriculture was more important to business, and advocated the new values that "merchants are not inferior to scholars" "scholars and merchants are comrades though they belong to different circles", and that "education, agriculture, industry and business are equally important". The propaganda and acceptance of new values relieved the psychological pressures for Huizhou people to engage in business, which is the ideological foundation for the formation of Huizhou business society in the Ming Dynasty and Qing Dynasty②. Second, take full advantage of blood relationship and geographical relationship to form a strong centripetal force and cohesive force. When Huizhou people did business, they usually did it with their fathers or brothers, relatives and good friends, or cooperated with people of the same clan or town, and they built business halls and houses in the place where they did business so that they can "communicate with each other", and "help each other", which had very distinctive industry blood relationship and industry geoborderition. Jin Sheng, who was from Shexian County in the end of the Ming Dynasty, said, "People of Shexian County and Xiuning county have no farmland, but their business is spread all over the country... Two people, due to same interests in business, cooperated with each other like what relatives and good friends did, so when one family succeeds, the family will not enjoy alone the success but lead hundreds and thousands of

---

① Li Linqi, *Huizhou Merchants and Huizhou Education in Ming and Qing*.

② Li Linqi, *Changes in Traditional Culture and the Minds of Huizhou Merchants*, Academic Monthly, No. 10.

families to make fortune, if not so, the family will at least benefit tens or several decades of families. "① This is the organizational foundation for the formation of the commercial society of Huizhou. Third, Huizhou merchants have the features that "merchants value Confucianism". Most Huizhou merchants can stick to the moral standards of honesty, credit, justice and benevolence, and are keen to public welfare undertakings and charity, carry forward moral principles, and are brave to undertake responsibilities. Thus, Huizhou merchants won certain reputation and credit, which provide advantageous social atmosphere for their development. And this is the moral foundation for the formation of the commercial society in Huizhou.

II. Summaries and Compacts of the Spirit of Huizhou Merchants

The spirit belongs to the category of social consciousness, but it is generated in the social existence, and meanwhile leads the carrying out of social practices as a kind of force and orientation. The spirit of a nation reflects the nationality of the nation, and thus is the foundation for the survival and development of the nation. Similarly, the spirit of a group also reflects the characteristics of the group, and is the foundation for the survival and development of the group. The fact that Huizhou merchants could emerge and dominate the business circles in Ming and Qing and acted as the leaders of the business circles for over three hundred years is undoubtedly due to the spirit of Huizhou merchants in a great degree.

Wang Shihua can be said to be the first scholar giving a systematic summary of the spirit of Huizhou merchants. In his book of the Rich Huizhou Merchants, he classifies the spirit of Huizhou merchants into five aspects: the patriotic spirit of overcoming national difficulties and seeking for race independence; the aggressive spirit of being persevering and not fearing difficulty; the competitive spirit of considering the situation and

---

① Jin Sheng, *Correspondence with Mr. She Ling* of *Collections of Jin Court Historian*, Volume 4, Collection of Qiankun Uprightness.

defeating one's opponent by a surprise move; the harmonious spirit of sailing on the same tack and helping each other; and the industrious and thrift spirit of being sparing no pains and being simple despite the richness[①].

Afterwards, a lot more other scholars made their respective summaries and descriptions of the spirit of Huizhou merchants in their works. Mr. Liu Boshan interprets the connotations of the spirit of Huizhou merchants into four aspects: the spirit of be unwilling to be poor and daring to blaze new trails; the spirit of not fearing frustrations, persistent pursuit and forging ahead; the spirit of sparing no pains, being industrious and frugal and hard struggle; and the spirit of having no internal frictions, having overall consistency and solidarity and cooperation[②].

Zhu Wanshu, etc. classify the spirit of Huizhou merchants into twelve aspects: Huizhou camel—the spirit of bearing hardships of Huizhou merchants; mountains beyond mountains—the pioneering spirit of Huizhou merchants; sincere earnings—the major tactics of the business operations of Huizhou merchants; "merchants love Confucianism"—the cultural pursuit of Huizhou merchants; stick to ethics—the dependence of Huizhou merchants on tradition; great expectations on children—the cherishment of Huizhou merchants on education; one sings, many chorus—the group awareness of Huizhou merchants; win the society—the life philosophy of Huizhou merchants; cultural investment—another kind of eyesight of Huizhou merchants; self-abasement and self-respect—the contradictory psychology of Huizhou merchants; serve the emperor—the great sadness of Huizhou merchants; nature returning—the destination of the life voyage of Huizhou merchants[③].

Mr. Fei Yuan summarizes the spirit of Huizhou merchants into seven

---

① Wang Shihua, *Rich Huizhou Merchants*.
② Liu Boshan, The Spirit of Huizhou Merchants, *Anhui Daily*, May 13, 1999.
③ Zhu Wanshu, Xie Xin, *The Spirit of Huizhou Merchants*, Hefei University of Technology Press.

aspects: the human-centered spirit of admiring culture and kindness and seeking truth; the hardworking spirit of being industrious and hardworking and pioneering with arduous efforts; the innovation spirit of daring to be the first and forging ahead; the professional ethics of valuing righteousness and honesty and doing business on the basis of morality; the team spirit of helping each other and being all of one mind; and the dedication spirit of being benevolent and loving home and country[①].

The research team of "Revive the Vigor of Huizhou Merchants" of the Development Research Center of People's Government of Anhui Province summarizes the essential connotation of the spirit of Huizhou merchants as the five aspects of being open-minded, honest, aggressive, innovative and harmonious, which are specifically stated as : the open-minded spirit of looking at and doing business in the outside world; the honest spirit of doing business under the guidance of morality and cherishing credit; the aggressive spirit of sparing no pains and being indomitable; the innovative spirit of daring to explore and being the first; and the harmonious spirit of staying in the same boat and helping each other [②].

From the above, we can get two basic points: first, almost all of them use such key words as opening-up, aggressive, competitive, harmonious, honest, patriotic, and there is no unique feature in wording; second, they all try to expand and upraise the connotations of the spirit of Huizhou merchants, so their summaries are almost the same as the spirit of the People's Republic of China, lacking pertinence and characteristics.

What are Huizhou merchants? Huizhou merchants refer to the merchant group formed in one prefecture and six counties of Huizhou in Ming and Qing. What is the spirit of Huizhou merchants? The spirit of Huizhou

---

① Fei Yuan, *The Spirit of Huizhou Merchants—the Essence of Huizhou Culture*, refer to *Papers on Huizhou Merchants* collected by the Center for Huizhou Studies of Anhui University, 2004.
② Wu Keming, *The Spirit of Huizhou Merchants-Selected Essays of the Research of Huizhou Merchants II*, University of Science and Technology of China Press, 2005.

merchants refer to the prevailing custom, belief, feelings and other ideology reflected in social activities. While summarizing the spirit of Huizhou merchants, we think that we must obey the following three principles: first, specifying the subject. It refers to the spirit of the particular group of Huizhou merchants, so it should not be generalized; second, specifying the evidence. The evidence of summarizing the spirit of Huizhou merchants should be the natural environment, social environment and the practical activities of Huizhou merchants. Third, inheritance and development. We should carry forward the summary of the previous scholar that is fine, and conduct contemporary explanation matter-of-factly.

According to the above principles, we think, the spirit of Huizhou merchants can be summarized and stated as: the aggressive spirit of "Huizhou Camel" and the humanistic spirit of "merchants love Confucianism", which are shortened as "Huizhou camel" and "Merchants love Confucianism".

First, the aggressive spirit of "Huizhou camel". It was summarized by Hu Shi, a famous scholar of previous Huizhou, who grew up in the influence of Huizhou culture. In 1945, after the victory of anti-Japanese war, Hu Shi inscribed the scroll of "Huizhou Camel" for the Xin'an Association at Liyang, Jiangsu; in 1953, Hu Shi inscribed the scroll of "Strive to Be Huizhou Camel" for Jixi Association in Taiwan. With the propaganda of Hu Shi, the expression of "Huizhou Camel" gradually enjoyed popular support, and "camel" was taken as the symbol of Huizhou people and the spirit of Huizhou merchants. We think, it is appropriate and fine for Hu Shi to compare Huizhou people and Huizhou merchants as "Huizhou Camel", and the connotations of which are profound. At first, "camel" stands for a kind of aggressive spirit, only when camel keep advancing and do not stop in the front of setbacks can it succeed. In this kind of aggressive spirit, there contains the belief of success at the same time, which is the belief of survival and development. A camel can only survive when it walks out of sand and develop when it meets green land. At the same time, it contains the collaboration awareness. While walking through the sand, camels usually go in groups, which contains the relationship among people, the relationship between people and camels, and the relationship among camels. Only with solidify and cooperation can the difficulties be overcome. And these are highly consistent with Huizhou people and Huizhou merchants. The reason that Huizhou people engaged in business was that "the land was too barren to produce enough food for local people" to survive and develop, so they should not only dare to go out of the mountain ranges, but have the belief of success. And this kind of belief needs the support of the spirit of being indomitable which is specifically reflected as "try again if you fail, and try again and over if you fail again, and try over and over again if you fail over and again"[①]. However, it is far from enough to have only the belief of success and the aggressive spirit, because of the fact that in ancient time, the traffic conditions were not very good, so was the social security, and people were exclusive, so it was impractical for people to do business and live alone in the outside world, this is why Huizhou people took advantage of existing blood relationships and geographical relationships, especially the clan kinships to form business group so that they could depend on each other to jointly achieve development, so Gu Yanwu said in the third volume of Record of Zhao Region, "Xindu (Huizhou) people…do business in the outside world where they meet town fellows so they struggle to help them as much as possible which is also for the benefit of themselves"[②].

Second, the humanistic spirit of "merchants love Confucianism". In the documents of Ming and Qing, there were lots of documents which associated "merchants" with "Confucianism". For example, in the Ming Dynasty, there was a merchant in Xiuning County called Wang Tan, he said, "we do

---

① *Form of Gaofeng Shuren and Hutai Shuren*, second volume of *Ni's Family Tree in Qimen*, Guangxu period.

② Quoted in *Selected Works on Huizhou Merchants in Ming and Qing*, co-authored by Zhang Haipeng and Wang Tingyuan.

business in the market, but we will not make dirty money. And we are honest and helpful to each other, we are merchants but we value Confucianism!"① In the Ming Dynasty, there was a merchant in Shexian County called Zheng Chaoji who said, "we do business in the outside world, but our hearts are still at home, wherever we go...we are merchants but we follow Confucianism."② Huang Changshou, a merchant in the Ming Dynasty, said, "After the death of my father, I went to the outside world to do business. I stuck to Confucianism while doing business which attracted people near and far. So it only took few years for my business to grow big...I did with merchants, but I strictly followed the Confucianism in my words and behaviors..."③ Jiang Shiluan, a merchant in Shexian County in the Ming Dynasty, said, "the merchant is respectful and cautious, just like a Confucian...famous scholars like to travel together."④ Jin Dinghe, a merchant of Xiuning in the Qing Dynasty said, "I engaged in business, but do well in classics and history, just like a Confucian."⑤ Dai Zhen, a famous scholar from Xiuning County in the Qing Dynasty, said, "In my county (Huizhou), there is little plain and wild field, we live in the mountains, merchants do business in the outside world to make a living...a merchant as he is, he is just like a Confucian."⑥ In today's words, such kind of "merchants but Confucians" or "businessmen

---

① *Wang's Genealogy*, Volume 168, Ming Dynasty Version; quoted in *Selected Works on Huizhou Merchants in Ming and Qing*, co-authored by Zhang Haipeng and Wang Tingyuan.

② Shexian County *Zheng's Genealogy—Epitaph of Zheng Jun of the Guqing Pavilion in the Ming Dynasty*, transcription of the Jiajing period in the Ming Dynasty.

③ Shexian County, *Autobiography of Mr. Wang Yun*, Volume 9 of *Huang's Genealogy in Tandu*, the ninth year edition of the Yongzheng period in the Qing Dynasty.

④ Shexian County, *Autobiography of Mr. Shi Luan, Intellectual of the Ming Dynasty*, Volume 9 *Jiang's Genealogy of Jiyang*, the eighteenth year edition in the Daoguang period of the Qing Dynasty.

⑤ *Figure—Knowledgeable*, Volume 6 of *Xiuning County Annal* in the Kangxi period.

⑥ Dai Zhen, *Family Story of Miss Dai Jie*, *Selected Works of Daizhen Collections*, volume 12, Shanghai Chinese Classics Publishing House, 1980.

but Confucians" express is just the humanistic spirit of Huizhou merchants. And this kind of humanistic spirit of Huizhou merchants, are specifically reflected in three aspects: first, the prevailing custom of valuing culture and emphasizing education. Huizhou merchants loved cultural education. They loved reading and were knowledgeable, and donated money to establish schools and spent money in repairing schools and building schools in addition to donating some education materials and providing scholarships, as well as funding collecting books and inscribing books, which greatly promoted the development of cultural education of Huizhou and the places where Huizhou merchants did business[1]. Second, stick to the morality of Confucian. Huizhou merchants regard the ethical morality of Confucians as the foundation of behaviors and actions. In the process of doing business, most of the Huizhou merchants can follow the ethnical morality of Confucians: "treat others honestly", "do business by credit", and "make profits by righteousness"[2]. Third, the feelings of social responsibilities. They like to join in charity activities and make donations to repairing bridges and building roads, helping disastrous areas, taking dangerous rescue and other social charities, which reflected the feelings of social responsibilities of Huizhou merchants[3].

3. On the Decay of Huizhou Merchants and Modern Transformation

As to the decay of Huizhou merchants, some senior scholars of Huizhou merchants and Huizhou study in the academic circle such as Fujii, Ye Xianen, Zhang Haipeng, Wang Tingyuan, Wang Shihua, etc. almost have

---

[1] Li Linqi, *Huizhou Merchants and Huizhou Education in Ming and Qing*.

[2] Zhang Haipeng, Tang Lixing, *On the Characteristics of "the Merchants Love Confucians" of Huizhou Merchants*, Journal of Chinese History Studies, No. 4, 1984.

[3] Bian Li, *Study on the Society of Huizhou Merchants in Ming and Qing*, Anhui University Publishing House, 2004.

the same understanding①. They think that after the middle of the Qing Dynasty, especially the Daoguang period, with the salt of Huaidong and Huaixi being changed into tickets which broke through the monopolistic sales system of the salt, and the influence of wars and the economic transformation under the impacts of external forces, the Huizhou merchants dominating the business circle for over three hundred years had decayed beyond any help.

However, after the 1990s, certain scholars began to question the above opinions. Some think: "the history circle thinks that Huizhou merchants began to decay in the Daoguang period of the Qing Dynasty... but if we examine the business circle of the People's Republic of China (1912—1949), we see that Huizhou merchants are still an important force in traditional activity areas and industries (except the salt industry). In other words, Huizhou merchants did not decay in the People's Republic of China (1912—1949), and did not withdraw from the historical stage."② Some other scholars think, "The fact that modern Huizhou merchants decay has been universally accepted by the academic circle, but if this kind of decay means disintegration and even retreat the business stage still calls for careful analyses. Lots of facts showed that contemporary Huizhou merchant group did not disappear but still existed not only in Huizhou but also in the areas where they did business, and they played very important roles in social and economic life." the saying that "Contemporary Huizhou merchant group

---

① Fujii, *Study of Xin'an Merchants*, quoted in *Selected Works of the Studies of Huizhou Merchants* edited by Jianghuai Forum; Ye Xian'en, *The Decay of Huizhou Merchants and Their Historical Roles*, Jianghuai Forum, No. 3, 1982; Zhang Haipeng, Wang Tingyuan, *The Decay of Huizhou Merchants* Chapter 11 of *The Study of Huizhou Merchants*; Wang Tingyuan, Wang Shihua *The Decay of Huizhou Merchants*, Chapter 12 of Huizhou Merchants.

② Zhang Chaosheng. *Huizhou Tea Merchants in Shanghai in the People's Republic of China (1912—1949): Concurrently Talk about the Decay of Huizhou Merchants*, Historical Research in Anhui, No. 2, 1996.

'collapse', or 'withdraw from the historical stage' are still worth further discussions; The existence of contemporary Huizhou merchant group is an undeniable fact". ①

Questions are hard to answer, but it is beneficial to the development of learning, worth advocating and encouragement. However, it should be based on comprehensive and correct understanding of the existing opinions. So, it is quite questionable when the above two scholars question the existing opinion that contemporary Huizhou merchants have declined. First, the senior scholars who thought contemporary Huizhou merchants have declined didn't say that contemporary Huizhou merchants have "withdrawn from the historical stage"②. On the contrary, some of them clearly pointed out that: "The fact that Huizhou merchants declined doesn't mean that Huizhou merchants have disappeared... the decay of Huizhou merchants' refers to the decay of the main body of the business groups rather than the decay of all Huizhou merchants" "original business groups in contemporary Huizhou have collapsed, but the custom of engaging in business here is still very popular."③ So, the questioning scholars don't have the factual premise of questioning.

Second, the "Huizhou merchants" in the dynasties of Qing and Ming are different from the "Huizhou group" frequently mentioned in contemporary documents. As Mr. Zhang Haipeng said, "Early in the Ming Dynasty, 'Huizhou' and 'merchant' are used together in documents, which means that 'Huizhou merchants' are a merchant team, namely the name of the merchant group"④; this "merchant group takes region as the center, the kinship and fellowship as the bond, and 'mutual help' as the purpose, and

---

① Feng Jianhui, *Studies on Contemporary Huizhou Merchants*.

② Only Mr. Li Zegang has similar opinion. Refer to *Profile of Huizhou Merchants*, Jianghuai Forum, No. 1 1982.

③ Zhang Haipeng, *Preface of Contemporary Merchants in Huizhou Merchants Series*, Huangshan Publishing House, 1996.

④ Ibid.

takes club house and guild as the gathering place, so it is a 'close' but loose merchant group formed spontaneously"[1]. That is, Huizhou merchants in Ming and Qing refer to the merchant group formed with Huizhou territory as the center. However, for the "Huizhou group" appeared in contemporary documents, on the one hand, it is the natural expression affected by traditional influences; on the other hand, "contemporary Huizhou merchants scattered in different places, they didn't take territory as the center to discuss some issues or help each other, but constitute a society to maintain business competition in the industry, so the merchant society or association in the same industry replaced previous guild in the same region. So, in contemporary Huizhou, there were only 'merchants' other than 'group'."[2] That is to say, contemporary "Huizhou group" refer to the merchant group developed by industry. As contemporary Liu Jinzao said, "Huizhou is adjacent to the upstream of Xin'anjiang River, at the back of Huangshan Mountain, where there produced too cereals to feed people and animals, so people went to the outside world to engage in business. No matter it was a business shop, money shop, tea house, painting or restaurant, it was named 'Huizhou Group', and emphasized good faith and enjoyed good reputation in the business circle."[3] As the contestant said, "Contemporary Huizhou merchants were quite influential in the salt industry, wood industry, pawn industry, ink industry, cloth industry, painting industry, sauce industry, department store industry, and some other traditional industries. And there were a group of famous merchants and firms. And Huizhou merchants in these industries also maintained the feature of doing business in groups."[4]

---

[1] Zhang Haipeng, Zhang Haiying, *China's Top Ten Merchant Group Preface*, Huangshan Publishing house, 1993.

[2] Zhang Haipeng, *Preface of Contemporary Merchants in Huizhou Merchants Series*, Huangshan Publishing House, 1996.

[3] Liu Jinzao. *Examination of Yudi No. 9, General Examination of Subsequent Document in the Qing Dynasty*, Volume 313.

[4] Feng Jianhui. *Studies on Contemporary Huizhou Merchants*.

Part V Huizhou Merchants

The "group" by industry of contemporary Huizhou merchants is different from the "group" by territory of Huizhou merchants in Ming and Qing. Therefore, questioning scholars had no logical foundation of questioning.

As to the transformation of contemporary Huizhou merchants, scholar studying contemporary Huizhou merchants claimed: "the research of Huizhou merchants has long been concerned with Huizhou merchant group in Ming and Qing, and neglected the transformation of contemporary Huizhou merchants... The occurrence of such a phenomenon is related to not only the academically accepted 'the decay of contemporary Huizhou merchants' but also 'the backwardness of contemporary Huizhou merchants'. No scholar has ever used the title of 'the backwardness of contemporary Huizhou merchants', but such connotations can be fully experienced."[1] Afterwards, this scholar quoted a paragraph from the *Huizhou Merchants* co-authored by Wang Tingyuan and Wang Shihua: "When western business has been incorporated into capitalism system, China's business is still rooted in feudal production method. Huizhou merchants have strong characteristics of feudalism, they continued to operate according to traditional operation modes and tried to make profits in the circulation field instead of investing on production. Under the double oppression of domestic feudal political power and western capitalism, it is inevitable for such a merchant group with strong feudal characteristics to decline."[2] And then, he said, "the discussion is quite representative... a backward merchant group was universally regarded as having been declined, so its transformation in contemporary times is hard to attract the interests of researchers, and even no scholar ever concerned whether or not Huizhou merchants had transformed in the contemporary times, which is completely understandable."[3] For the above three statements, there are three problems: first, the statements of Wang Tingyuan and Wang Shihua in

---

[1] Feng Jianhui. *Studies on Contemporary Huizhou Merchants*.
[2] Wang Tingyuan, Wang Shihua. *Huizhou Merchants*.
[3] Feng Jianhui. *Studies on Contemporary Huizhou Merchants*.

Huizhou Merchants are concerned with the Huizhou merchants in Ming and Qing, completely irrelevant with "the backwardness of contemporary Huizhou merchants". Second, the statement "scholars studying Huizhou merchants have been concerned with the Huizhou merchant group in Ming and Qing for quite a long time, and neglected the transformation of contemporary Huizhou merchants", is entirely inconsistent with the fact. In the *Research of Huizhou Merchants*, ten years before the publishing of Huizhou Merchants, the author clearly mentioned, "although Huizhou merchants as a feudal merchant group... has thoroughly declined after the middle of the Guangxu period in the Qing Dynasty, but a part of Huizhou merchants have kept up with the pace of times and developed commercial capital. From the early of the People's Republic of China (1912—1949) to the time before the liberation of the People's Republic of China, in cities in the south of the Yangtze River, merchants of Huizhou nationality were still very active.

In the economic life of various places, merchants of Huizhou nationality were still a force to be reckoned on, and some even became members of "the national bourgeoisie".[1] Third, the statement "even no scholar concerns whether or not Huizhou merchants have transformed in contemporary times" is also not entirely consistent with the fact. Early in 1996, Zhang Haipeng had delicately stated, "most of the Huizhou merchants can keep up with the trace of the times and advance forward in the business tides of the era...Facts show that in contemporary merchants of Huizhou, the operating activities of some people have been connected with "foreign"... Since the middle of the nineteenth century, some of the Huizhou merchants had withdrawn from the commodity circulation field, but invested their commercial capitals in industries, finance and real estate."[2]

Indeed, as to Huizhou merchants in Ming and Qing, the research on

---

[1] Zhang Haipeng, Wang Tingyuan. *Studies on Huizhou Merchants*.
[2] Zhang Haipeng. *Preface of Contemporary Merchants in Huizhou Merchants Series*.

contemporary Huizhou merchants has just started, and needs to be further strengthened. But, the research of contemporary Huizhou merchants must be based on the comprehensive and accurate understanding of the studies on contemporary Huizhou merchants in the dynasties in Ming and Qing. Only in this way can we scientifically and systematically understand the development history of all the Huizhou merchants and make positive contributions to the profound development of the research of Huizhou merchants.

Published in *Anhui History Studies*, No. 2, 2014
Written by Li Linqi
Translated by Gu Kui

Chapter 13   On the Formation and Development of the Huizhou Merchant Group

In recent years, the research of Huizhou merchants has aroused more concerns among scholars at home and abroad, the reason of which is not only because Huizhou merchants have played an important role in China's social and economic fields, but also that its emergence, development and evolution are closely related to the social and economic conditions at that time. Through studies on Huizhou merchants, we can see the whole social and economic overview from one side.

Ⅰ. When Did Huizhou Merchants Emerge?

For this question, there are different opinions. Some say, Huizhou merchants emerged in Dongjin, some say they appeared in the dynasties of Tang and Song, and some even say they formed in the middle of the Ming Dynasty. We think that the business history of Huizhou people can be traced back to early ages, but the history of Huizhou merchants should start from the middle of the Ming Dynasty. Huizhou merchants refer to Huizhou merchant group formed by the bond of native clan community. Like Shanxi merchants, Shaanxi merchants, Fujian merchants, and Guangdong merchants, it is only the title of a merchant group. So the question of the origin of Huizhou merchants is in fact the question of the origin of Huizhou merchant group. As to the formation of Huizhou, there must be two conditions: first, there are a big group of wealthy Huizhou merchants who constituted the backbone elements of merchant group; second, the business competition is increasingly fierce. In order to defeat competition opponents, it is necessary for Huizhou merchants to form a merchant group. And only in the middle of the Ming Dynasty did it have the two conditions.

In the pre-capitalism, the accumulation of commercial capital is indispensible to the development of long-distance transportation trading. In Europe in the middle age, big merchant groups just developed in international trade. So Engels said, "At least in the beginning, merchant capital can only make profits from foreigners who purchased Chinese commodities or domestic buyers who purchased foreign commodities."[1] China's commercial capital mainly developed in domestic trade, but its accumulation and the formation of big merchant group are inseparable from the development of long-distance transportation trade. In China, the phenomenon of "rich merchants dispersed around the world" has existed ever since ancient times, however, in the eras that natural economy had fixed domination position, there were not too many categories of commodities suitable for long-distance transportation which greatly restricted the scale of transportation trade. On the basis of this kind of trade, there were some rich merchants, but the number was not too big, and the competition among merchants was not too fierce. So at that time, merchants at different places had no power and necessity to form merchant group. Till the middle of the Ming Dynasty, some changes happened to this situation.

Since the middle of the Ming Dynasty, with the development of commodity currency economy, some changes also happened to the tax system of feudal country. From the taxation of golden flower silver to the implementation of single whip law, the levy of currency took up more proportions and even most proportions of the total tax. This change is not only a reflection of the development of commodity economy, but also an important factor that promoted the development of commodity economy. The result is that it forced producers to sell more products to change for currency. The fact that a big batch of commodities emerged into market must make it difficult for commodities to be sold in local place, and so merchants had to turn to other places for the market which greatly promoted the development of long-distance transportation trade. Especially that the farmers turning in taxes were forced by the taxation duration and had to sell their products at lower

---

[1] Supplement to Volume III of Capital.

prices for urgent needs, which artificially caused the deviation of the commodity prices away from the values. And situation provided advantageous chances for transportation merchants to cut down the commodity prices so as to make exorbitant profits. In this situation, long-distance transportation trade developed at unprecedented speed, and its scale was increasingly expanded, and the transportation route also gradually prolonged. Towns and cities gradually became the gathering places of large batches of commodities and the starting and ending points of long-distance transportation trade. Lots of rural fairs also gradually changed routine isolation state and had associations with remote markets. With the commodity change "breaking local restrictions", precious metal silver also became the main currency prevailing in the whole country.

Due to the development of long-distance transportation trade, the commercial capital of Huizhou merchants expanded at unprecedented speed. In Jiajing period, Wu Ke, a person of ancient Shexian County, claimed that "Only 10% of the scholars can succeed, but 90% of merchants finally succeed", so some scholars entered into the business circle and so really "made a fortune"[①]. The success rate of getting rich by doing business was not necessarily so high, but the expansion of the commodity circulation at that time provided very good chances for merchants to make profits. Huizhou merchant Pan Kan said, "if merchants want to make profits, they had to go to the outside world to do business."[②] It can be said that Pan Kan spoke out the secrecy that Huizhou merchants built up the family fortunes. Most of the Huizhou merchants became rich through long-distance transportation activities. "Huizhou Shexian County dominated the left side of the Xin'anjiang River, while rich merchants usually transported their goods to a place one thousand miles away, made speculative profits, and thus

---

① *Annals of Fengnan*, Book 5 & Book 10.
② *Collections of Tai Han*, Volume 14.

made a big fortune"①, which was really the situation at that time. In the Annals of Shexian County in Wanli period of the Ming Dynasty, "moving business" was listed as the first of the five business methods of Huizhou merchants. They valued transportation trade, just because this kind of activity could bring them with seductive profits. Huizhou was adjacent to the most economically advanced areas in the southeast, and Huizhou people had rich business experiences, which caused them to lead the custom, and distinguished themselves early in business activities. They took advantage of canals, the Yangtze River and southeast maritime transportation to ship to all over the country the silk and cotton cloth of the five prefectures, the salt of Yangzhou, china of Jingdezhen, and the bamboo, wood, tea, painting, paper, ink, and ink-stone produced in Huizhou area, and ship to Jiangsu and Zhejiang the cotton and soybean of the northern China, the rice of Jiangxi and Huguang, as well as the wood in the upstream of the Yangtze River, so as to make great profits in the transportation trade. This situation caused a great batch of merchants with big fortunes to emerge from Huizhou people. For example, Wu of Shangshan in Xiuning County "made a fortune though he was not an official"②, Sun of Yancao "made more money than his neighbors"③, Wang of Fenghu "made big fortunes together with his neighbors"④, almost all Huang families of Latang of Shexian County were "rich merchants, and even had more reputation than officials"⑤. In other family clans, there were countless merchants who made a fortune in business, so that the Huizhou at that time enjoyed the reputation of "being the richest in the world"⑥. Facts have showed that in the middle of Ming Dynasty, there had been a big batch

---

① *Xu's Clan*, Volume 6.
② *Collections of Jin Court Historian*, Volume 7.
③ *Collections of Tai Han*, Volume 52.
④ *Annals of Famous Clans in Xiuning, Xin'an*, Volume 1.
⑤ Shexian County, *Huang's Clans in Latang*, Volume 5.
⑥ *Huizhou Prefecture of Jiang'an Eleven of Annals of Zhao Yu*.

of rich merchants. And Huizhou merchant group just developed from the backbone of a big group of rich merchants. While Huizhou merchants emerged, merchants in Shanxi, Shaanxi, Fujian, and Guangdong and other places had also developed in the long-distance transportation trade, and became strong opponents of Huizhou merchants in the markets all over the country. In order to adapt to fierce competition situation, they all had the need to form a merchant group. So, as a kind of combination form of merchants, merchant group came into being. Wang Shixing said, "Huizhou merchants did business in the outside world. When they met with town fellows, they usually made no efforts to help them, and the merchants receiving help would help other Huizhou merchants who needed help, in fact they helped themselves while helping others. And people in the right side of the River also imitated their behaviors"①. This showed that the formation of Huizhou merchant group was really due to competition. In that times, only by using their natural clans and town fellowships and mutual support could merchants maintain their own interests in competitions. It was also true with other merchants, and even Jiangxi merchants that started late also struggled to imitate Huizhou merchants. It could be seen that merchant group was the product of a time, and Huizhou merchant group was one of the few merchant groups that formed in early time.

Ⅱ. The Signs of the Formation of Huizhou Merchant Group

First, the formation of the custom that Huizhou people engaged in business. Only when multiple merchants invited their relatives and families to engage in business could they form merchant groups in various places. When did Huizhou people have the custom of engaging in business? Different people had different opinions. The *Annals of Shexian County* in the Wanli period of the Ming Dynasty pointed that before the Zhengde period, the folk was still the situation of "women wove cloth, men planted crops". In the

---

① *Explanation of Guangzhi*, Volume 3.

late Zhengde period and early Jiajing period, the custom of engaging in business began to prevail: "lots of people engaged in business, neglected their work in the fields, collected money to invest in business, and rose and fell in the business world". Xu Chengyao, Laoyu Huizhou boss ever disagreed with this record. He said, "Xu's family clan recorded, my ancestors had gone out of Juyongguan to engage in tea business in the Zhengtong period, so it seemed that the business custom had long formed, but gave very brief introduction about it in the *Annals of Shexian County*"[①]. What Xu said was reasonable, because most of the deeds of Huizhou people doing business in the outside world before the Zhengde period had been recorded in books. According to our examination, the business custom of Huizhou people roughly generated in the Chenghua and Hongzhi period. According to *Xin'an Jiang's Genealogy*, Jiang Cai determined to engage in business in his early childhood, but lacked funds. His wife Zheng encouraged him by saying, "In our town, ninety percent of the people are merchants, do you really want to quit the business due to the shortage of funds?" Jiang Cai was born in the tenth year of Chenghua period, and went to Hua Bei after he grew up, did business there and thus made a big fortune. If the encouragement of Zheng happened when Jiang Cai was about 20 years old, then early in the beginning of Hongzhi, the business custom had been prevailing in Xin'an at Shexian County. Huang Bao, a person in La Tang of Shexian County, was poor in his childhood. "Seeing so many rich merchants in Yi Zhong, wearing a martial hat and sword-fully armed, riding horse or taking carriage, making friends with officials, and having many servants at home, he really thought they were in high spirits. He sighed, 'they are also local people, but they live a complete different life'!" So he determined to engage in business, and finally got rich[②]. Bao was born in the 22ed year of the Chenghua period. His childhood was just in the beginning of the Hongzhi period. It was clear

---

① *About Affairs in Shexian County*, Book 1.
② *Huang's Clans in Latang*, Volume 5.

that rich merchants in Latang area had been showing off their wealth in the hometown, and engaging in business has attracted lots of people. Wanli *Preface of Annals of Shexian County* 5 showed "the elder said, before the Chenghong period, there were few intellectuals in the countryside, people were content with their quiet life, busy with their farm work, and were modest and thrifty. But nowadays, every family had been very rich, and they gave little importance to farm work and attached more importance to business, some even learned calligraphy and dancing, taking carriage and riding horse. Such changes are unpreventable even by the waters of the Yangtze River". That is to say, ancestors in Shexian County thought that the critical period when changes happened to the customs was in the Hongzhi period. And in the *Annals of Xiuning County* written in the beginning of Hongzhi, there were also records of "people rarely worked hard in the fields but strived to do business". It was clear that in some places of Xiuning County and Shexian County, the business custom in the countryside had developed in a real sense in the Hongzhi period.

Second, it was universal that Huizhou merchants did business in groups. In the Jiajing period, a big Huizhou merchant Cheng did business in Guangdong and Guangxi, "had several thousand workers under his leadership. Cheng helped farmers to choose proper business site and suitable business, which benefited everyone and made them very happy. If they failed to have a harvest, he would forgive them; and if they had a good harvest, he would get few returns from them and let them enjoy most of the earnings. So they were willing to follow him, and since he had become a great merchant, all of his clans had benefited a lot from him."[1] It can be seen that at that time Huizhou people often did business in great groups which usually had more than one thousand members. This kind of group was established with clan and village relationship as the bond. In the group, the chief supported merchant members in finance, guided them in business; while the merchant

---

[1] *Four Series of Qizhou Volume.*

members followed the command of the chief and coordinated with him in actions. Since the Mid-Ming Dynasty, a lot of similar situations had been recorded. As Jin Sheng said, people in Xiuning and Shexian County usually did business with their relatives and friends, so when one family got successful, the family would not enjoy the happiness of success alone. A big merchant could support hundreds and thousands of families, or decades of families, and at least several families[①]. It was noticeable that the activity mode of Huizhou people had appeared in the Chenghua and Hongzhi period. According to records, Xu Zeng, a merchant with Huizhou nationality, had engaged in business in Zhengyang for over twenty years. He "had harmonious relationship with his relatives and former friends who often made a success due to his help, and so the market of Zhengyang was getting more prosperous because of his leadership"[②]. It can be known that when Xu Zeng did business in Zhengyang, there had been a big group of merchants under his leadership. Xu Zeng was born in the fifth year of the Jingtai period, and died in the seventeenth year of the Hongzhi period in Zhengyang. And the time when he was chief of Huizhou merchants just belonged to the Chenghua and Hongzhi period. Wang Xuanyi, the grandfather of Wang Daokun, ever travelled northward to Yan Dai to do salt business, "tens of his disciples followed his leadership, and travelled outside to do business according to the decision jointly made"[③]. The time when he led his disciples with the surname of Kun northward to do business also belonged to the Hongzhi period.

  Third, "Hui" and "merchants" have been connected into a phrase, becoming a noun phrase expressing a particular concept and being widely applied. Since the middle of Ming Dynasty, "Huizhou merchants" and "Huizhou businessmen" had frequently appeared in records. At that time,

---

① *Collections of Jin Court Historian*, Volume 1.
② *Profile of Chu Shi Mr. Meng Jie of Xu's Traditional Clans*.
③ *Sub-writing of Tai Han*, Volume 1.

whey people used the expression of "Huizhou merchants", the characteristics of a single Huizhou merchant were not so important. What were important were the common characteristics of Huizhou merchants which were quite different from those of other merchants, so they were a particular group of merchants. That is, "Huizhou merchant" was a general concept abstracted out of lots of single Huizhou merchants, and was a species concept from generic concept. Although at that time, "Huizhou merchant" was not used as a special noun to express a single concept, Huizhou merchants had their common features as well as advantages and disadvantages, they usually did business in groups and made joint actions, so people had taken Huizhou merchants as a special group in actual life. Wanli *Annals of Jiading County* showed, "In Nanxiang Town lived lots of Huizhou merchants, and the market was filled with goods, better than other towns. But rogues encroached on Huizhou merchants, which led to its deterioration." Here, whether Huizhou merchants stayed or left was based on unified action. Rogues in Nanxiang Town deliberately nibbled up Huizhou merchants and did not affect other merchants. For all the Huizhou merchants, they just nibbled them up without any hesitation. The author of the *Annals of Jiading County* summarized the reasons of the decay of Nanxiang Town as the leaving of Huizhou merchants. They all treated Huizhou merchants as a group. In this sense, the expression of "Huizhou merchants" had been endowed with the connotations of the merchants with Huizhou nationality, this was just the reflection of the formation of Huizhou merchant group on the concept of people. Interestingly, early in the Chenghua period, the expression of "Huizhou Merchants" had been popular in the Songjiang Area. *Cloud Markings* showed, "At the end of Chenghua period, a prominent official returned home with honor, and old man came to kneeled down before him. The official as astonished, asked him why. The old man answered, 'most of the wealth of local people was earned by Huizhou merchants. Now, you are back, I should show you my gratitude.'" Song Jiang was the most active place of Huizhou merchants in early days, and so it was reasonable for the expression of "Huizhou merchants" to prevail here.

Fourth, Huizhou salt merchants, the backbone of Huizhou merchants, had got advantageous positions in the salt industry of Huaidong and Huaixi. In the beginning of Ming Dynasty, Kaizhong Law was implemented. At that time, Huizhou people went to the borderland to collect grains and sell salt, but they were incapable of competing against Shanxi merchants and Shaanxi merchants due to the restrictions of geological conditions. Till the end of Chenghua and the beginning of Hongzhi, the Kaizhong Law was gradually implemented which made salt merchants free from the pains of collecting grains at the borderland, and thus provided conveniences for Huizhou merchants to engage in the salt industry. So, in the beginning of implementing the Kaizhong Law, Huizhou people took advantage of the geographical advantages to swarm into Yangzhou and dominated the salt market over there. At that time, Shanxi merchants and Shaanxi merchants also went southward to compete against Huizhou people, but they were away from hometown and so their spirit was willing but the flesh was weak. As a result, they had to subordinate to Huizhou merchants. Wanli *Annals of Shexian County* said, "Nowadays, the so-called big merchants are nearly all in our town. Although there were also some merchants in Qin and Jin, there were not so many after all." The advantageous position of Huizhou people in the salt industry of Huaidong and Huaixi was about formed in the Chenghua and Hongzhi period. Huang of Latang of Shexian County and other clans had dominated the salt market in Huaidong and Huaixi. For example, Huang Chongde engaged in salt business in Yangzhou, "he was very knowledgeable... enquired to Jian Si, and listed the advantages and disadvantages. Jian Si thought it reasonable, and so issued relevant law to the south and north of the Huaihai Sea. At that time, most merchants near Huaihai Sea were Guanzhong People, loved giving advice and suggestions. Heaving what Huang said, they all followed Huang, and promoted the law proposed by Huang as the code"①. Huang Chongjing emigrated to Yangzhou and engaged in the salt industry over there, "On the day when Huang died, merchants stopped all the business and cried over his death."② Both the two made a success in the time of Chenghong period. It can be seen that Huizhou people had eminent positions among the salt merchants in Huaidong and Huaixi, and could decide the salt policy of the country. They were too powerful so that Shanxi merchants and Shaanxi merchants had no ways to compete against them. In the Ming Dynasty, Huaidong and Huaixi made the largest profits in salt. After Huizhou merchants got advantages in the salt industry in Huaidong and Huaixi, they rapidly expanded their financial resources. They either involved in other businesses while engaging in the salt business, or support their relatives and town fellows to engage in various business activities. This was of great significance to the formation and development of the Huizhou merchant group.

In a word, Huizhou merchant group should have formed in the Chenghua and Hongzhi period. At this time, the signs of the formation of Huizhou merchant group had emerged.

III. Booming and Decay

Over the four hundred years from the formation of Huizhou merchant group to its collapse, no obvious changes happened to its operation form, but the booming and decay of its advantages experienced four different stages.

1. The one hundred years from the Chenghua and Hongzhi period to the middle of Wanli period belonged to the development stage of Huizhou merchant group. Its development is mainly reflected in the following aspects:

(1) Huizhou people had strong custom in business. Huizhou had lots of

---

① Shexian County *Huang's Clans in Latang*, Volume 5.
② Ibid.

mountains and little farmland, and the population kept increasing. As soon as the road for engaging in business to make a living, people emerged out of their hometown to make a living in the outside world. Huizhou "had a saying that people did business to make a living, or they would have no hope"①. So, "people would leave their hometown to do business at the age of sixteen"②. In the six counties of Huizhou, except for Yixian County and Jixi where the business custom developed at a later time, the other four counties had formed the custom of engaging in business in the middle of Ming Dynasty. For example, in Shexian County, "seventy percent of people engaged in business"③; in Xiuning, people "took goods as their permanent properties"④; in Qimen, "thirty percent of local people worked in the field, and merchants took up seventy percent of the local people"⑤; in Wuyuan, transporting wood and tea has become an important method for people to make a living. The prevailing business custom was also reflected in the changes in the values of people. At that time, the saying that "Confucians are superior to merchants' was widely accepted, and the profits that a merchant earned became the main evidence of evaluating whether a person showed filial obedience or was a sage".

(2) Lots of operation industries. The operation range of Huizhou merchants was very abroad, "including all the goods". With the expansion of social division of labor, the salt, tea, wood, grains, cloth, silk, china and other industrial and agricultural products required in people's routine life gradually became the main commodities that they provided. Due to the development of commodity currency economy, more Huizhou merchants opened pawnshops or engaged in currency business. In the industries mentioned above, there had never been so many Huizhou merchants and the

---

① Wanli, *The Trading of Annals of Shexian County*.
② *Talks in Bea Shed*, Chapter 3.
③ *Collections of Tai Han*, Volume 16.
④ *Annals of Yudi of Annals of Xiuning County*.
⑤ Wanli, *Annals of Qimen County*, Volume 4.

business scale was unprecedentedly big. Especially, the prosperity of the four industries of salt, pawn, tea and wood were beyond the imagination of all other merchant groups. And some other Huizhou merchants belonged to no fixed industries. They either engaged in more than one industries, or changed their operation contents according to different time and place, and earn higher profits in a more flexible way. Of course, this practice was related to the insufficiency of the development of markets, but also reflected the vitality of Huizhou merchants in a certain degree.

(3) Wide range of activity. Due to the expansion and extension of commercial route and the further development of market network, the activity range of Huizhou merchants also continued to expand accordingly, the "traces of whom are spread all over the country". They either went northward along the canal and run business in north China; or walked along the Yangtze River, did business in Sichuan, Hubei, Wu and Yue areas; or walked past the Ganjiang River, crossed the Dayu Ridges, and went into Guangdong; or sailed over the sea and did business in coastal cities. Nanjing and Beijing and the capitals of some provinces were the gathering places of Huizhou merchants. In addition, Huizhou merchants were found everywhere else, even in "remote villages and mountains". So at that time, there was a saying, "Huizhou merchants are here and there"[①].

(4) Deep pockets. Some Huizhou merchants were born in rich families, but most of the Huizhou merchants were small traders forced to make a living in the outside world. Although these small traders had few funds, they had very rich business experience and hardworking and enterprising spirit, while the development of commodity economy provided them with good opportunities to earn profits and make a fortune, so some of them "made a fortune overnight". And this caused the whole Huizhou merchant group to have strong strength rapidly. At the Wanli period, Huizhou

---

① *Ancient and Modern Anecdote*, Volume 3.

merchants had been as famous as Shanxi merchants and dominated the national markets. Xie Zhaozhe said, "as to the richest place, it should be Xin'an in the south of the Yangtze River, and Shanyou in the north of the Yangtze River. In Xin'an, big merchants took fish and salt as their business. Some big merchants had been millionaires, and even the modest merchants also got two hundred thousand yuan①." From this, we could see the deep pockets of Huizhou merchants.

2. The one hundred years from the late Wanli to the beginning of Kangxi was the period in which the development of Huizhou merchants suffered setbacks. In this stage, Huizhou merchants suffered from the following blows, which greatly weakened their strength:

(1) Extort excessive taxes and levies. In the Wanli period, tax leviers extorted here and there, and so Huizhou merchants suffered a great deal. The places where tax leviers extorted much were all the gathering places of Huizhou merchants. Naturally, Huizhou merchants became the object of their blackmail. Officials such as Chen Zeng etc. "did bad things" in the south and north of the Yangtze River and Zhejiang, which caused lots of Huizhou merchants to go bankrupt. Li Weizhen said, "Some officials brought disasters to local people, especially the Huizhou merchants in Xin'an"②, this was really the case. In the Tianqi period, Wei Zhongxian checked the old case of Huangshan, sent Lv Xia to ask the official positioned in Shexian County, "find out the rich families all over the county and impose severe punishment on them,"③ which affected "Huai, Yangzhou, Tianjin, Xiangfu, Dexing, Renhe, Qiantang, and other counties"④. In this disaster, the consumption of the wealth of Huizhou merchants was hard to estimate.

(2) The blow of peasant uprising troops in the end of the Ming Dynasty

---

① *Five Gossips*, Volume 4.
② *Collections of Damishan*, Volume 69.
③ *Annals Manuscript of Yanzhen Town*.
④ *Annals of Fengnan*, Book 5 & Book 10.

on Huizhou merchants. The peasant uprising troops led by Li Zicheng implemented the policy of "fair buying and selling" and protecting merchants, but gave strict blow to the rich but selfish merchants. And the attitude that Huizhou merchants turned against the peasant uprising troops increased their hatred to peasant uprising troops. So wherever the peasant uprising troops went, they must levy severely on Huizhou merchants. After the Dashun troop overcame Beijing, "Huizhou merchants were severely robbed and nearly one thousand Huizhou merchants died"[①]. Wang Ji, giant Huizhou merchant, just died in this disaster. Due to the formidable force of peasant resistance, some other Huizhou merchants told themselves not to "hide goods and wealth", so they burned the bonds, and dispersed their wealth. As a result, they were penniless and stopped all the business activities[②].

(3) The damage of wars in Ming and Qing. When the soldiers of the Qing Dynasty went to the south, Su Zhe and Hu Guang suffered a great lot from the wars, while the two places were just the places where most Huizhou merchants gathered together. So it was not difficult to imagine their sufferings. In the beginning when the power of Hongguang was established, the town general took soldiers to attack Yangzhou, "the houses out of the town were burned down"[③], and the villas of lots of Huizhou merchants were reduced to the ground. Duo Ze led soldiers to attack Yangzhou, Huizhou merchant Wang Wende donated three hundred thousand silver, begging the soldiers of Qing "not to kill the innocent mass", only to get the disaster of "Yangzhou was slaughtered within ten days". In the early years of Shunzhi period, the soldiers of Qing oppressed the fights of citizens in southeast cities, which caused a big batch of Huizhou merchants to lose wealth and even lives. The area of Hu-Guang was the main battle where the

---

① *Annals of Pingkou*, Volume 10.
② Yi County, *Ye Clan of Nanping*, Volume 1.
③ *Profile of Ming Jinan*, Volume 23.

soldiers of Ming fought against the soldiers of Qing, where "half of the people died", and "there were no people in a thousand miles". The warlords of the Nanming, in the name of collecting silver, "hired treacherous man to inform against rich Huizhou merchants, and so robbed them of great wealth which caused them to go bankrupt"①, and the Huizhou merchants naturally became the main levy objects, In the transition period from the Ming Dynasty to Qing Dynasty, there were countless wars, which greatly damaged production activities, and resulted in the decline of the purchasing power, and the blocks of commercial routes, all of which greatly affected the commercial activities of Huizhou merchants. Jin Sheng said, half of the Xin'an people got crippled②. Zhao Jishi also said, "In the end of the Ming Dynasty, Huizhou merchants were the richest people. After the damages of wars, Huizhou merchants gradually declined, and were not as ten percent rich as before."③ Their words summarized the overall situation of the setbacks of Huizhou merchants in Ming and Qing.

3. The over one hundred years from the middle of Kangxi period to the Jiajing period and Daoguang period belonged to the booming stage of Huizhou merchants. In this period, with the recovery and development of production, and social stableness, Huizhou merchants came alive again. Their strength recovered, and surpassed the Ming Dynasty in many aspects:

(1) The business custom of Huizhou people was more common. In the Qing Dynasty, the business custom in Xiuning, Shexian County, Qimen and Wuyuan was more prevailing, so was that of Yi County and Jixi County. In the Ming Dynasty, people of Yi County "were plain, read books and worked hard in the field, and did not engage in business", but in the Qing Dynasty, "people began to travel far away, and knew properties could be pawned. They often got properties and paid relevant interests" in order to support

---

① *Record of Yongli*, Volume 7.
② *Collections of Jin Court Historian*, Volume 8.
③ Kangxi, *Annals of Huizhou Prefecture*, Volume 2.

themselves to buy clothes and food①. Till the beginning of Qianlong period, people of Jixi County still "stuck to agriculture, and neglected business"②, but after the middle of Qianlong, more and more people did business in the outside world, and left their traces all over the world. Hu Shi thought the migrant business of Jixi people constituted the "big Jixi" outside the border of Jixi, "if there was no big Jixi, the small Jixi had deteriorated long ago"③. Jixi was the hometown of Hu Shi, so what he said was reliable. In the six counties of Huizhou, the business custom was quite prevailing, which naturally expanded the team of Huizhou merchants, and enhanced the strength of Huizhou merchant group.

(2) The development of the influence of Huizhou salt merchants. The Salt Law was implemented in the end of Wanli period, which endowed Huizhou salt merchants with the privilege of selling salt for generations. However, soon after the Law was carried out, the big turmoil happened in the end of the Ming and Qing Dynasties, and Yangzhou where the salt merchants gathered suffered a great deal. So, at that time, Huizhou merchants did not benefit from the Salt Law in a real sense. In the periods of Kangxi, Yongzheng and Qianlong, due to the recovery of production and the growth of population, the sales of salt also grew a lot accordingly. In addition, the court of the Qing adopted some measures to "favor merchants", so it was quite profitable to engage in the salt business. A great many of Huizhou merchants with great wealth frequently took root in the salt industry and occupied the salt profits. In Huizhou, the prominent families in the salt industry were mostly Huizhou people. "eight major merchants in Huaidong and Huaixi, four of which were people of Yi (She)"④. With the support of officials, Huizhou salt merchants enjoyed high monopoly profits, and

---

① Kangxi *Annals of Yixian County*, Volume 1.
② Qianlong, *Annals of Jixi—Tax*.
③ *First Report of Jixi Annals Museum*.
④ *Annals of Shexian County*, Volume 1, Volume 9.

suddenly had much wealth. In the period of Qianlong, the capital of some people even reached up to ten million. If the factors leading to the reduction of the purchasing power of silver, their capitals had grew by four to five times than that in the Ming Dynasty.

(3) The expansion of the business activities of Huizhou merchants along the Yangtze River. In the Ming Dynasty, most of the domestic transportation trade focused on the south-north trade alongside the canal. Till the Qing Dynasty, the south-north trade continued to expand, and the east-west trade along the Yangtze River also developed rapidly. In the Ming Dynasty, there were altogether eight Chao Guan all over the country, seven of which were established along the canal, with only one Chao Guan in Jiujiang alongside the Yangtze River. In the Wanli period, Jiujiang Chao Guan only collected no more than 25 thousand pieces of silver, taking up only 8% of the revenues of the seven Chao Guan alongside the Yangtze River[1]. While in the Qing Dynasty, according to *General Codes of the Qing Dynasty* compiled in the Qianlong period, there were altogether six Chao Guans which were established in the Yangtze River basin such as Wuhu Guan, Jiujiang Guan, Gan Guan, Wuchang Guan, Jing Guan and Kui Guan, collecting nearly one million pieces of silver every year, about 85% of the revenues of the Guans alongside the Yangtze River[2]. The rapid increase of the tariffs in the Yangtze River basin showed the rapid expansion of the east-west trade scale. The Yangtze River basin was just the place where Huizhou merchants took the lead, and most of the trade along the Yangtze River had left in the hands of Huizhou merchants. The expansion of the riverside trade was inseparable from the increase of the strength of Huizhou merchants.

(4) The universal establishment of Huizhou guild. In the Jiajing Wanli period of the Ming Dynasty, Huizhou people had established Shexian County

---

[1] *General Examination of Subsequent Documents*, Volume 18.
[2] *General Code of the Qing Dynasty*, Volume 8.

Guild and Xiuning Guild in Beijing. But the two were "especially established for provincial graduates to attend examinations in Beijing", and were not allowed to be used by merchants①. Changshu Meiyuan Guild established in the Ming Dynasty was actually built by Huizhou merchants for their own uses, but there were not so many houses, and the houses were only used for placing coffins. And even such guilds were rarely seen in the Ming Dynasty. After it entered the Qing Dynasty, there established Huizhou guild almost in all the industries all over the country, most of which became the activity centers of Huizhou merchants. The Guilds built by Huizhou merchants in Shangxin River of Nanjing and Jingdezhen of Jiangxi were directly named as "Huizhou Merchants Guild", showing that Huizhou merchants played a dominant role in guilds②. Some guilds were very big and were equipped with Xin'an pier, Yixue Lecture Hall for Huizhou merchant to transport goods and train disciples to read books③. The universal establishment of Huizhou Guild played an important role in strengthening the cohesion of Huizhou merchant groups.

(5) Huizhou merchants were more closely associated with feudal political forces. Since the middle of the Ming Dynasty, it became common for Huizhou merchants to associate with bigwigs and bribe government. After the Qing Dynasty, the association between officials and merchants were more closely. On the one hand, donation was prevailing in the Qing Dynasty, which provided conveniences for Huizhou merchants to seek for official titles. At that time, lots of rich merchants took a position in government, and even middle-class families took some official positions by the way of donation. On the other hand, with the increase of the strength of Huizhou merchants,

---

① *Subsequent Collections of Re-annals of Shexian County Guild by Daoguang.*
② Guangxu *Annals of Wuyuan County*, Volume 33 & Volume 35.
③ *Facts about Mr. Peng Yuan of Revision of Ping's Clan of Ancient Shexian County*—*Facts about Mr. Peng Yuan.*

there were more and more people who got official positions by "making contributions". In order to praise the salt merchants in Huaidong and Huaixi for their "donations", the Qing Government frequently endowed them some of them with official positions and promoted them, which almost "benefited" every salt merchant in Huaidong and Huaixi. Jiang Chun, a merchant of Shexian County, were entitled with the title of provincial administrative commissioner, and "associated with the emperor as an ordinary person"[①]. And this showed that the combination between Huizhou merchants and feudal political forces had reached the peak of perfection.

4. The nearly one hundred years from the middle of Daoguang period to the end of Qing Dynasty belonged to the decay and collapse period of Huizhou merchant groups. The decay of Huizhou merchant group started from the failure of the salt merchants of Huizhou. In the twelfth year of the Daoguang period, the Qing Dynasty abolished the Gang Law and implemented the Ticket Law, which caused Huizhou merchants to lose their inherited salt business patents. Because of financial difficulty, the Qing Dynasty recollected the salt taxes that they should have paid in previous years, which caused a great many salt merchants to go bankrupt. Huizhou salt merchants had always been the backbones of Huizhou merchant group, the failure of Huizhou salt merchants forced the forces of the whole Huizhou merchant groups to decline greatly. During the revolutions of Taiping Revolution, Huizhou merchants suffered a lot. At that time, the lower dream and middle dream of the Yangtze River became the main battlefields, the channels of the Yangtze River were blocked so the riverside trade could not be conducted normally, which caused "previous big merchants turn into poor peasants, and previous small traders changed into beggars"[②], and some of these small traders were just Huizhou people. Huizhou was a place which rarely served as the

---

① *Annals of Shexian County*, Volume 1 & Volume 9.
② *Sequel of New Classics*, Volume 43.

battlefield, but now had been a place where Taiping soldiers fought against Qing soldiers. Some villages and towns where Huizhou rich merchants gathered were severely damaged by war. When Zeng Guopan stationed troops in Qimen, "he indulged his soldiers to rob the natives of all their materials"①. After this disaster, "In one hundred people, there was no more than two males, and women and servants were ready for being chosen as long as they were fed on"②, which can fully showed the suffering of Huizhou merchants. The aggression of western great powers brought heavy attacks to Huizhou merchants. Due to the increasing imports of foreign cotton gauze, foreign cloth, foreign colors as well as wood imported from the Southeast Asia, the cloth merchants and wood merchants of Huizhou suffered a lot. The emergence of money shops and the banking industry caused Huizhou pawnbrokers to lose their positions in the finance industry. Only tea merchants and silk merchants could save the situation. After the opening up of the five ports, the export sales of silk and tea increased a great lot and became the major commodities. Huizhou merchants had solid foundation in operating Huizhou tea and Hu silk, while Shanghai at that time had replaced Guangzhou as the major port of the exports of silk and tea, providing conveniences for Huizhou merchants to do business nearby, so Huizhou tea merchants and silk merchants enjoyed certain prosperity in a certain period of time. However, after a short period of time, due to the increasing taxation, the international competitiveness of China's tea and silk was weakened. Foreign merchants took the chance to manipulate the market, cut down the price to collect goods, which caused Chinese merchants to "lose in consecutive years", and formed the situation "that nine out of ten merchants were in difficulty"③. In the middle of Guangxu period, Huizhou tea

---

① *Five Gedanite*.
② *Qing Bai Lei Chao Book 15 , About Marriage*.
③ *Memorials of Mr. Zeng Wenxiang*, Volume 25.

merchants and silk merchants had lost too much money to support their business. In order to adapt to changes in economic situations, some Huizhou merchants changed their traditional operation modes, and took the road of developing enterprises. They tried in tea-making, reeling off raw silk from cocoons, weaving cotton, exploiting porcelain clay, and china-making and other industries. However, under the oppression of imperialism and feudal forces, they gained a little and failed to get out of the dilemma. When Huizhou merchants increasingly declined, the combination forms of Chinese merchants also changed gradually. After the Daoguang period, there were more and more merchant guilds developed according to industries. In the end of the Qing Dynasty and the beginning of the People's Republic of China (1912 — 1949), merchant guilds involved into industry association, and developed chamber of commerce. The peer relationship gradually weakened the countrymen relationship, so the Huizhou merchant group developed with township family relationship as the tie gradually collapsed. Afterwards, there were still some Huizhou merchants in different industries, but Huizhou merchant group had become a name in history, and its traces of boom and decay immediately became the research subject of some historians.

Through out the history of Huizhou merchant groups, it is not difficult to find that the traces of emergence, development and decay were consistent with the evolutions of the political and economic situations of the Ming Dynasty and Qing Dynasty. Huizhou merchant group was a product of the commodity economy which developed to a certain stage in the late stage of China's feudal society. Its development had played a positive role in promoting the development of commodity economy and the prosperity of the markets. However, it was after all a merchant group combined with the township family relationship as the tie, and their capitals were mainly accumulated by feudal political power in the circulation field, so it had always been attached to feudal political forces and failed to take on the road of independent development, and the increases and decreases of their power had to be greatly affected by political situations. When the social nature of China changed fundamentally, it inevitably tended to collapse with the decline of the feudal system.

Published in *Chinese History Studies*, No. 3, 1995
Written by Wang Tingyuan
Translated by Gu Kui

Information of the Original Passages

序号	作者	论文题目	出版物	出版时间	译者
1	张海鹏	徽学漫议	光明日报	2000年3月24日	方传余
2	赵华富	论当代徽学	安徽大学学报	2004年第5期	汪杨文
3	唐力行	徽州学研究的对象、价值、内容与方法	史林	1999年第3期	汪杨文
4	刘伯山	徽学研究的多学科价值	探索与争鸣	2004年第9期	汪杨文
5	刘伯山	徽州文化的基本概念及历史地位	安徽大学学报	2002年第6期	程洪珍
6	栾成显	徽州文化的形成与演变历程	安徽史学	2014年第2期	程洪珍
7	叶显恩	徽州文化的定位及其发展大势——《徽州文化全书》总序	黄山学院学报	2005年第2期	程洪珍
8	赵华富	关于徽州宗族制度的三个问题	安徽史学	2003年第2期	周青
9	周晓光	明清徽州家谱与徽州社会风俗	安徽史学	2011年第6期	周青
10	阿风	徽州文书研究十年回顾	中国史研究动态	1998年第2期	李峤
11	周绍泉	徽州文书与徽学	历史研究	2000年第1期	李峤
12	李琳琦	论徽商研究中的几个问题	安徽史学	2014年第2期	顾奎
13	王廷元	论徽州商帮的形成与发展	中国史研究	1995年第3期	顾奎